MW

A Day in the Country

A Day in the Country

John Gooders

ILLUSTRATED BY
DAVID THELWELL

ANDRE DEUTSCH

First published 1979 by
André Deutsch Limited
105 Great Russell Street London WC1

Copyright © 1979 by John Gooders

Printed in Great Britain by
Ebenezer Baylis & Son Ltd
The Trinity Press, Worcester, and London

ISBN 0 233 97082 7

Contents

List of Maps

14

Preface

The British countryside is rich, varied and beautiful and has too long been locked away out of reach of people. The nation is itself the largest single landowner, and has been for some time, but even our own land has been made 'communally private' by organizations that have inherited a squire-like approach from the private landowners that surround them. Gradually, as is our way, things are changing. Countryside Acts have brought pressure on public bodies to open their 'estates' to the public for various recreational activities. The Forestry Commission, the largest landowner of all, has responded. The various water authorities have allowed access to yachtsmen, anglers and birdwatchers. There are National Parks where the emphasis is on people enjoying themselves and the countryside, and Country Parks where access is freer still. A network of long distance footpaths has been established drawing people's attention to what, in many cases, were already rights of way. Even bodies as notoriously secretive as the Nature Conservancy Council have become aware that people have rights and that they want to see and enjoy the wildlife that the NCC seeks to protect on their behalf. A rash of nature trails and even, in some places, longer mountain trails seek to guide the visitor to areas of interest.

Private landowners too have opened their estates to visitors, though usually as a source of extra income or as a result of some agreement regarding death duties. Among the largest such landowners are the National Trust and the Scottish National Trust, independent bodies that receive large quantities of land by gift of government but over which we seem to have little, if any, control. Yet they consist, to quote their own literature, of 'a body of responsible private citizens who . . . act as trustees for the nation in the acquisition and ownership of land and buildings worthy of . . . preservation'.

In the specific field of nature the Wildfowl Trust has shown the way; others are following. The Trust has instituted the 'turnstile' approach to nature conservation, and it has worked. Suddenly there are more bird gardens than one thought there were bird-watchers,

15

though not all have such lofty aims as the Wildfowl Trust. The admirable Royal Society for the Protection of Birds has opened its gates on an increasing scale. There are no turnstiles, but access is much easier than it was a few years ago.

The most important of all the 'private' nature reserve owners are the various County Naturalists' Trusts, a mass of organizations as diverse as one could ever imagine. Most are administered on a shoestring by local do-gooders with varying degrees of efficiency. First to be established, in 1926, was the Norfolk Naturalists' Trust, often said to be the model for the genre, though judging by those that followed such a statement could be taken as an insult. The Norfolk NT is a paradigm, a well-run, go-ahead organization with excellent educational and access facilities to some of the most important reserves in Britain. Other trusts are close by, but the majority are unbelievably tenacious in protecting their properties against visitors. 'No visiting', 'members only', 'no publicity' – these are the sorts of notes that mark their literature (if they have any). It is a staggering thought that there is no full list of the nature reserves in this country because many of the trusts refuse to supply details of their properties. No doubt things will change, but meanwhile thousands of acres of nature reserves remain unknown, unvisited except by the esoteric few.

This then is the background against which *A Day in the Country* is written. Its function is simple – to pick out those areas where people who wish to can enjoy our countryside and the natural life that lives there, and to make their visits as straightforward and as pleasurable as possible. Such a task is not without its problems. Masses of people can damage fragile plant communities, disturb birds and mammals and destroy what they came to see. Many 'delicate' natural history sites have been omitted on this score, but I have worked on the assumption that visitors (and plenty of them) should be allowed unless a good reason could be found for not doing so. Unfortunately, altogether too many reserve managements work exactly the other way around. It is this attitude – 'stop all access unless forced to concede' – that is the major stumbling block to the progressive education of the public (and their children) in the use and value of our countryside. If this guide helps to open more reserves to public access, then its aim will have been achieved. We need more enjoyment of the countryside, much more, not a plethora of 'keep out' notices.

JOHN GOODERS

Introduction

A Day in the Country is just that – a guide to places nearby where you can get a breath of fresh air and see wildlife in its many forms. Of course you can see wildlife anywhere – in city centres, sewage farms, on municipal rubbish dumps and so on. But this is a guide to wildlife, where the enjoyment of the surroundings is as important as the animals and plants themselves. Specialists may do what they like – even if it means a day at Perry Oaks Sewage Works near Heathrow Airport, where the thundering jets take off every two minutes and the stench dulls your sense of smell for days to follow – but for most of us the enjoyment of the countryside is the break we require.

But wildlife is not confined to the countryside. Many animals live in zoos and parks in captive conditions that are far from their normal homes. Yet they are wildlife, are worth seeing, and give us just a taste of the unattainable wild country that we shall never be able to visit.

So this guide is a mixture, but hopefully one that will enable those with an interest in wild animals and plants to find somewhere handy to visit, and give those with no interest whatsoever the opportunity to expose themselves to the risk of being fascinated. There are nature trails through forest and marsh; safari parks where, with a little imagination, you could be on safari in deepest Africa; zoos with rare and strange animals from around the world; bird reserves with Britain's rarest wild animals; sea cliffs teeming with birds that are the envy of the rest of Europe; and quiet country walks where you may see much or little depending on your skill as an observer.

I shall not (indeed could not) hide the fact that my speciality is birds. As a result I have leaned over backwards to try to bring a balanced picture of Britain's wildlife to these pages. Perhaps I have over-compensated, but birds are the most obvious, numerous and most easily seen members of our wildlife community. Flowers too are numerous and obvious, and it is my great regret that, despite having had the good fortune to meet some of the country's best botanists, I am still a botanical duffer. However, my good friend Allen Paterson, Curator of the Chelsea Physic Garden, has laboured his way through the manuscript in an attempt to eliminate the most glaring errors, and I am grateful to him both for his efforts and for the amusement we both enjoyed as he pointed them out. Many others have given of their time and energy to make this book both more accurate and complete. But at the end I am totally responsible for its inaccuracies and shortcomings.

In Part One I have listed all of the reserves of the major national bodies, whether or not they can be visited, together with notes on the British Tourist Authority, and on the Country Code. In Part Two (the major section) I have chosen those places and areas able to cope with visitors and where there is something positive for the visitor to see. The choice of such places is entirely personal, as indeed is the choice of places throughout this guide. Some may disagree, but as the boom in conservation effort and interest in our countryside develops, more and more prime wildlife areas are brought into the nature reserve system. Many such reserves are small, unwardened and unable to provide the necessary supervision and facilities for visitors, but progressively more are being opened up so that people can enjoy them.

Thus I have needed to be selective. The wildlife areas that are described at length can all be visited fairly easily – they vary from the open-to-all-for-free to the book-ahead-permit-only system. Details of access and what to look for are provided for each, with a checklist of species of main interest. The test of such a guide is that it should work, and I would be pleased to hear of inaccuracies in this respect.

The major specialities of each reserve are indicated by symbols. Thus a sandpiper, a daisy, a deer and a butterfly signify the particular attractions of birds, flowers, mammals and insects respectively in each reserve or area. The absence of a symbol does not indicate a total absence of the life form, simply that there is no subject of special attraction. Anthony Chapman of the Royal Society for the Protection of Birds has kindly advised me on access to nature reserves by the physically disabled. In areas where access by wheelchair is practical, a symbol is given next to the place name. This does not mean that the disabled cannot enjoy other areas – from the windows of a car, for instance. The symbols are as follows:

The law of trespass is remarkably ancient and remarkably vague. By and large, access to the countryside is restricted, and all users of this guide would be well advised to check access before entering any area. But the areas covered in the guide can be entered without let or hindrance other than as described. In all cases visitors should respect the Country Code detailed in Part One. Nothing is more likely to restrict our enjoyment of the British countryside than the misuse of privilege where it has been granted. Read the Country Code, obey it to the letter, and then perhaps we can all go on enjoying ourselves for our days in the country.

Finally, I am grateful to Hazel Cooper, who has laboured over my manuscript to produce a finished typescript fit to delight the eye of any printer; and to my publishers André Deutsch, who have shown the most extraordinary patience during the long gestation period.

JOHN GOODERS

Wildcat

Part One

National Parks

The National Parks were established in the 1960s by what has since become the Countryside Commission. There are ten Parks in all, covering over five thousand square miles of some of the most splendid countryside in Britain. Yet the land itself remains in private hands, and visitors have no more right of access than they do elsewhere in the countryside. This apparent contradiction may lead some to question the validity of the National Park system, while others may simply wonder what is the point. However the Countryside Commission has the function of maintaining and improving the landscape of the Parks by tidying up eyesores and encouraging visitors by supplying information and improving access. The fact that an area is a National Park may facilitate its defence against intrusive development, but it is doubtful whether any regulations or agreements would, in the long term, prevent economic exploration and production of oil, copper, coal or what have you.

To the visitor from overseas the National Park system is particularly strange. He is used to such Parks being lonely wilderness areas devoid of permanent human habitation and often full of wildlife. The United Nations have laid down a set of rules that govern the declaration of an area as a National Park. Not surprisingly no British Parks are included in their official list. No, the British have once more defined their terms in their own way and for their own purposes. Who is to say that we are wrong to do so?

For convenience a list follows:

	area in square miles
Brecon Beacons	524
Dartmoor	365
Exmoor	265
Lake District	866
Northumberland	398
Peak District	542
Pembrokeshire Coast	225

	area in square miles
Snowdonia	838
Yorkshire Dales (North Riding)	553
Yorkshire Dales (West Riding)	680

Red squirrel

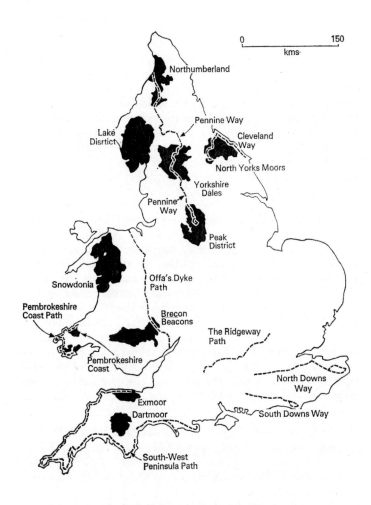

NATIONAL PARKS AND LONG DISTANCE ROUTES

National Long Distance Routes

Several of the Long Distance Routes are included in the main body of this book, not because visitors are recommended to walk their entire length but because of the splendid countryside through which they pass and the access they give to many areas of wildlife interest. The idea of such routes is excellent, and the Countryside Commission is performing a valuable function in their establishment. Several are already open for their full length, while others are gradually progressing towards completion. Unfortunately many other footpaths and rights of way are disappearing from our countryside, mainly it must be said from lack of use, which is partly the result of automobilization. A footpath kept open by country people for generations soon disappears when the car makes the short-cut redundant. Yet as more and more people seek relaxation in the countryside they are progressively hard put to locate the very walks that they could legally use. Local people know (or knew) where the footpaths were. The visitor not only lacks this local knowledge but finds it almost impossible to locate rights of way where they do exist. There are few signposts or marks, and even where such signs are found the paths themselves often disappear. Perhaps the Countryside Commission should have obligations in this area as well. But the Long Distance Routes are in the main well marked, and publicity ensures that continued usage keeps them open. A full list follows:

1 *The Pennine Way* (250 miles). A hill walk from Edale in Derbyshire along the Pennines and over the Cheviots to the Scottish border.
2 *The Cleveland Way* (93 miles). Over the North York Moors and the Cleveland Hills from Helmsley to Saltburn and thence along the coast to Filey.
3 *The Pembrokeshire Coast Path* (167 miles). From Amroth to St Dogmaels, almost entirely within the Pembrokeshire Coast National Park.
4 *The Offa's Dyke Path* (168 miles). From the Severn to Prestatyn, running through the borders of England and Wales.
5 *The South Downs Way* (80 miles). From Beachy Head to the

Hampshire boundary. The first long distance bridleway to be created, it caters for riders and cyclists as well as walkers.

6 *The Cornwall Coast Path* (268 miles). Encircling the entire coast of Cornwall, it forms part of the South-West Peninsula Coast Path (515 miles) from Minehead in Somerset to Studland in Dorset.

7 *The Ridgeway Path* (85 miles). From Ivinghoe Beacon in Buckinghamshire to Overton Hill, near Avebury in Wiltshire, within the Chilterns and North Wessex Downs Areas of Outstanding Natural Beauty. The western section is open to riders and cyclists as well as walkers.

8 *The North Downs Way* (141 miles). From Farnham in Surrey to Dover in Kent it follows or runs parallel to the Pilgrims' Way over part of its length. The section between Hollingbourne and Dover (43 miles) is already open for use.

9 *The South Devon Coast Path* (93 miles). From Turnchapel, near Plymouth, to the Dorset boundary at Lyme Regis.

10 *The Dorset Coast Path* (72 miles). From Lyme Regis to Studland.

11 *The Somerset and North Devon Coast Path* (82 miles). From Minehead in Somerset to Marsland Mouth on the Devon/Cornwall boundary.

These last three routes form the remaining sections of the South-West Peninsula Coast Path which is still not fully operative. Most of the paths are the subjects of individual guidebooks published by HMSO and which are available locally.

Military orchid

Monkey orchid

Areas of Outstanding Natural Beauty

Thirty-two areas of Britain have been declared to be Areas of Outstanding Natural Beauty (AONB). They vary in size from the tiny Dedham Vale (22 square miles), on the Essex–Suffolk border, to the North Wessex Downs (676 square miles). Such a declaration makes little difference to the would-be visitor, who is as free to visit as he would be anywhere else in the countryside, i.e., not at all apart from rights of way. So two significant questions arise. First, what is the point? Second, how do such areas differ from National Parks? Taking the second first: the difference seems to be that National Parks are administered centrally by the government and have the aim to encourage recreation and access, whereas AONBs are locally administered to no public advantage. What then is the point? Here the answer seems to be that being declared an AONB confers a certain amount of protection to an area when it comes to planning development. A list follows:

	area in square miles
Anglesey	83
Arnside and Silverdale	29
Cannock Chase	26
Chichester Harbour	29
Chilterns	309
Cornwall	360
Cotswolds	582
Dedham Vale	22
Dorset	400
East Devon	103
East Hampshire	151
Forest of Bowland	310
Gower	73
Isle of Wight	73
Kent Downs	326
Lincolnshire Wolds	216

	area in square miles
Lleyn	60
Malvern Hills	40
Mendip Hills	78
Norfolk Coast	174
North Devon	66
Northumberland Coast	50
North Wessex Downs	676
Quantock Hills	38
Shropshire Hills	300
Solway Coast	41
South Devon	128
South Hampshire Coast	30
Suffolk Coast and Heaths	151
Surrey Hills	160
Sussex Downs	379
Wye Valley	125

Bee orchid

Spring gentian

Country Parks

Country Parks are areas where people may relax and enjoy themselves, study natural history, walk and explore and generally be at home in the countryside. There are about a hundred recognized by the Countryside Commission, often located near large towns, and in general they are open throughout the year and offer parking, toilet and other facilities. Some have nature trails, wardens and information centres, though there is much variation. Entry to some is subject to a charge and some charge a parking fee. The vast majority are administered by the local authority, though some belong to the National Trust and others still are in private hands. A list follows:

1 The Wirral, Cheshire, Merseyside
2 Elvaston Castle, Derbyshire
3 Barton Farm, Wiltshire
4 Beacon Fell, Lancashire
5 Normanby Hall, Humberside
6 Emberton Park, Buckinghamshire
7 Keynes Park, Gloucestershire
8 Pow Hill, Durhamshire
9 Sherwood, Nottinghamshire
10 Bradgate Park, Leicestershire
11 Bayhurst Wood, Greater London
12 Berry Head, Devon
13 Yateley Common, Hampshire
14 Worsbrough, South Yorkshire
15 Mapledurham, Oxfordshire
16 Farley Mount, Hampshire
17 Llyn Padarn, Gwynedd
18 Burton Dasset Hills, Warwickshire
19 Etherow Park, Greater Manchester
20 Camer Park, Kent
22 Windmill and Waseley Hills, Hereford and Worcester
23 Holme Pierrepont, Nottinghamshire
24 Clare Castle, Suffolk
25 Kingsford, Herefordshire and Worcestershire

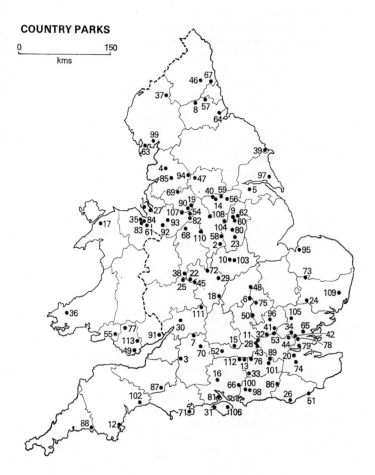

COUNTRY PARKS

0   150

kms

26 Seven Sisters, East Sussex
27 Eastham Woods, Merseyside
28 Black Park, Buckinghamshire
29 Coombe Abbey, West Midlands
30 Robinswood Hill, Gloucestershire
31 Fort Victoria, Isle of Wight
32 Aldenham Reservoir, Hertfordshire
33 Frensham Common, Surrey
34 Weald Park, Essex
35 Moel Arthur, Clwyd
36 Llys-y-Fran Reservoir, Dyfed
37 Talkin Tarn, Cumbria
38 Highgate Common, Staffordshire
39 Church Cliff, North Yorkshire
40 Cannon Hall Park, South Yorkshire
41 Great Wood, Hertfordshire
42 Thorndon Park, Essex
43 Langley Park, Buckinghamshire
44 Hainault Forest, Greater London
45 Lickey Hills, West Midlands
46 Bolam Lake, Northumberland
47 Penistone Hill, West Yorkshire
48 Irchester, Northamptonshire
49 Porth Kerry Park, South Glamorgan
50 Stockgrove Park, Bedfordshire
51 Hastings, East Sussex
52 Snelsmore Common, Berkshire
53 Trent Park, Greater London
54 Lyme Park, Cheshire
55 Afan Argoed, West Glamorgan
56 Cusworth Park, South Yorkshire
57 Derwent Walk, Durham
58 Shipley, Derbyshire
59 Howell Wood, South Yorkshire
60 Rufford Abbey, Nottinghamshire
61 Waun-y-Llyn, Clwyd
62 Clumber Park, Nottinghamshire
63 Bardsea, Cumbria
64 Hardwick Hall, Durham
65 Danbury Park, Essex
66 Queen Elizabeth, Hampshire
67 Plessey Woods, Northumberland
68 Greenway Bank, Staffordshire
69 Jumbles Reservoir, Greater Manchester
70 Barbury Castle, Wiltshire

71 Durlston, Dorset
72 Kingsbury, Warwickshire
73 Brandon Park, Suffolk
74 Manor Park, Kent
75 Stewartby Lake, Bedfordshire
76 Lightwater, Surrey
77 Dare Valley, Mid Glamorgan
78 Langdon Hills West, Essex
79 Langdon Hills East, Essex
80 Burnstump, Nottinghamshire
81 Lepe and Calshot Foreshores, Hampshire
82 Tegg's Nose, Cheshire
83 Moel Fammau, Clwyd
84 Loggerheads, Clwyd
85 Witton Park, Lancashire
86 Ditchling Common, East Sussex
87 Ham Hill, Somerset
88 Mount Edgcumbe, Cornwall
89 Horton, Surrey
90 Chadkirk, Greater Manchester
91 Caldicot Castle, Gwent
92 Little Budworth Common, Cheshire
93 Marbury Park, Cheshire
94 Wycoller, Lancashire
95 Sandringham, Norfolk
96 Knebworth, Hertfordshire
97 Burton Constable, Humberside
98 Goodwood, West Sussex
99 Fell Foot, Cumbria
100 Weald and Downland Open Air Museum, West Sussex
101 Box Hill, Surrey
102 Farway Countryside Park, Devonshire
103 Wanlip, Leicestershire
104 Hardwick Hall, Derbyshire
105 Hatfield Forest, Essex
106 Robin Hill, Isle of Wight
107 Styal, Cheshire
108 Longshaw, Derbyshire
109 Easton Farm Park, Suffolk
110 Ilam, Staffordshire
111 Broadway Tower, Herefordshire and Worcestershire
112 Wellington, Hampshire
113 Parc Cefn Onn, South Glamorgan

National Nature Reserves and Wildfowl Refuges

The Nature Conservancy, a government department, is directly responsible for the administration of National Nature Reserves and National Wildfowl Refuges. It is not, except in an unofficial consultancy capacity, concerned with local or private nature reserves, of which there are a considerable number owned and/or administered by a variety of conservation bodies in the UK. National Nature Reserves have been established throughout the country for a variety of purposes and for many differing reasons. In each, protection and conservation are of prime importance together, in some cases, with the opportunities provided for research. Indeed the Conservancy is primarily a scientific body. Though called 'National' Nature Reserve this does not mean that the public (although they own or lease the land through the State) have right of access. Indeed in most cases access is restricted to *bona fide* scientists, a strange contrast to the 'private' nature reserves which, by and large, encourage visitors and do their best to educate the visitor to an appreciation of the value of what they are doing. No doubt this exclusiveness is essential in many cases, but it seems strange that the country's major conservation body should take so little interest in showing nature to the public.

The Conservancy has separate headquarters for England, Scotland and Wales, and within each country a network of regional offices responsible for the national nature reserves. The addresses follow, together with a complete list of National Nature Reserves and details of conditions of access. The figures in square brackets refer to those in the accompanying map.

England

Headquarters for England:
1 Cambridge Gate,
Regent's Park,
London NW1 4JY.
Tel. 01-935-5533.

NATIONAL NATURE RESERVES AND WILDFOWL REFUGES

0 _____ 200
kms

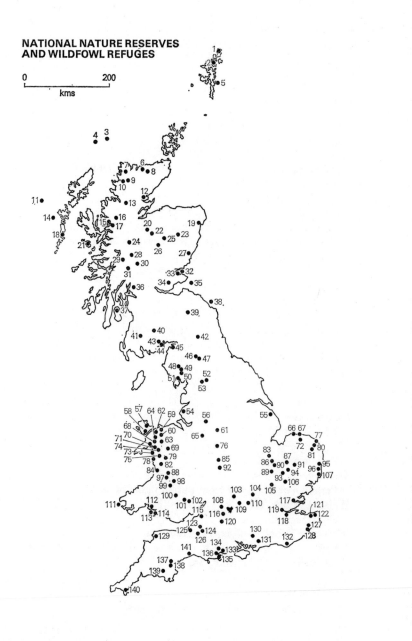

A DAY IN THE COUNTRY

East Anglia Region

The Regional Officer for East Anglia,
Nature Conservancy Council,
60 Bracondale,
Norwich,
Norfolk NOR 58B.

Bure Marshes, Norfolk, 1018 acres [81]
  Permit required, except for nature trail.
Cavenham Heath, Suffolk, 376 acres [94]
  Permit required to visit Ash Plantation and Tuddenham Heath.
Hales Wood, Essex, 20 acres [106]
  Permit required.
Hickling Broad, Norfolk, 1204 acres [80]
  Navigation unrestricted. Permits to visit available from: Norfolk
  Naturalists' Trust, 72 The Close, Norwich NOR 16P.
Holkham, Norfolk, 9700 acres [67]
  Unrestricted access, except to farmland.
Leigh, Essex, 634 acres [117]
  Permit required.
Orfordness–Havergate, Suffolk, 556 acres [107]
  Permit required to visit Havergate Island, available from: Royal
  Society for the Protection of Birds, The Lodge, Sandy, Beds.
  Restricted access to some parts of Orford Beach.
Scolt Head Island, Norfolk, 1821 acres [66]
  Access to ternery restricted during breeding season (May–July
  inclusive).
Swanton Novers Woods, Norfolk, 149 acres [72]
  Permit required.
Thetford Heath, Suffolk, 243 acres [91]
  Permit required.
Walberswick, Suffolk, 1270 acres [95]
  Permit required away from public rights of way.
Weeting Heath, Norfolk, 338 acres [87]
  Permit required.
Westleton Heath, Suffolk, 117 acres [96]
  Permit required away from picnic area and public rights of way.
Winterton Dunes, Norfolk, 259 acres [77]

East Midland Region

The Regional Officer for the East Midlands,

36

Nature Conservancy Council,
Monks Wood Experimental Station,
Huntingdon.

Castor Hanglands, Cambs., 221 acres [83]
  Permit required except for Ailsworth Heath.
Chippenham Fen, Cambs., 258 acres [93]
  Permit required. Restricted access April–July inclusive.
Holme Fen, Cambs., 640 acres [86]
  Permit required.
Knocking Hoe, Bedfordshire, 22 acres [105]
  Permit required.
Monks Wood, Cambs., 387 acres [89]
  Permit required.
Saltfleetby–Theddlethorpe Dunes, Lincolnshire, 1088 acres [55]
  Unrestricted access, except during Ministry of Defence operations.
Woodwalton Fen, Cambs., 514 acres [90]
  Permit required.

North Region

The Regional Officer for North England,
Nature Conservancy Council,
Merlewood Research Station,
Grange-over-Sands,
Cumbria LA11 6JU.

Ainsdale Sand Dunes, Merseyside, 216 acres [54]
  Permit required away from public rights of way and concessionary
  paths.
Blelham Bog, Cumbria, 5 acres [48]
Colt Park Wood, North Yorkshire, 21 acres [53]
  Permit required.
Coom Rigg Moss, Northumberland, 88 acres [42]
  Permit required.
Glasson Moss, Cumbria, 143 acres [45]
Lindisfarne, Northumberland, 8101 acres [38]
Ling Gill, North Yorkshire, 12 acres [52]
Moor House, Cumbria, 9956 acres [46]
  Permit required away from public rights of way.
North Fen, Cumbria, 5 acres [49]
Roudsea Wood, Cumbria, 287 acres [51]
  Permit required away from public rights of way.

Rusland Moss, Cumbria, 59 acres [50]
  Permit required.
Upper Teesdale, Durham, 8642 acres [47]
  Permit required away from public rights of way.

South Region

The Regional Officer for South England,
Nature Conservancy Council,
Foxhold House,
Thornford Road,
Crookham Common,
Newbury, Berks. RG15 8EL.

Aston Rowant, Oxfordshire, 259 acres [110]
  Permit required away from paths.
Cothill, Oxfordshire, 4 acres [109]
  Permit required.
Fyfield Down, Wiltshire, 612 acres [116]
  Permit required away from paths.
North Meadow, Cricklade, Wiltshire, 92 acres [108]
  Permit required away from public rights of way.
Old Winchester Hill, Hants., 151 acres [130]
Pewsey Downs, Wiltshire, 188 acres [120]
Wychwood, Oxfordshire, 647 acres [103]
  Permit required.

South-East Region

The Regional Officer for South-East England,
Nature Conservancy Council,
'Zealds',
Church Street,
Wye, Ashford, Kent TN25 5BW.

Blean Woods, Kent, 164 acres [121]
  Permit required away from paths.
Ham Street Woods, Kent, 240 acres [128]
  Permit required away from paths.
High Halstow, Kent, 130 acres [118]
  Permit required away from paths.
Kingley Vale, West Sussex, 351 acres [131]
  Permit required for Bow Hill.

Lullington Heath, East Sussex, 155 acres [132]
  Permit required away from paths.
Stodmarsh, Kent, 402 acres [122]
  Permit required away from paths.
Swanscombe Skull Site, Kent, 5 acres [119]
  Permit required.
Tring Reservoirs, Herts., 49 acres [104]
  Permit required away from paths.
Wye and Crundale Downs, Kent, 250 acres [127]
  Permit required away from paths and open access area on Broad
  Downs.

South-West Region

The Regional Officer for South-West England,
Nature Conservancy Council,
Roughmoor,
Bishops Hull,
Taunton, Somerset TA1 5AA.

Arne, Dorset, 9 acres [134]
  Permit required.
Avon Gorge, Avon, 156 acres [115]
Axmouth–Lyme Regis Undercliffs, Devon, 793 acres [141]
  Permit required away from paths.
Bovey Valley Woodlands, Devon, 180 acres [137]
  Permit required away from paths.
Braunton Burrows, Devon, 1492 acres [129]
  Unrestricted access on foot.
Bridgwater Bay, Somerset, 6323 acres [125]
  Permit required to visit Stert Island.
Dendles Wood, Devon, 73 acres [139]
  Permit required.
Ebbor Gorge, Somerset, 101 acres [124]
  Permit required away from marked paths.
Hartland Moor, Dorset, 637 acres [136]
  Permit required.
The Lizard, Cornwall, 103 acres [140]
  Permit required.
Morden Bog, Dorset, 367 acres [133]
  Permit required.

Rodney Stoke, Somerset, 86 acres [123]
  Permit required.
Shapwick Heath, Somerset, 546 acres [126]
  Permit required.
Studland Heath, Dorset, 429 acres [135]
Yarner Wood, Devon, 372 acres [138]

West Midland Region

The Regional Officer for the West Midlands,
Nature Conservancy Council,
Attingham Park,
Shrewsbury, Salop SY4 4TW.

Chaddesley Woods, Hereford and Worcester, 252 acres [92]
  Permit required away from public rights of way and concessionary
  paths.
Chartley Moss, Staffordshire, 104 acres [76]
  Permit required.
Derbyshire Dales, Derbyshire, 294 acres [61]
  Permit required.
Rostherne Mere, Cheshire, 377 acres [56]
  Permit required.
Wren's Nest, West Midlands, 74 acres [85]
  Permit required to carry out scientific work and collect specimens.
Wybunbury Moss, Cheshire, 26 acres [65]
  Permit required.

Scotland

Headquarters for Scotland:
12 Hope Terrace,
Edinburgh EH9 2AS.
Tel. 031-447-4784/6.

North-East

The Regional Officer for the North-East,
Nature Conservancy Council,
Caledonia House,
63 Academy Street,
Inverness IV1 1BB.

Cairngorms, Grampian and Highland Regions (Moray, Kincardine and Deeside, Badenoch and Strathspey Districts), 64,118 acres [22]
Access restricted to parts of the Reserve August–October.

Craigellachie, Highland Region (Badenoch and Strathspey District), 642 acres [20]

Dinnet Oakwood, Grampian Region (Kincardine and Deeside District), 33 acres [23]
Permission required to visit.

Haaf Gruney, Shetland Islands, 44 acres [2]

Hermaness, Shetland Islands, 2383 acres [1]

Morrone Birkwoods, Grampian Region (Kincardine and Deeside District), 557 acres [26]
Access by indicated paths only.

Noss, Shetland Islands, 774 acres [5]
Between 1 May and 28 August the National Conservancy Council operates a ferry service to island.

St Cyrus, Grampian Region (Kincardine and Deeside District), 227 acres [27]

Sands of Forvie, Grampian Region (Gordon District), 1774 acres [19]
Permission required to visit parts of the Reserve.

North-West

The Regional Officer for the North-West,
Nature Conservancy Council,
Caledonia House,
63 Academy Street,
Inverness IV1 1BB.

Allt Nan Carnan, Highland Region (Ross and Cromarty District), 18 acres [17]

Beinn Eighe, Highland Region (Ross and Cromarty District), 11,757 acres [16]

Corrieshalloch, Highland Region (Ross and Cromarty District), 13 acres [13]

Glen Roy, Highland Region (Lochaber District), 2887 acres [24]

Gualin, Highland Region (Sutherland District), 6232 acres [7]
Written permits required to visit.

Inchnadamph, Highland Region (Sutherland District), 3200 acres [9]
Permission required to visit the Reserve in late summer and autumn.

Invernaver, Highland Region (Caithness District), 1363 acres [6]

Inverpolly, Highland Region (Ross and Cromarty District), 26,827 acres [10]
  Permission required to visit Drumrunie in late summer and autumn.
Loch Druidibeg, Western Isles Islands Area (South Uist), 4145 acres [18]
  Permission required during the bird breeding season.
Monach Isles, Western Isles Islands Area, 1425 acres [14]
  Permission to land must be obtained from either North Uist Estate, Lochmaddy, Isle of North Uist, or Loch Druidibeg Warden.
Mound Alderwoods, Highland Region (Sutherland District), 659 acres [12]
  Permission required to visit.
North Rona and Sula Sgeir, Western Isles Islands Area, 320 acres [3, 4]
  Permission to land must be obtained from Barvas Estates Ltd., c/o Smiths Gore, Edinburgh, and the Regional Officer informed.
Rassal Ashwood, Highland Region (Ross and Cromarty District), 209 acres [15]
Rhum, Highland Region (Lochaber District), 26,400 acres [21]
  Permission required to visit parts of Reserve away from Loch Scresort area.
St Kilda, Western Isles Islands Area, 2107 acres [11]
  Permission to stay on the island must be obtained from National Trust for Scotland, 5 Charlotte Square, Edinburgh 2.
Strathy Bog, Highland Region (Caithness District), 120 acres [8]
  Road impossible for vehicles.

South-East

The Regional Officer for the South-East,
Nature Conservancy Council,
Headquarters for Scotland,
12 Hope Terrace,
Edinburgh EH9 2AS.

Caenlochan, Tayside Region (Angus, Perth and Kinross, Kincardine and Deeside Districts), 8991 acres [25]
  Permission required to visit the Reserve in late summer and autumn.
Isle of May, Fife Region (North-East Fife District), 140 acres [35]
  No permission required for day visits.
Loch Leven, Tayside Region (Perth and Kinross District), 3946 acres [34]

Access to the Reserve confined to Kirkgate Park, Findatie, Burleigh Sands and Loch Leven Castle.

Meall Nan Tarmachan, Tayside and Central Regions, 1142 acres [30]

Morton Lochs, Fife Region (North-East Fife District), 59 acres [33]
Permits required to visit hides on the Reserve.

Rannoch Moor, Tayside Region (Perth and Kinross District), 3704 acres [28]

Tentsmuir Point, Fife Region (North-East Fife District), 1249 acres [32]
Wheeled transport on the Sands within the Reserve and access to the Abertay Sands are prohibited.

Whitlaw Mosses, Border Region (Ettrick and Lauderdale District), 38 acres [39]
Written permits required to visit.

South-West

The Regional Officer for the South-West,
Nature Conservancy Council,
The Castle,
Loch Lomond Park,
Balloch,
Dunbartonshire.

Ben Lui, Strathclyde Region (Argyll and Bute District); Central Region (Stirling District), 1972 acres [31]
Access to Reserve by permit only.

Caerlaverock, Dumfries and Galloway Region (Nithsdale District), 13,514 acres [44]
Access to part of the Reserve by permit only. Wildfowling by permit only.

Glasdrum Wood, Strathclyde Region (Argyll and Bute District), 42 acres [29]
Permission required to visit.

Glen Diomhan, Strathclyde Region (Cunninghame District), 24 acres [37]

Kirkconnell Flow, Dumfries and Galloway Region (Nithsdale District), 383 acres [43]
Permission to visit should be obtained from the owner.

Loch Lomond, Central and Strathclyde Regions (Stirling and Dumbarton Districts), 624 acres [36]

Access to islands is unrestricted. Permission to visit parts of the mainland and to camp on whole Reserve is required.

Silver Flowe, Dumfries and Galloway Region (Stewarty and Wigtown Districts), 472 acres [41]

Tynron Juniper Wood, Dumfries and Galloway Region (Nithsdale District), 12 acres [40]

Wales

Headquarters for Wales:
Ffordd Penrhos,
Bangor,
Gwynedd LL57 2LQ.
Tel. Bangor (STD 0248) 4001/5.

North Wales

The Regional Officer for North Wales,
Nature Conservancy Council,
Headquarters for Wales,
Penrhos Ffordd,
Bangor,
Gwynedd LL57 2LQ.

Cader Idris, Gwynedd (Meirionnydd), 969 acres [82]

Coed Camlyn, Gwynedd (Meirionnydd), 157 acres [71]
 Permit required.

Coed Cymerau, Gwynedd (Meirionnydd), 65 acres [69]
 Permit required away from rights of way.

Coed Dolgarrog, Gwynedd (Aberconwy), 170 acres [60]
 Permit required away from rights of way.

Coed Ganllwyd, Gwynedd (Meirionnydd), 59 acres [79]

Coed Gorswen, Gwynedd (Aberconwy), 33 acres [59]
 Permit required away from rights of way.

Coed y Rhygen, Gwynedd (Meirionnydd) 68 acres [74]
 Permit required.

Coed Tremadoc, Gwynedd (Dwyfor), 50 acres [70]
 Permit required, and special permit for rock climbing.

Coedydd Maentwrog, Gwynedd (Meirionnydd), 169 acres [68]

Cors Erddreiniog, Gwynedd (Ynys Mon), 78 acres [57]
 Permit required.

Cwm Glas Crafnant, Gwynedd (Aberconwy), 38 acres [63]
  Permit required.
Cwm Idwal, Gwynedd (Aberconwy and Arfon), 984 acres [62]
Morfa Dyffryn, Gwynedd (Meirionnydd), 500 acres [78]
  Permit required away from rights of way.
Morfa Harlech, Gwynedd (Meirionnydd), 1214 acres [73]
  Permit required.
Newborough Warren/Ynys Llanddwyn, Gwynedd (Ynys Mon),
  1565 acres [58]
  Permit required away from rights of way.
Rhinog, Gwynedd (Meirionnydd), 1478 acres [75]
Y Wyddfa–Snowdon, Gwynedd (Dwyfor), 4145 acres [64]

Central Wales

The Regional Officer for Central Wales,
address as for North Wales.
Allt Rhyd y Groes, Dyfed (Dyfed/Powys), 153 acres [99]
  Permit required away from rights of way.
Coed Rheidol, Dyfed (Dyfed/Powys), 107 acres [88]
  Permit required away from rights of way.
Cors Tregaron, Dyfed (Dyfed/Powys), 1898 acres [97]
  Permit required away from rights of way.
Dyfi, Dyfed, Gwynedd and Powys (Dyfed/Powys), 3973 acres [84]
Nant Irfon, Powys (Dyfed/Powys), 336 acres [98]
  Access to permit holders only.

South Wales

The Regional Officer for South Wales,
address as for North Wales.
Craig Cerrig Gleisiad, Powys (Dyfed/Powys), 698 acres [100]
  Landowner's permission required.
Craig y Cilau, Powys (Dyfed/Powys), 157 acres [101]
  Permit required to visit caves.
Cwm Clydach, Gwent (South), 50 acres [102]
Gower Coast, West Glamorgan (South), 116 acres [113]
  Part Statutory Bird Sanctuary.
Oxwich, West Glamorgan (South), 646 acres [114]
  Permit required away from rights of way.
Skomer, Dyfed (Dyfed/Powys), 760 acres [111]
  Access may be restricted to certain parts of the island.
Whiteford, West Glamorgan (South), 1932 acres [112]

Local Nature Reserves

Under Section 21 of the National Parks and Access to the Countryside Act 1949, various levels of local authority were empowered to establish local nature reserves. The response to such enabling powers has varied immensely. Some authorities have taken the opportunity to create several reserves covering hundreds of acres, others have done nothing at all – there are, for instance, only two local nature reserves in the whole of Scotland, although parts of England are just as badly served. A list follows:

England

Berry Head, Brixham, Devon; Torbay BC; 107 acres.
Breydon Water, Norfolk and Suffolk; Norfolk CC, Suffolk CC and Great Yarmouth BC; 1120 acres.
Brocton, Staffordshire; Staffordshire CC; 120 acres.
Castle Eden Denes, Durham; Durham CC; 517 acres.
Chobham Common, Surrey; Surrey CC; 368 acres.
Cooper's Hill, Cranham, Gloucestershire; Gloucestershire CC; 140 acres.
Drigg Dunes and Gullery, Ravenglass, Cumbria; Cumbria CC; 946 acres.
Fairburn Ings, North Yorkshire; North Yorkshire CC; 618 acres.
Farlington Marshes, Portsmouth, Hampshire; Portsmouth BC; 294 acres.
Farndale, North Yorkshire and West Yorkshire; West Yorkshire CC; 2500 acres.
Gibraltar Point, Lincolnshire; Lincolnshire CC; 1000 acres.
Hackhurst Downs, Gomshall, Surrey; Surrey CC; 73 acres.
Hilfield Park Reservoir, Elstree, Hertfordshire; Hertfordshire CC; 195 acres.
Hothfield Common, Kent; Ashford BC; 143 acres.
Lytham St Annes, Lancashire; Fylde BC; 38 acres.
Newton Marshes, Isle of Wight; Isle of Wight CC; 300 acres.

Nore Hill Chalk Pinnacle, Worms Heath, Chelsham, Surrey; Surrey CC; $\frac{1}{3}$ acre.
North Common, Chailey, East Sussex; East Sussex CC; 429 acres.
Pagham Harbour, West Sussex; West Sussex CC; 1100 acres.
Parndon Wood, Harlow, Essex; Harlow DC; 52 acres.
Perivale Wood, London; London Borough of Ealing; 27 acres.
Queendown Warren, Kent; Swale DC; 18 acres.
Red Hill, Goulceby, Lincolnshire; Lincolnshire CC; 9 acres.
Ruislip, London; London Borough of Hillingdon; 11 acres.
Rye Harbour, East Sussex; East Sussex CC; 244 acres.
Sandal Beat, Doncaster, South Yorkshire; Doncaster BC; 170 acres.
Screech Owl, Bridgwater, Somerset; Somerset CC; 29 acres.
Seaford Head, East Sussex; East Sussex CC; 76 acres.
Snipe Dales, near Winceby, Lincolnshire; Lincolnshire CC; 124 acres.
South Bank of the Swale, Kent; Kent CC; 1038 acres.
Staffhurst Wood, Limpsfield, Surrey; Surrey CC; 93 acres.
Stanpit Marsh, Christchurch, Dorset; Dorset CC; 145 acres.
Street Heath, Somerset; Somerset CC; 21 acres.
Sugar Loaf Hill and Saltern Cove, Goodrington, Devon; Torbay BC; 39 acres.
Temple Ewell Downs, Kent; Dover DC; 53 acres.
Thatcham Reed Beds, Berkshire; Newbury DC; 35 acres.
Therfield Heath, Hertfordshire; Hertfordshire CC; 417 acres.
Titchfield Haven, Fareham, Hampshire; Hampshire CC; 211 acres.
Totternhoe Knolls, Bedfordshire; Bedfordshire CC; 32 acres.
Ufton Fields, Warwickshire; Warwickshire CC; 79 acres.

Scotland

Aberlady Bay, Lothian Region; East Lothian DC; 1439 acres.
Castle and Hightae Lochs, Lochmaben, Dumfries and Galloway Region; Dumfries and Galloway Regional Council; 339 acres.

Wales

Cleddon Bog, Gwent; Gwent CC; 37 acres.
Cliff Wood, Barry, South Glamorgan; Vale of Glamorgan BC; 12 acres.

The Forestry Commission

The Forestry Commission owns large areas of the countryside which, under government pressure, it has increasingly opened up to public use and recreation. This does not mean that the public have the right to enter all forests or that they can do what they will in those that are opened. However the Commission is aware of its duties and is taking a more active role in providing information not only about its work but also about the nature of the areas under its care. Information centres and nature trails are the most obvious outward signs, but in many of its forests the Commission has opened up the forest drives and paths for those who care to explore for themselves. Several of the larger and more obvious areas controlled by the Forestry Commission are detailed in this book. The New Forest is, for example, justifiably famous as both a recreation centre and a haunt of wildlife.

With forests at various stages of growth spread throughout the length and breadth of the land, there are few who are not well placed to visit one or more of the Commission's lands. In some parts it has created Forest Parks, large areas where among its various woodlands the Commission has established camp sites, picnic places and forest trails and walks. It has offices, study centres and sometimes even a shop. All of its forests are summarized in its publication *Guide Map to Your Forests*, a full and cheap source of information to those who would explore the woodlands of Britain. Each forest is marked and symbols show the kinds of facilities provided. It is staggering just how much of Britain has been opened up to the people in a span of just ten years.

While the map is the key to exploring the Commission's lands, it also publishes guides to major individual forests and to several important ecological aspects of forestry in its relationship with the wild creatures that live there, and a good series of tree identification guides.

All publications are available from The Forestry Commission, 231 Corstorphine Road, Edinburgh EH12 7AT, or from local offices and information centres.

Field Studies Council

The FSC exists to promote a better understanding of our environment and the way we use it. It runs nine residential centres in England and Wales and a day centre in Epping Forest. Residential centres provide accommodation for up to sixty visitors in single, twin and dormitory rooms. Each centre is strategically sited to provide ample opportunities for field research and each is staffed by a warden, a director of studies and teaching staff. Visitors, whether groups or individuals, are free to follow a centre course or pursue their own interest as they will. Facilities for advanced work up to university level are provided, including lecture theatres, laboratories, maps and reference books. Among a wide range of one-week courses are plant and animal ecology, geography, geology, environmental studies, field teaching methods, conservation, land use, meteorology, archaeology, birds, photography and art.

Glancing through the season's programmes there are courses as varied as Ecology of Seabirds, Underwater Photography, Plant Drawing and Painting, Nature Photography, History in the Hedgerow, Insects, Old Buildings, Summer Scenery, Freshwater Algae, Ecology of Bogs and Fens, Flies, Midges and Gnats, Bird Identification, Lichens, Mountain Weather, Spiders of South Devon, and Butterflies and Moths.

Recognizing that not all of us wish to return to sixth form (or even third form) level, the Council organizes many courses specifically for adults. Many of these are for complete beginners, so that those just starting a hobby do not have to look silly by being shown the way by a load of know-all kids.

The Field Centres are:

1 Dale Fort Field Centre, Haverfordwest, Dyfed; Tel. Dale 205. Dale lies on the old Pembrokeshire coast on a narrow peninsula at the mouth of Milford Haven. It boasts a good list of little-known plants and the cliffs are of great interest in May and June. It is very handy for the bird islands that lie offshore and is particularly strong on marine biology.

FIELD CENTRES

0   150
kms

● Malham Tarn

● Drapers

● Preston Montford

Flatford Mill ●

Dale Fort ●
● Orielton

Epping Forest ●
Juniper Hall ●

● Leonard Wills

● Slapton Ley

2 The Drapers Field Centre, Rhyd-y-crenau, Betws-y-coed, Gwynedd; Tel. Betws-y-coed (069-02) 494. The Field Centre is situated in the Conway Valley and is more or less placed over the fault between pre- and post-Silurian rocks. In fact a wide range of geological formations are within easy reach, providing excellent opportunities for study. The effects of glaciation are easy to see and the long history of human occupancy provides further opportunities. Botany and birds are interesting and varied.

3 Flatford Mill Field Centre, East Bergholt, Colchester, Essex

CO7 6UL; Tel. East Bergholt (0206-29) 283. Flatford is perhaps the most attractive of all the field centres in a physical sense – a mellow old watermill and mill house at the head of the Stour estuary in the heart of Constable country. The Stour runs under, through and around Flatford and provides excellent opportunities for aquatic biology both marine and freshwater. The surrounding landscape of east Suffolk is immensely varied and rich.

4 Juniper Hall Field Centre, Dorking, Surrey RH5 6DA; Tel. Dorking (0306) 3849. Situated in an old mansion on the chalk escarpment of the North Downs overlooking the Mole Gap, Juniper Hall offers a large range of geological phenomena. The corresponding land use is so dependent on the underlying structure that the Centre is well used by geography classes from nearby London. The association with chalk and its rich flora of orchids and other open ground flowers dominates the non-geological interest.

5 The Leonard Wills Field Centre, Nettlecombe Court, Williton, Taunton, Somerset; Tel Washford (098-44) 320. A house has stood here since the thirteenth century and the Field Centre is only the last in a line of conversions and alterations to this charming old mansion. It lies in the Nettlecombe Valley, which joins the Vale of Stogumber in separating the Quantock from the Brendon Hills. Visitors dine in the Great Hall – with a log fire in winter. The unspoilt character of the landscape and the nearness of the Brendon Hills and Exmoor make the Centre an excellent site for studying a wide variety of disciplines. Facilities exist for the pursuit of almost every branch of field study, from marine and freshwater biology to human and economic geography.

6 Malham Tarn Field Centre, Settle, Yorkshire BD24 9PU; Tel. Airton (072-93) 331. Malham lies near Malham Tarn at an altitude of 1230 feet on a Carboniferous Limestone plateau in the Pennines. Nearby are the famous Malham Cove and Gordale Scar, the Three Peaks and the varied geology of the Pennines. The 'karst' limestone scenery is unique and the botanical interest rich and diverse. There are a few moorland birds, including numerous curlew, and a long history of human settlement to be investigated.

7 Orielton Field Centre, Pembroke, Dyfed; Tel. Castlemartin 225. Orielton lies on a peninsula between the gentle mud flats of Milford Haven and the harsh waves of the open Atlantic. Its geology is interesting, showing accordant drainage and inverted relief, and both coast-lines show both submergence and emergence. Geologically this is classic ground, but there are woods and grasslands, salt marshes and

mud flats, rocks and limestone cliffs all providing a wealth of botanical interest. Nearby the Prescelly Hills are where the bluestones of Stonehenge originated.

8   Preston Montford Field Centre, Montford Bridge, Shrewsbury SY4 1DX; Tel. Montford Bridge (0743-71) 380. This Field Centre overlooks the River Severn some four miles west of Shrewsbury and is situated among one of the classic grounds of British geology. The highly varied landscape is based on an underlying structure of igneous and volcanic rocks, grits, shales and limestone. The Stiperstones area has old lead mines, and an excellent view can be had from the Long Mynd. Ancient remains litter the landscape and at Coalbrookdale there are numerous monuments to the early industrial revolution, including the iron bridge at Ironbridge.

9   Slapton Ley Field Centre, Slapton, Kingsbridge, Devon TQ 7 2QP Tel. Torcross (054-858) 466. The Field Centre is housed in a charming and rambling old farmhouse at the eastern end of Slapton village. The 'Ley' is a beach-enclosed lagoon with a rich growth of reeds about 2½ miles in length. The Field Studies Council leases a 460-acre nature reserve which includes the Ley as well as two large areas of deciduous woodland. Outstanding are wild otters (as well as foxes and badgers) and there is a rich avifauna. Bird-watchers search for the rare aquatic warbler in late summer – this is almost its only regular haunt in Britain. The shingle beach is interesting for succession of coastal plants.

10   Epping Forest Conservation Centre, High Beech, Loughton, Essex; Tel. 01-508-7714. Situated on the edge of one of the largest open spaces left near London, and with the varied geology of Epping Forest, this Field Centre is a magnet to the children and educationalists of North London. Once the Royal Forest of Essex, Epping has been a public open space since 1878 under the care of the City of London. Over four hundred cattle still graze the Forest, though this is the only right of common that is still maintained. There are fallow deer and a rich avifauna that includes very reliable hawfinches. The Centre has a permanent Conservation Exhibition catering for the casual visitor.

The Field Studies Council is a registered charity dependent on membership, donations and fees charged for the courses it organizes. It welcomes members. Write to 9 Devereux Court, Strand, London WC2R 3JR; Tel. 01-583-7471.

Royal Society for the Protection of Birds

The Royal Society for the Protection of Birds (RSPB) is one of the fastest-growing conservation bodies in Britain. It is supported entirely by its members' subscriptions, by appeals and by the sale of bird-based knickknacks of which Christmas cards are probably the most significant item. From its headquarters in Bedfordshire it administers a series of regional offices, a continually growing number of nature reserves and a nationwide organization of members' groups. From its tiny, somewhat amateurish beginnings the RSPB has become a fully professional conservation body with a progressive policy towards conservation. If it has a major fault it is that it is solely concerned with birds, and 'British' birds at that.

Most of its reserves are open to visitors by a permit system. These are usually booked in advance and are considerably cheaper to members. In fact if you wish to visit an RSPB reserve or two, it quickly becomes cheaper to join the Society and gain the advantages of smaller entrance fees. The Society issues a quarterly magazine, *Birds*, which is an excellent production full of pictures, news and interesting articles on birds and the places they live. It is not on public sale, but comes free to members. The local organizations, with which new members are put in touch, run regular meetings, film shows and outings in search of birds.

The reserves owned or run by the Society grow in number year by year. The name of many reserves is followed by a map reference to the appropriate 1:50,000 Ordnance Survey sheet and grid reference, the size in acres and the address from which permits can be obtained. In all cases it is a good idea to write in advance to the RSPB for their current *Reserves Visiting* leaflet, stating whether or not you are a member.

National Headquarters:
The Royal Society for the
  Protection of Birds,
The Lodge,
Sandy,
Bedfordshire SG19 2DL.
Tel. 0767 80551.

Scottish Office:
17 Regent Terrace,
Edinburgh EH7 5BN.
Tel. 031-556 5624.

Wales Office:
18 High Street,
Newtown,
Powys SY16 1AA.
Tel. Newtown 26678.

North of England Office:
'A' Floor,
Milburn House,
Newcastle-upon Tyne NE1 1LE.
Tel. 0632 24148.

South-East England Office:
Abinger House,
Abinger Road,
Portslade-by-Sea,
Brighton,
Sussex.
Tel. 0273 410200.

South-West England Office:
42 St David's Hill,
Exeter,
Devon.
Tel. 0392 32691.

RSPB Reserves as at 1977

Numbers in square brackets refer to the map on p. 55.

England

Arne, Dorset: SY/972875. 739 acres. Permit from Warden, Syldata, Arne, Wareham BH20 5BJ. [1]

Barfold Copse, Surrey: SU/920318. 13 acres. Details from Reserves Dept, The Lodge. [2]

Bempton Cliffs, North Yorkshire: TA/197741. 60 acres. Access all times via public footpath. [3]

Blacktoft Sands, Humberside: SE/843232. 460 acres. Access at all times via public footpath along sea wall, starts opposite Ousefleet Primary School. More details from Warden, Hillcrest, Whitgift, Nr Goole. [4]

Chapel Wood, Devon: SS/483413. 14 acres. Free permit, all year, from Warden, Sherracombe, Raleigh Park, Barnstaple, EX31 4JD. [5]

Church Wood, Buckinghamshire: SU/973873. 34 acres. Open all year, no permits required. [6]

Coombes Valley, Staffordshire: SK/005530. 261 acres. No permits but

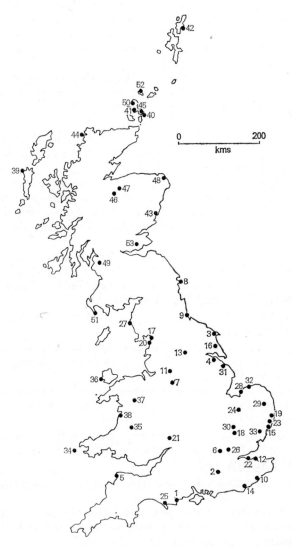

ROYAL SOCIETY FOR THE PROTECTION OF BIRDS RESERVES

report Information Centre on arrival. Large parties write in advance to Warden, Six Oaks Farm, Bradnop, Leek, ST13 7EU. [7]

Coquet Island, Northumberland: NU/294047. 16 acres. No visiting. [8]

Cowpen Marsh, Cleveland: NZ/507250. 160 acres. Details from Reserves Dept, The Lodge. [9]

Dungeness, Kent: TR/063196. 1193 acres. All year, Sat., Wed. No permit. Report to reception centre 10.30 to 17.00 hrs. Parties by prior arrangement with Warden, Boulderwall Farmhouse, Dungeness Road, Lydd TN29 9PN. [10]

Eastwood, Cheshire: SJ/972977. 12 acres. No permit but write in advance to Warden, 12 Fir Tree Crescent, Dukinfield, Cheshire, SK16 5EH, for more details. [11]

Elmley, Kent: TQ /938679. 3300 acres. Sat. and Wed. only, 1 Apr. to 31 Aug. Assemble Kingshill Farm 10.00 hours. Any queries, write to Warden, Kingshill Farm, Elmley, Sheerness, Isle of Sheppey, Kent ME12 3RW, or phone Sheerness 5969 before 18.00 hrs. [12]

Fairburn Ings, West Yorkshire: SE/549275. 620 acres. Access at all times to part of reserve with Public Hides. Coach parties by prior arrangement with Warden, Fairburn Ings Reserve, Caudle Hill, Fairburn, Knottingley, West Yorkshire. [13]

Fore Wood, East Sussex: TQ /753128. 135 acres. Open all year, no permit required. [14]

Havergate Island, Suffolk: TM/425496. 267 acres. Permit and further information from Permit Secretary, 30 Mundays Lane, Orford, Woodbridge IP12 2LX. [15]

Hornsea Mere, Humberside: TA/188471. 580 acres. Escorted only. Apply to Warden, The Bungalow, The Mere, Hornsea, North Humberside. [16]

Leighton Moss, Lancashire: SD/478751. 321 acres. Permit and further information from Warden, Myers Farmhouse, Silverdale, Carnforth, LA5 oSW. [17]

The Lodge, Bedfordshire: TL/188478. 104 acres. No permit required. [18]

Minsmere, Suffolk: TM/473672. 1350 acres. Permit from Permit Secretary, Minsmere Reserve, Westleton, Saxmundham IP17 3BY – specify a.m. or p.m. [19]

Morecambe Bay, Lancashire: SD/460700. 6000 acres. No formal visiting yet, but good views at Hest Bank at high tide. [20]

Nagshead, Gloucestershire: SO/608090. 378 acres. Access via way-marked path, always open, across part of reserve. Inquiries to Warden, c/o Post Office, Parkend, Lydney, Glos. [21]

Northward Hill, Kent: TQ /784761. 130 acres. Open daily all year, access from Northwood Avenue, High Halstow. Further details from Warden, Swigshole Cottage, High Halstow, Rochester ME3 8SR. [22]

North Warren, Suffolk: TM/455587. 220 acres. Open all year. Access strictly limited to public footpaths. [23]

Ouse Washes, Cambridgeshire: TL/478871. 1714 acres. No permit. Parties of ten or more advise Warden, Limosa, Welches Dam, Manea, PE15 oND of date and time of arrival. [24]

Radipole Lake, Dorset: SY/676796. 192 acres. Open daily all year. [25]

Rye House Marsh, Hertfordshire: TL/386100. 18 acres. No permit. For further information apply Warden, 32 Caxton Road, Hoddesdon EN11 9PG. [26]

St Bees Head, Cumbria: NX/959118. 55 acres. Access at all times via public footpath from St Bees Village. [27]

Snettisham, Norfolk: TF/648333. 3250 acres. No permit. Access along beach overlooking reserve. Large parties by prior arrangement with Warden, School House, Wolferton, King's Lynn PE31 6HD. [28]

Strumpshaw Fen, Norfolk: TG/342063. 438 acres. Visiting only by prior arrangement with Warden, Staithe Cottage, Strumpshaw, Norwich, Norfolk. [29]

Sutton Fen, Bedfordshire: TL/212478. 91 acres. Visits for educational purposes by arrangement with the Warden at The Lodge. [30]

Tetney Marshes, Lincolnshire: TA/360037. 2900 acres. No visiting at present – details to be announced in due course. [31]

Titchwell, Norfolk: TF/757437. 420 acres. No permit. Access only from east sea wall from A149 between Titchwell/Brancaster or west sea wall from A149 between Thornham/Titchwell. [32]

Wolves Wood, Suffolk: TM/155440. 92 acres. Open all year. [33]

Wales

Grassholm, Dyfed: SM/599093. 23 acres. Inquiries to Wales Office, 18 High Street, Newtown, Powys SY16 1AA. [34]

Gwenffrwd and Dinas, Dyfed: SN/749460. 1366 acres. No permit. Report to Warden's House, Troedrhiwgelynen, Rhandrimwyn. [35]

South Stack Cliffs, Gwynedd: SH/205823. 780 acres. Access via public footpath [36]

57

Lake Vyrnwy, Powys: SH/985215. 16,000 acres. No regular facilities as yet, but some access via public footpaths. [37]

Ynys-hir, Gwynedd: SN/683963. 630 acres. Permit at least two weeks in advance from Wales Office. [38]

Scotland

Balranald, North Uist: NF/707707. 1625 acres. No permit required. [39]

Copinsay, Orkney: HY/610010. 375 acres. Access unrestricted. Day trips by boat crossing from Newark Bay, contact boatman (Tel. Deerness 245). [40]

Dale of Cottasgarth, Orkney: HY/370195. 2713 acres. Access unrestricted. [41]

Fetlar, Shetland: HU/603917. 1694 acres. For information contact Warden at Bealance on arrival. [42]

Fowlsheugh, Kincardineshire: NO/880798. No permit. [43]

Handa, Sutherland: NC/130480. 766 acres. No permit. Day visits via local boatman from Tarbet. [44]

Hobbister, Orkney: HY/381067. 1875 acres. Access unrestricted. [45]

Insh Marshes, Speyside: NH/775998. 1150 acres. No permit. Report to reception on arrival. Large parties by prior arrangement with Warden, Ivy Cottage, Insh, by Kingussie, Inverness-shire. [46]

Loch Garten, Speyside: HN/977185. 1517 acres. Open in season, no permit required. Observation hide and visitor centre. [47]

Loch of Strathbeg, Aberdeenshire: NK/073590. 2300 acres. Permit must be obtained in advance from Warden, The Lythe, Crimonmogate, Nr Fraserburgh, Aberdeenshire. [48]

Lochwinnoch, Renfrewshire: NS/355583. 388 acres. Details from Warden, The Barony, Kirkland Road, Kilbirnie, Ayrshire. [49]

Marwick Head, Orkney: HY/228245. 40 acres. Access at all times by path northward from Marwick Bay. [50]

Mull of Galloway, Wigtownshire: NX/157305. 40 acres. Access unrestricted. [51]

Noup Head, Westray, Orkney: HY/392500. 35 acres. Access at all times from road to Noup Head lighthouse. [52]

Vane Farm, Kinross: NT/160993. 458 acres. No permit, visitor centre. Further information from Warden, Vane Farm, Kinross. [53]

* The RSPB has acquired 5000 acres of the Dee Estuary as we go to press.

Wildfowl Trust

Established as the Severn Wildfowl Trust by Peter Scott in 1946, the Wildfowl Trust is dedicated to the study and conservation of wildfowl. To this end it has established the most comprehensive collection of wildfowl in the world and opened a number of refuges where wild birds can be seen. Each is dealt with individually, but for convenience all are listed here.

Arundel. The most recent wildfowl refuge, covering 55 acres just north of Arundel. Tel. Arundel 883355.

Caerlaverock. An exciting refuge on the Solway Firth seven miles from Dumfries. Tel. Glencaple 200.

Martin Mere. One of the most exciting conservation projects in the North-West, only five miles from Southport. Tel. Burscough 895181.

Peakirk. These beautiful gardens are a charming combination of woodland and water, blending to form an intimate and peaceful haven five miles from Peterborough. Tel. Peterborough 252271.

Slimbridge. The world's largest and most varied collection of wildfowl, and headquarters of the Wildfowl Trust. Tel. Cambridge (Glos.) 333.

Washington. A new centre covering 103 delightfully landscaped acres on the north bank of the River Wear three miles from Sunderland. Tel. Washington 465454.

Welney. The Welney Refuge occupies 700 acres on the famous Ouse Washes, which constitute one of the most important areas for wildfowl in Europe. Tel. Ely 860711.

Scottish Wildlife Trust

The Scottish Wildlife Trust is the national body concerned with the conservation of all forms of wildlife in Scotland – there is no equivalent body in other parts of Britain. By purchase, lease or agreement the Trust has established thirty-five nature reserves of which six are open to the general public. It is a voluntary charitable organization with a membership of 7000 and a go-ahead policy towards education and publicity. Though some 30,000 visitors a year flock to the hides at Loch of Lowes where ospreys can be seen, the Trust makes no charge at this site. The aim is to persuade visitors to become members, and very successful it is too.

As elsewhere, it is advisable before visiting any reserve to inquire from the Trust's headquarters:

The Scottish Wildlife Trust,
8 Dublin Street,
Edinburgh EH1 3PP.

Reserves as at 1977

Enterkine Wood, Ayrshire. 12 acres. Mixed woodland; nature trail and badgers.

Hare and Dunhog Mosses, Selkirkshire. 10 acres. Two small mosses and pools.

Duns Castle, Berwickshire. 190 acres. Mature woodland, loch and marsh.

Gordons Moss, Berwickshire. 101 acres. Peat bog and birchwood.

Ardmore, Dunbartonshire. 479 acres. Promontory with extensive mudflats and foreshore on north bank of the Clyde.

Doire Donn, Argyll. 70 acres. Oakwood on Lock Linnhe.

Ballagan Glen, Stirlingshire. 12 acres. Sedimentary rock exposure, ashwood and gorge.

Bankhead Moss, Fife. 9·5 acres. Raised bog, heather, birch and pine.

Fontainbleu and Ladypark, Dumfries. 14 acres. Birchwood and wetlands; willow tits.

Pepper Wood, Kirkliston, West Lothian. 2·8 acres. Small deciduous wood with rare flowering plants.

East Lammermuir Deans, East Lothian. 55 acres. Wooded gorges in the Lammermuir Hills.

Yetholm Loch, Roxburghshire. 65 acres. Loch, wildfowl and interesting marsh plants.

Corehouse, Lanarkshire. 65 acres. Woodland by 'Falls of Clyde'; rocky gorge.

Bemersyde Moss, Berwickshire. 67 acres. Flooded hollow with marshland in the Border hills.

Loch of Lowes, Perthshire. 242 acres. Open to the public. Loch and wooded fringe; varied habitats; water birds and ospreys; hide and visitor centre.

Ballantrae, Ayrshire. 55 acres. Open to the public. NX 080820. Shingle bank with nesting terns at mouth of River Stinchar.

Loch Fleet, Sutherland. 1750 acres. Large tidal basin, dune grassland and pinewoods with seabirds, seals and rare plants.

Keltneyburn, Perthshire. 77·5 acres. Wooded burn; rough meadow with orchids.

Knowetop Lochs, Kirkcudbrightshire. 68 acres. Acid moorland with small lochs.

Eilean na Creige Duibhe, Wester Ross. 2·8 acres. Open to the public. NG 824335. Wooded island with a heronry.

Loch of Craiglush, Perthshire. 88 acres. Adjoining Loch of Lowes, with nesting ospreys.

Bawsinch-Duddingston, Edinburgh. 15 acres. Addition to Duddingston Loch Bird Sanctuary.

Hoselaw Loch and Din Moss, Roxburghshire. 50 acres. Wildfowl (particularly winter); bog plants.

Flanders Moss, Perthshire. 110 acres. Raised valley bog, close to River Forth.

Aberfoyle Bat Reserve, Perthshire. Hibernating bats in mine tunnel now sealed with grille.

Talich, Easter Ross. 33 acres. Alder wood and wet grassland with orchids.

Carradale, Argyll. 173 acres. Open to the public. NR 817372. Coastal grassland and low cliffs; wild goats.

Loch Libo, Renfrewshire. 44 acres. Nutrient-rich loch; water plants; woodland; birds.

Farigaig, Inverness-shire. 12 acres. Mixed scrub woodland near to Loch Ness.

Loch of Lintrathen, Angus. 400 acres. Wintering wildfowl on reservoir; hide available special open days.

Glen Muick and Lochnagar, Aberdeenshire. 6350 acres. Open to the public. NO 250850. Mountain habitats and wildlife: part of Balmoral Estate: red deer.

Drummains Reed Bed, Kirkcudbrightshire. 13·7 acres. Reed bed and meres on Solway; wildfowl and waders.

Rhunahaorine Point, Kintyre. 698 acres. Winter feeding ground for geese; coastal birds in summer.

Seaton Cliffs, Arbroath. Open to the public. NO 667416.

Red Deer

British Tourist Authority

The British Tourist Authority publishes and distributes information and guidance covering the whole range of leisure activities from its headquarters at:

Tourist Information Centre,
64 St James's Street,
London SW1A 1NF.
Tel. 01-629-9191.

Though designed for holidaymakers and travellers, some of the BTA's material is of considerable use to even the most dedicated of countryside enthusiasts. An up-to-date list of publications (prices are usually nominal) can be obtained from the authority. Recommended are:

Nature Trails: a list with information, access, etc., of many of the trails now open throughout Britain, treated region by region. Ideal for planning a holiday as well as a day in the country.
Activity Holidays: covers many outdoor pursuits mostly of the sporting type, but a little nature walking creeps in here and there.
Pony-Trekking and Riding: a useful guide for those who prefer to explore the countryside in style.

The Country Code

The Country Code was created to help reduce or prevent the un-intentional damage that occurs every year, particularly at public holidays. Too many visitors to the countryside are unfamiliar with its ways. They forget that a single careless act – a gate left open, a fence or hedge weakened, a dropped cigarette end – can mean a lot of extra work and expense for farmers, foresters and other country folk.

The Code is a series of ten reminders based on common sense – and common failings. So when in the country remember:

Guard against all risk of fire. Plantations, woodlands and heaths are highly inflammable: every year acres burn because of casually dropped matches, cigarette ends or pipe ash.

Fasten all gates. Even if you found them open. Animals can't be told to stay where they're put. A gate left open invites them to wander, a danger to themselves, to crops and to traffic.

Keep dogs under proper control. Farmers have good reason to regard visiting dogs as pests; in the country a civilized town dog can become a savage. Keep your dog on a lead wherever there is livestock about, also on country roads.

Keep to the paths across farmland. Crops can be ruined by people's feet. Remember that grass is a valuable crop too, sometimes the only one on the farm. Flattened corn or hay is very difficult to harvest.

Avoid damaging fences, hedges and walls. They are expensive items in the farm's economy; repairs are costly and use scarce labour. Keep to the recognized routes, using gates and stiles.

Leave no litter. All litter is unsightly, and some is dangerous as well. Take litter home for disposal; in the country it costs a lot to collect it.

Safeguard water supplies. Your chosen walk may well cross a catchment area for the water supply of millions. Avoid polluting it in any way. Never interfere with cattle troughs.

Protect wildlife, wild plants and trees. Wildlife is best observed, not collected. To pick or uproot flowers, carve trees and rocks or disturb wild animals and birds destroys other people's pleasure as well.

Go carefully on country roads. Country roads have special dangers: blind corners, high banks and hedges, slow-moving tractors and farm machinery or animals. Motorists should reduce their speed and take extra care; walkers should keep to the right, facing oncoming traffic.

Respect the life of the countryside. Set a good example and try to fit in with the life and work of the countryside. This way good relations are preserved, and those who follow are not regarded as enemies.

Cross bill

C

Part Two

REGIONS OF GREAT BRITAIN

0   200

kms

Highlands
and Islands

South
Scotland

North-East

North-
West

East
Midlands

Wales

Heart of
England

East Anglia

Thames

West Country

London and
South-East

West Country

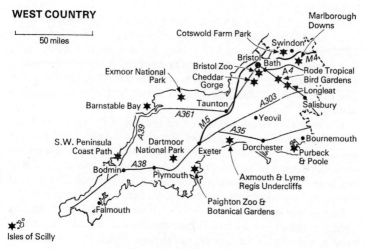

WEST COUNTRY

50 miles

Marlborough Downs
Cotswold Farm Park
Swindon
Bristol
Bath
M4
Bristol Zoo
Exmoor National Park
Cheddar Gorge
A4
Rode Tropical Bird Gardens
Longleat
Salisbury
Barnstable Bay
Taunton
A361
Yeovil
A303
M5
A35
S.W. Peninsula Coast Path
Dartmoor National Park
Exeter
Dorchester
Bournemouth
Purbeck & Poole
Bodmin
A38
Plymouth
Axmouth & Lyme Regis Undercliffs
Falmouth
Paighton Zoo & Botanical Gardens
Isles of Scilly

★ *localities mentioned in text*

Axmouth to Lyme Regis Undercliffs

Extending for five miles from Lyme Regis westward to the mouth of the River Axe, this landslip area has created one of the most magnificent stretches of coastal scenery to be found in Britain. It was established as a National Nature Reserve in 1958, and covers 800 acres.

The upper cliffs consist of chalk and these overlay greensand. Both are permeable. But below them lies an impermeable layer of gault clay. It is the action of water seeping through the top layers and running off over the clay that creates the small landslips that occur every year. The whole rests on the older beds of the Jurassic and Triassic periods, which consist of marls, clays and limestones. The exposed beds are all rich in fossils, and it is these glimpses into prehistory that are responsible for the importance of the cliffs.

The most impressive of all modern landslips occurred on Christmas Eve 1839 when twenty acres of land slid toward the sea between Bindon and Dowlands. A chasm opened separating the so-called Goat Island from its original position. Though the most famous fossil to emerge from the Undercliffs is a 25-foot-long ichthyosaur found in 1809, the

69

most common fossils are molluscs, especially large ammonites and nautiloids. As in other NNRs, collecting without a permit is strictly forbidden.

The Reserve is not open to the public and access is confined to the beach and to the rough and slippery public footpath that leads all the way from Underhill Farm just outside Lyme Regis to Bindon Cliffs. Unfortunately there are no intermediate escape routes, so the visitor is committed to retracing his steps or walking the full tiring five miles. The route is often difficult to find, but the authorities have done their best to mark it.

The natural woodland is interesting because of its regenerative and colonizing qualities, and includes the only naturally developed ash wood to colonize virgin soil over the last half century. Flowers are good in places, and wall-pepper, Carline thistle, rockrose, birdsfoot trefoil and creeping fescue quickly colonize fresh soil. Other good species include bog pimpernel and fen orchid in the damper areas.

Though 120 species of birds have been recorded, this total includes passing seabirds and waders. Those species that actually depend in some way on the Undercliffs are rather fewer. They include buzzard, sparrowhawk and kestrel, as well as woodpeckers, nightingale, stonechat and jackdaw, herring gull and possibly pure rock doves. Badgers are common and roe deer elusive.

Visiting: by the beach or public footpath out of Lyme Regis. Make a day of it; but do not dig.

Botany: wild madder, everlasting pea, dog's mercury, wood spurge, yellow archangel, slender false-brome, giant horsetail, water-mint, purple loosestrife, fen orchid, bog pimpernel, wall-pepper, Carline thistle, rockrose, birdsfoot trefoil, creeping fescue.

Birds: buzzard, sparrowhawk, kestrel, herring gull, stock dove, green woodpecker, great spotted woodpecker, long-tailed tit, treecreeper, stonechat, blackcap, lesser whitethroat, chiffchaff, willow warbler, nightingale, goldcrest, rock pipit, jackdaw, carrion crow.

Barnstaple Bay

Only a few minutes' drive south from the teeming holiday resorts of Ilfracombe and the north Devon coast lies an area of wilderness that is an oasis of life away from the beach and surf. The twin rivers Torridge and Taw form a joint estuary at the head of the Bay enclosed to the north by the massive dunes of Braunton Burrows. The old

towns of Barnstaple and Bideford lie nearby and there are views westward to the monolithic shape of Lundy, Isle of Puffins. The estuaries
are not easy to work, but those who wish to see waders and wildfowl
are seldom disappointed with the views from Appledore in the south.
A small flock of white-fronted geese has established a home here and
they, along with other wildfowl, sometimes flight to the Braunton
Burrows for retreat.

The Burrows are a National Nature Reserve sublet from the Ministry
of Defence. Sometimes military training takes place, and access is not
allowed while red flags proclaim their warning. However at the
southern point (Crow Point) there is a car park and excellent views
over the estuary. The dune system here is one of the most extensive
in the country and botanists will enjoy searching out the colonizing
glasswort and sea samphire as well as creeping willow in the slacks.
Unfortunately the delicate balance of the dunes is easily upset, and
visitors must confine themselves to the boardwalks that funnel them
to the beach. Here they can see wigeon, shelduck, turnstone, black-
tailed godwit and the scuttling sanderling, depending on season.

Visiting: free access at Braunton Burrows (but beware of red flags)
and at Appledore.
Birds: shelduck, wigeon, white-fronted goose, redshank, dunlin,
sanderling, whimbrel, black-tailed godwit, common tern.
Botany: dune colonizers.

Bristol Zoo

Though covering only twelve acres, Bristol Zoo has earned itself a high
place in zoo rankings. It is a charming spot, with well laid out gardens
and a number of notable tree specimens surrounding a lake. Its park-
like tranquillity is broken only by the calls of birds and other exotic
animals, a complete contrast to the bustling city of Bristol that surrounds it. The Zoo exhibits a fine range of species from all parts of the
world, and has achieved a considerable degree of fame in its path-
finding efforts to breed from stock. Whereas almost anyone can breed
lions – so much so that the surplus lion population in the country is
something of an embarrassment – many other species prove much
more difficult. As one of today's main justifications for the existence of
zoos at all is to provide a breeding basis to support the wild stock of
endangered animals, the efforts of institutions like Bristol are to be
encouraged. Way back in 1934 Bristol bred the first chimpanzee in

captivity in Europe. This was followed by the first lowland gorilla born in Britain in 1971, and the first successful rearing later the same year. There are now breeding groups of both of these species, as well as orang-utans and other species. A new ape house was completed in 1976. Altogether the collection of apes and monkeys is one of the most representative in the world. A troop of rhesus monkeys is housed in a temple reminiscent of the temples in India and Nepal where, being regarded as sacred, these animals live a privileged semi-domestic life and proliferate.

Among the more spectacular species there is a good collection of big cats, including the only white tigers in Europe. These are, of course, only a mutant of the normal Bengal tiger and the Bristol animals, like all others, are descended from the stock established by the Maharajah of Rewa.

Other significant achievements at Bristol include the breeding of polar bear, okapi, black rhinoceros and peccary, some of which have been passed into zoo commerce and conceivably saved a few animals for the wild. There is an excellent bird collection, including a few rarities like Manchurian crane, peacock pheasant and ocellated turkey – the smaller of the two wild species of turkey found only in central America. There is a good aquarium and a fine reptile house, where this much-maligned and generally endangered group is well represented.

In addition to the main zoo the Bristol, Clifton and West of England Zoological Society, to give its full name, also owns Hollywood Towers, a secluded retreat where breeding rather than display comes first.

Visiting: Bristol Zoo is located in the Clifton area of Bristol and is served by bus and train (Clifton Down). It is open throughout the year. Tel. Bristol 38951. Restaurant, cafeteria, shop, etc.

Mammals: gorilla, chimpanzee, orang-utan and other primates; white tiger, black rhinoceros, polar bear, okapi, African elephant, Indian elephant, hippopotamus, giraffe, zebra.

Birds: good collection from all parts of the world.

Botany: good plantings around the animal pens. Chilean fire-bush (*Embothrium*) flowers in June.

Cheddar Gorge

One of the most famous of all 'days-in-the-country'. Thronged by tourists from an increasing number of countries, it is little surprise that Cheddar, a small sleepy village in the Mendip Hills of Somerset south of Bristol, has been spoilt. If not an actual tourist trap, then at least the 'trappings' are there. It's difficult to get away without paying something and, with so much on offer, easy to spend a great deal. But just down the road from this commercialism is some of the finest scenery in southern England. A vast, rolling, little-inhabited landscape full of attractive villages and woods, downland and copses, dry-stone walls and hedgerows full of flowers.

Two particularly fine areas right next to Cheddar are managed by the Somerset Trust for Nature Conservation. Black Rock Nature Reserve lies along the B3135, the road that runs along the Gorge itself. Over 500 feet up among the hills, its heart is the old Black Rock Quarry. The area is now largely wooded along the scarp, but with open downland with scrub beyond. At Black Rock Gate a track leaves the road eastward to the start of a nature trail that in one way or another covers the whole of the reserve. It leads along the limestone cliffs where the usual rich flora of such areas may be found. Orchids, lady's smock, the fine spleenwort and hosts of other wild flowers can be sought, but not picked. There is a badger sett in the reserve, and a variety of birds.

To the north, and reached by the same track, the Long Wood Nature Reserve, also boasts a useful wide-ranging nature trail. En route you pass Velvet Bottom, where the Romans mined lead and silver.

The reserve boasts a typical limestone community of mature trees including wych elm, ash and yew. It harbours a good collection of mammals, including roe deer, rabbit, badger, fox, grey squirrel, stoat, weasel, hedgehog and wood mouse – though one is fortunate to see more than a couple of these. Birds are generally common species, though there is a good population of summer migrants, including garden warbler and redstart. Buzzard and sparrowhawk may also be seen overhead.

Progressing through the reserve (and according to season) one may see early purple orchid, cuckoo-pint, meadow saffron, broad-leaved garlic, spotted orchid, hemp agrimony, herb Paris and toothwort. There is a plethora of ferns and lichens and a wealth of butterflies including brimstone, comma, small tortoiseshell and peacock. Some areas are locked and others roped off – remember this is limestone country and full of caves and swallowholes.

Continuing by road over the Mendips you drop down to the huge Chew Lake, a reservoir beloved by bird-watchers and anglers alike. Duck, terns, waders and a host of small birds throng this water and its natural banks. It is accessible at several spots, and bird-watchers gather in numbers at some of the best vantage points along the public highway. Anglers can fish for trout from both boat and bank, and the average size is excellent. Just a couple of miles to the west lies the magnificent Blagdon Reservoir, where trout fisherman gather on those balmy summer evenings hoping for the rare 'Blagden Boil' – a moment of true magic, I am told, when trout appear feeding at the surface in unbelievable numbers.

Visiting: take the B3135 from Cheddar up the Gorge and beyond. Watch for the footpath on the left at Black Rock Gate. Walk up the valley and explore Black Rock Nature Reserve on the right via the marked nature trail. Continue up the track to Long Wood Wildlife Reserve, where another nature trail will be found.

Birds: willow warbler, chiffchaff, garden warbler, redstart, marsh tit, buzzard, sparrowhawk, kestrel, tree sparrow, great spotted woodpecker, lesser spotted woodpecker, green woodpecker.

Botany: wych elm, ash, yew, early purple orchid, spotted orchid, cuckoo-pint, meadow saffron, broad-leaved garlic, hemp agrimony, herb Paris, toothwort, Cheddar pink.

Insects: brimstone butterfly, comma butterfly, tortoiseshell butterfly, peacock butterfly.

Cotswold Farm Park

This Farm Park is run by the Rare Breeds Survival Trust and forms part of Bemborough Farm between Stow-in-the-Wold and Winchcombe in deepest Cotswold country. There are the usual visitor facilities, including a cafeteria and information centre. The aim of the Park and Trust is to exhibit breeds of domestic animals that disappeared from our countryside as a result of the agrarian revolution of the eighteenth century. By regressive breeding, old breeds have been re-created where necessary while others have been collected from various parts of the country. Cattle include the longhorn and white; sheep include Portland and Jacob; there are unusual chickens, lop-eared rabbit and much else besides.

Visiting: take the B4077 westwards from Stow to Ford, then turn off southward on to minor roads to the Farm Park.

Mammals: rare breeds of domestic stock.

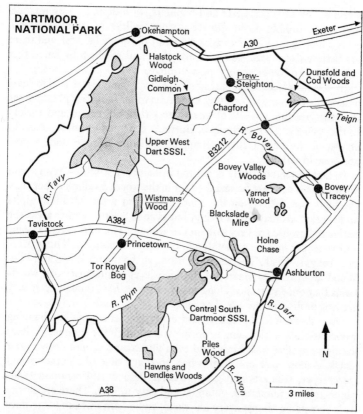

Dartmoor National Park 🦅 🐦 🌿 ♿

Amounting in all to 365 square miles, Dartmoor National Park co-incides more or less exactly with the geographically distinct upland area of Dartmoor. Thus it includes H.M. Prison and a huge and dangerous firing range, as well as some of the finest countryside in the whole of Britain. It also includes several Sites of Special Scientific Interest (SSSI's). The hills do no more than scrape the 2000 foot mark, but can be dangerous for the ill-prepared and inexperienced nevertheless. The high tops, often capped with an igneous pinnacle, are called 'tors' and are generally covered with bracken and rough grasses rather than heather. The green pastures, all neatly hedged, stretch up the hillsides, in many cases almost to the top. Fast-running

75

streams, full of white water and boulders, with dippers, grey wagtails and trout, tumble down the steep-sided valleys in every direction. At the foot of the hills they are crossed by old stone bridges, and there are little villages scattered here and there, all reached by lanes that cut deep into the land they pass through.

In several places these streams have been dammed at a high level among the open moors creating large reservoirs. Judicious planting has created screening coverts of mixed trees that add colour and variety to the scenery. The reservoir of Burrator is a good example; it could almost be the Lake District. Being at moderate altitude, such waters are poor in wildlife.

In fact Dartmoor really is not too brilliant for wildlife anyway, and what there is can best be searched for in the wooded valleys rather than the high tops. There, on the windswept open areas, meadow pipits and ring ousels may find a living, but even in strong heather areas the native red grouse are very thin on the ground. The odd raven, curlew and wheatear may be encountered, but only occasionally. Things were not always so bleak. There are remnants, at Wistman's Wood and Piles Wood at Black Tor Beare, of the high-level pedunculate oak woodlands that once stretched along many of the valleys, though even they are not prolific in the life they support.

Drop down into the valleys and everything changes. The hanging woods are full of bird song in spring and through the summer. Village gardens are alive with birds, and even the streams cannot drown their songs. Willow warblers, chaffinches, great and blue tits, nuthatch and treecreeper, redstarts and grey wagtails, dippers and common sandpipers, all are numerous, common and easy to find. There are tawny owls occupying almost every old wood, and a barn owl can sometimes be seen drifting over the meadows. There are kestrels, and that indicates voles, though you do not see many small mammals unless you look very hard. And above all else there are buzzards – perhaps as numerous among the wooded valleys of Dartmoor as anywhere in the country. Overhead they soar on wings held still in a shallow 'V'; at rest they sit on tree or fencepost awaiting their chance to pounce on small prey among the grass.

The valleys are the home of Dartmoor's mammals too. Fox and badger are both numerous and viewable. Otters still play in the streams, but they are becoming more scarce and increasingly nocturnal in habit. They were still hunted in the traditional way, by otter hounds and men on foot until a recent Act granted the full protection of the law to this endangered native mammal.

The Dartmoor ponies are hardy little creatures that live on the open moors that are one of the largest unenclosed common lands in England, and in the same way as the ponies have the right to wander at will over some 100,000 acres of the central section of the Moor, so too do we. This is the Dartmoor Forest proper, together with the adjacent Commons of Devon. However some 30,000 acres are used for military training, and noticeboards and white posts with two red bands indicate the danger zones. Firing times can be obtained from local police stations and post offices and a red flag indicates firing in progress. This section is mainly in the north-west.

The Dartmoor National Park offers fine countryside with hill walking or valley strolling to naturalist, fisherman and rambler. There are so many superb spots for a day that personal preference is bound to vary. A list of favoured tourist spots would include: Buckland-in-the-Moor, the most photographed village in Devon; Buckland Abbey, once a monastery, later owned by Sir Francis Drake, now leased by the National Trust to Plymouth Corporation as a maritime museum; Buckfast Abbey; Dartmeet, the most famous of all the Moor's beauty spots; Sticklepath, near Okehampton, with its museum of rural industries; Postbridge, for its old drovers' clapper bridge; and Widecombe-in-the-Moor, for its fair held on the second Tuesday of September and made famous by 'Uncle Tom Cobleigh and all'.

For walks through the Park the following is a highly selective bunch:

(a) Leave Okehampton westward on the A30 and near *Fowley* follow the West Okement River upstream to the oak woods at Black Tor Beare. Keep left across the open moor to High Willhays, where the heather may produce red grouse, then on to Yeo Tor and West Mill Tor. Turn north to Okehampton Camp and the road across the railways. Turn left and follow the southern river bank back to Fowley. A good long hard day's walk – map and compass essential.

(b) Leave the tourists at *Dartmeet* and walk downstream along the south bank of the River Dart through delicious oak woods. This soon becomes the National Trust property called Holne Woods. Continue to New Bridge and then walk the A384 to Holne Bridge and cut off southward along the west bank of the Dart to Buckfastleigh. About half a day.

(c) Follow the valley of the West Dart northward from *Two Bridges* to the high-level oaks of Wistman's Wood. Venture no further – this is military country. Also from Two Bridges take the B3212 northward and after passing the pine plantations on the right turn right to Bellever and explore southward along the East Dart River. No permits are required to visit these woods, but visitors are requested to keep to the marked routes and to remain outside the experimental plots. About half a day each.

(d) Yarner Wood Nature Trail through the National Nature Reserve of the same name starts above *Bovey Tracy* at Yarrow Lodge. It leads through some fine old woodland and lasts about a couple of hours. The fortunate might glimpse badgers, but all should see redstart and pied flycatcher in summer.

Visiting: easy access with plentiful accommodation of every type.

Birds: buzzard, kestrel, red grouse, raven, common sandpiper, ring ousel, redstart, whinchat, stonechat, grey wagtail, dipper, willow warbler, chaffinch.

Mammals: otter, fox, badger, ponies.

Botany: varied and interesting at all levels. Because of the continued grazing in this area, meadow flowers continue to prosper.

Exmoor National Park

Compared with the starkness of the high tors of Dartmoor, Exmoor is gentle, its appeal less obvious, its landscape less of a contrast to the surrounding countryside. But Exmoor has a beauty all its own, with its little villages all thatch and plaster, tumbling streams lined with thick woodlands alive with bird song, market towns that seem to echo the words of a bygone age – Withypool, Simonsbath. The highest spot is Dunkery Beacon at a mere 1707 feet above sea level – no more than a hill. This is Lorna Doone country, with a traditional way of life and an intimate social system. The coast has changed. Lynton and Lynmouth were once national headlines when destroyed by floods, but they have rebuilt themselves to cope with the tourists, but much is just the same as it was a hundred years ago.

Wildlife is not outstanding, save for the blackcock that here find their southern outpost in Britain, and the red deer which are a local pride and joy. But there are red grouse and merlins on the moors, and dippers and many small birds along the streams.

The National Park authorities have produced three guides to 'Way-marked Walks' within the Park, and these excellent little booklets take the visitor through fine and beautiful countryside some of which has been specially opened to provide continuity away from the rights of way.

Visiting: booklets available from Exmoor National Park Information Centre, Market House, The Parade, Minehead, Somerset TA24 5ND.
Mammals: red deer, badger.
Birds: black grouse, red grouse, moor and valley species.

Longleat 🐾 ♿

The 'Lions of Longleat' was the first of the modern safari parks to be opened in the world and has set the style for those which followed this new approach to displaying animals. It centred its attraction on the fact that most customers would arrive by car, and provided they stayed inside them they would be safe from the ravages of animals and so could observe these without bars. The vast number of imitators has proved the success of the idea. Large paddocks, simply designed to keep predator and prey (rather than man and animal) apart, can be driven through, giving as genuine a taste of a wild safari as can be had outside Africa. Lions, of course, are the favoured stars of the show, and what a contrast to the old barred and fenced lions they provide. Perhaps unfortunately, the various safari parks that followed the lead of the Marquis of Bath and Jimmy Chipperfield at Longleat felt bound to offer more, with an inevitable increase in the demand for wild animals as stock. As seen on television, Mr Chipperfield is an inveterate animal collector, and his capturing trips are taking their toll on wild animals in East Africa, where the herds are progressively confined to National Parks and Game Reserves.

Now at Longleat you can see lions, tigers, giraffes, zebras and baboons, with a special island reserve for chimpanzees and the surrounding lake for sealions and hippo. There are eland, white rhinoceros, ostrich, wildebeest, in fact a good cross-section of the great mammal populations of the African savannahs. Of course, many of the animals do breed, but apparently not in sufficient numbers to produce the quantity required by zoos and safari parks, so the capturing goes on.

Nevertheless the grounds of Longleat are a major wildlife attraction, and well worth a visit. As elsewhere it is advisable to avoid holiday weekends.

Visiting: Longleat is well signposted off the A362 four miles south-west of Warminster. It is open throughout the year and there are the usual catering facilities and shops. Tel. Maiden Bradley 328.

Mammals: lion, tiger, giraffe, eland, wildebeest, zebra, chimpanzee, hippo, sealion, baboon, Ankole cattle.

Marlborough Downs and Fyfield Down

The Marlborough Downs lie at the western end of the chalk to the north and south of the A4 west of Marlborough, which itself follows the River Kennet – one of those famous chalk streams in which trout grow fat and about which anglers dream. Much of the downland is still as empty as ever, for settlements line the valleys and hug the spring

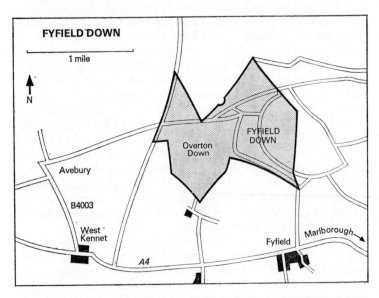

line below. But much has also been taken under the plough, destroying the association of sheep and grassland that once made the area rich and prosperous. The Downs are not unknown. Thousands of visitors flock to see the White Horse of Pewsey and take little notice of the wealth of other early human remains. Fewer still appreciate the rich flora typical of the chalk that can be found where agriculture and scrub have not destroyed it. To the south of the A4 between Lockeridge and Alton Barnes lies the Pewsey Downs National Nature Reserve, a farm that has been in the hands of the Stratton family for almost a hundred years and owned by New College Oxford for six hundred years. The area includes the White Horse. The NNR seeks to maintain the character of the area as one of the finest pieces of downland remaining in Britain.

Here one can find an excellent and comprehensive collection of the typical chalk flora. Orchids including the burnt-tip, eyebright, rock rose, chalk milkwort, harebell, round-headed rampion, early gentian, bastard toadflax, snakeshead fritillary and others. Butterflies too proliferate, including the chalk hill blue, which is the subject of experiment regarding the trampling of its habitat by livestock. The reserve is open along many rights of way, but it is not a public open space. Do not pick flowers – it is illegal, and in any case will destroy the attraction of this fine area for others.

To the north across the Kennet and the A4 lies Fyfield Down NNR, another major chalkland site where early gentian, chalk milkwort, frog orchid and other plants may be found. This offers a more variable landscape, and both long-eared and short-eared owls may be found, along with interesting birds like sparrowhawk and wheatear.

Until the 1930s sarsen stones were excavated and cut here for use in all parts of the country. Many thousands remain, particularly at Clatford Bottom, where their tough sandstone quality can be seen.

Visiting: Pewsey Downs is reached from the Lockeridge–Alton Barnes road which leaves the A4 a mile west of Marlborough. Access is by marked footpaths on either side of the road. Fyfield Down lies to the north, reached from the hamlet of Fyfield (see map), which is just a little west of Lockeridge, by an unclassified road. For leaflets on both, contact the Nature Conservancy Southern Office.

Botany: burnt-tip orchid, frog orchid, early gentian, chalk milkwort, eyebright, rock rose, harebell, round-headed rampian, bastard toadflax.

Birds: short-eared owl, long-eared owl, sparrowhawk, wheatear, corn bunting.

Paignton Zoo and Botanical Gardens

Paignton can, with some justification, claim to be Britain's most beautiful zoo; certainly it is the only one that combines wildlife with botany with such success. To many the trees and shrubs are just a backdrop for the animals, but the Zoo houses an excellent collection of plants that are of interest in their own right. There is a tropical house designed by Herbert Whitley, the Zoo's founder, to resemble nothing

81

more than a backwater in the Amazon jungle, with epiphytic ferns and orchids clinging to the trees, and creepers weaving their way upward. From time to time animals are displayed in the house. There is also a subtropical house in which flowering plants can be seen throughout the year.

The Zoo has an aquarium, a reptile house, numerous aviaries, and ponds holding cranes, storks and herons and penguins – the latter living in the luxury of a specially created Brooke-Bond Pool. There are lions, tigers, cheetahs, lynx, leopard, serval, ocelot and jaguar, a good collection of primates, and a specialized display of South American rodents, as well as the usual elephant, giraffe, rhinoceros and Barbary sheep. Large paddocks house antelopes and horses, as well as bison and deer. A group of gibbons live on a large island in one of the two lakes, and there are good numbers of birds wandering freely about the grounds.

Facilities include restaurants, a bar, and the Jungle Express miniature railway, which really does get visitors out into the grounds and among the trees and animals. Chusan palms grow luxuriously and there are Katsura trees (*Cercidiphyllum japonicum*) from Japan, a Mediterranean rockery, Atlas cedars, gunnera and hundreds of other plants.

Visiting: the Zoo is open throughout the year and is reached via the A385 inland from the town. There is a large car park.
Mammals: tiger, lion, jaguar, rhinoceros, elephant, giraffe, seals.
Birds: penguins, emu, rhea, macaws, flamingoes.
Botany: outstanding gardens with many interesting specimens.

Purbeck and Poole

Littered with place names like Worth Matravers and Creech Bottom, the Isle of Purbeck is England at its best. From Bournemouth eastwards the coast is built up and boring: westward there is Poole Harbour, a natural playground, and the delightful countryside of the Purbeck Hills. There is Studland Heath, a National Nature Reserve, and Durlston and St Aldhelm's Heads, white chalk cliffs that drop to the sea and which support the most westerly mainland colonies of fulmars and auks along the south coast. There is Arne, the Royal Society for the Protection of Birds' Reserve, with its free nature trail at Shipstal Point, and Poole Harbour itself, with its own nature reserve at Brownsea Island boasting the only strong colony of red squirrels in the deep south. The Island can be visited via a ferry from Sandbanks

Quay; there is a landing fee and escorted tours can be arranged to see a multitude of birds as well as the red squirrels.

The main artery is the A351 from Wareham to Swanage through the tourist attraction of Corfe Castle. After half an hour of tourism take the B3351 to Studland and take an optional detour to The Foreland to see the chalk stacks of Old Harry and his Wife. Wild flowers flourish away from the well-worn paths and are worth an hour in May and June. Continue on the minor road towards the Sandbanks Ferry. A sign shows the headquarters of the Studland NNR with a good display and a hide overlooking the Little Sea.

A nature trail leads around the south of Little Sea to the dune systems on the seaward side. This starts 100 yards north of the Knoll House Hotel, itself north of Studland village. Here is Knoll car park, and the trail leads from the seaward side of an old concrete pillbox on the left. Descend the old cliff to the beach and walk northward to a yellow-topped post. The trail then leads inland. It is possible that, in crossing the dunes, you may be fortunate enough to spot some of the reasons for establishing Studland NNR – the fact that all six British reptiles live here. Sand lizard, common lizard, slow-worm, adder, grass snake and smooth snake may all be seen. Insects are interesting and the giant royal fern grows in places. The adjacent Little Sea often holds good numbers of duck.

Durlston Head is excellent territory for birds, and kittiwake, fulmar and guillemot can be seen from the car park of this small Country Park. Tilly Whim caves are an attraction to young and old.

If one animal dominates the Purbeck scene it is the Dartford warbler, our only resident warbler and a rarity partly because it is highly vulnerable to severe weather. The Arne Reserve is the only spot in the country where this shy and skulking little bird can reasonably be expected to show itself. Visit in early spring and contact the Warden, Syldata, Arne, Wareham BH20 5BJ for a permit (small fee) in advance.

One of the finest cliff walks in Britain extends along the coast from Durlston Head westwards to Winspit, a deep sheltered valley thick with bushes, where a path leads upwards to Worth Matravers. There are orchids among the grasses and some very beautiful scenery. This is the eastern end of the South-West Peninsula Coast Path which will eventually extend all the way round the coast of Dorset, Devon and Cornwall to Minehead in Somerset.

Visiting: Studland Heath National Nature Reserve; **Arne Bird Reserve** (RSPB); Durlston Head; Brownsea Island.

Birds: kittiwake, fulmar, guillemot, Dartford warbler, stonechat, duck and waders in Poole Harbour.

Botany: heath and dune colonizers.

Other: all six British reptiles: sand lizard, common lizard, slow-worm, adder, grass snake, smooth snake.

Rode Tropical Bird Gardens 🐦 ♿

First opened to the public in spring 1962, the Gardens house an excellent collection of birds of over 180 different species. As far as possible they are kept under 'natural' conditions allowing free flight but relying on the food and shelter provided by the Gardens to pull back would-be wanderers. The result is several hundred birds in large, airy enclosures several of which can be walked through. As elsewhere the macaws of several species are the most obvious of the free fliers, and these colourful additions to the Somerset avifauna are a major attraction.

Pools house the usual waterfowl and flamingoes, and there are pheasants, cassowaries and ibises wandering around as well. Hornbills, owls and vultures are kept in large displays and there is a good collection of smaller birds including parrots, mynahs, toucans and weavers.

This is a good collection and, set in the heart of the Somerset countryside near Trowbridge, is an ideal day out for the people of Bristol.

Visiting: take the A361 between Trowbridge and Frome, or the A36 between Bath and Warminster, and watch for signs to Rode before Beckington. Admission charges are reasonable and there is a cafeteria. Tel. Beckington 326.

Birds: macaws, parrots, weavers, wildfowl, flamingoes, pelicans, peafowl.

Other: George Inn at Norton St Philip believed to be the oldest continuously licensed premises in the country.

Isles of Scilly 🐦 🌿 ♿

Though they can be visited within the day, the Isles of Scilly deserve a longer stay. They enjoy one of the mildest climates in Britain, are the centre of an early flower industry and have a character very much their own. The group consists of numerous islands and rocks, all but a handful of which are uninhabited. They have some cliffs, but these are generally not very high, and the low-lying nature supports the impression of gentleness. St Mary's, the largest and most densely populated, is the arrival point both for ferry and plane, and has developed something of a tourist industry, but is remarkably unspoilt away from Hugh Town. There are some interesting areas of shoreline and a few marshes which are interesting to botanist and ornithologist alike.

To the south lies the delightful island of St Agnes, formerly the site of a bird observatory, and its sister island of The Gugh, to which it is connected at low tide. At Horse Point, Manx shearwaters breed, but it is in the autumn that bird-watchers invade the island en masse to search out the rare vagrants that arrive from all points of the compass. Transatlantic waifs are the speciality, but anything may turn up. Accommodation in September and October is virtually unobtainable, but day trips from St Mary's allow full exploration. Follow bird-watchers for the birds of the day. Spring in the islands is delightful, with breeding birds arriving and a regular passage of migrants. Generally there are few rarities, but there are advantages in having the islands to oneself, and of course the flowers are marvellous.

Such is the unofficial inter-island communication system that St Agnes may be totally deserted as the seasonal residents head off to some other island in search of a reported rarity. The most likely is Tresco, where the freshwater pool regularly holds transatlantic waders. In fact some bird-watchers make this island their base. Tresco Abbey is the most remarkable subtropical garden in Britain, with palms, mimosas, gum trees, cacti, giant agaves and almost anything that one would expect to see in, say, the Canary Islands.

Annet, just west of St Agnes, is a Bird Reserve with puffins and gulls, but it is difficult to land and visitors must confine their visit to a cruise offshore. Such trips depart regularly from Hugh Town during the summer and are well worthwhile. Common seals are invariably seen.

Visiting: by ferry or air (helicopter service in summer) from Penzance to Hugh Town. Excellent inter-island ferries connect. Plentiful accommodation on St Mary's. St Agnes must be booked in advance, particularly for the autumn bird season. There are nature trails: Higher Moors Trail leads through a marsh with hides for watching birds; and Lower Moors Trail through an old withy plantation; and there is a third trail at Holy Vale. Guides from Frank Gibson's shop in Hugh Town.

Birds: puffin, razorbill, guillemot, Manx shearwater, fulmar, storm petrel, cormorant, shag, common tern, rock pipit, interesting migrants and autumn rarities.

Botany: cultivated daffodil fields, varied wild flower communities, naturalized agapanthus, mesembryanthemums, fuchsia.

South-West Peninsula Coast Path

This 515-mile-long path starts at the entrance to Poole Harbour at Studland and runs along the varied coast, over cliff and heath, along beach and marsh until it reaches the Somerset coast at Minehead. At present there are several stretches over which rights of way do not exist and, of course, there are several large urban areas where breaks will for ever be inevitable. Nevertheless the path is an admirable project, leading through some of the finest cliff scenery in Britain. It passes close to two national parks, Dartmoor and Exmoor, and through several Areas of Outstanding Natural Beauty: the Dorset coast and heathlands, the east and south Devon coasts, the south Cornwall coast and the Lizard Peninsula and the north-east Cornwall and north Devon coasts. Additionally the Path passes through, or close by, three Country Parks at Farway south of Honiton, at Berry Head and at Mount Edgcumbe west of Plymouth.

The Path starts at Poole Harbour and immediately heads through Swanage into the Isle of Purbeck (see p. 82). It then continues westward through the geologically interesting and tourist-attracting Lulworth Cove to Weymouth where there is a small group of wildlife haunts (mainly bird). It then follows the Chesil Beach past the Swannery and the subtropical garden, on the landward side of the Fleet at Abbotsbury. There is an alternative inland route via Osmington Mills to the White Horse about Sutton Poyntz, the Hardy Monument and over the downs to West Bexington. Both routes pass through the charming village of Burton Bradstock and follow the coast to Lyme Regis, where they pass through the great landslip with its immense wealth of fossils. The path then continues to Exmouth, where a ferry is taken to Dawlish and the footpath that runs just inland of the railway is followed. There then follows what is known as the 'Devon Riviera' which leaves Torquay and Paignton to the beach-lovers before the path starts once again leading to Brixham, Berry Head, and on to Kingswear and the ferry to Dartmouth.

Berry Head is a limestone outcrop rich in flowers and birds. It is something of a tourist attraction, but the environment is nevertheless protected. Fellwort, samphire, Portland spurge, rock sea lavender, pink thrift, white sea campion, autumn squill and wild rock rose can all be found, and there are rarities such as goldilocks, restharrow, hare's ear and honewort. Birds include a good community of seabirds – fulmar, kittiwake, guillemot and the occasional razorbill.

Southward from Dartmouth the beach of Slapton Ley leads onward around the coast to Prawle Point. Thereafter each of the sunken estuaries is crossed in turn to pass into Cornwall beyond Plymouth. All of these estuaries from the Exe to the Tamar are of ornithological interest, and in season and at the right point of the tide each can be full of birds and worthy of a lengthy stop. The Exe is probably the best for waders on a rising tide throughout the year, but the Tamar is the only regular wintering haunt of avocet in Britain. Cargreen is the spot to view with a charming, handy pub.

Within Cornwall the Path hugs the coast, giving sections of outstanding beauty and interest and passing through quaint old fishing villages. Looe, for instance, is an attractive little village that now finds itself the centre of the British shark-fishing business. Being sunken, the coast is highly indented, and more and more ferry crossings are necessary, until at the mouth of the Fal there is virtually more ferrying than walking. The Path skirts round the Lizard, passes through Penzance and then onward to Land's End, where it turns northward and then north-eastward to St Ives. It then crosses that delightful and bird-rich little estuary, the Hayle, before heading out to Godreavy Point, where guillemots and kittiwakes still breed. Along the north coast to Newquay, across the Camel, through villages that have become resorts, household names that have lost some of their magic, onward through Tintagel, Bude, Clovelly and northward to Appledore, where a gap can be bridged by ferry or bus to Braunton Burrows.

Northward the coast is marked by excellent views toward Lundy and the path continues to Bull Point, where it turns eastward to Ilfracombe, Combe Martin, and then skirts Exmoor to Minehead. What a walk! But better still, what a lovely series of walks for those who would choose the part that they wish and have the time to spend.

Visiting: a number of youth hostels serve the path, and by and large there are no long stretches without a variety of available accommodation. In particular there are many small inns which make the passing walker welcome, and in south Cornwall in the stretch between Looe and St Mawes they are particularly thick on the ground. In comparison the north coast is poorly served: no doubt it is the excellent harbours of the south coast that account for the difference.

Birds: estuaries in the south and seabird cliffs in the north. Make a point of visiting Slapton Ley, the Exe, the Tamar and the Hayle; and Godreavy Point, St Agnes Head, the Torridge-Taw confluence and Porlock Marsh.

Botany: some really outstanding haunts: slender mullein (*Verbascum virgatum*) is confined to the south-west. The Lizard Peninsula is especially fine – notice the Cornish heather.

Insects: the large blue butterfly is found only in northern Cornwall, and the Jersey tiger moth is best spotted between Exeter and Teignmouth.

Puffins

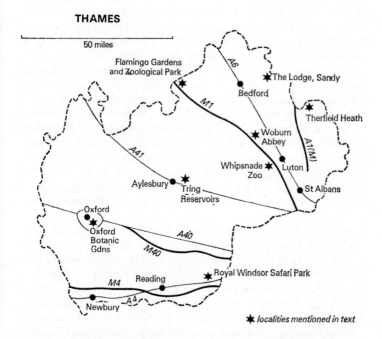

THAMES

50 miles

Flamingo Gardens and Zoological Park

The Lodge, Sandy

Bedford

A6

M1

Therfield Heath

Woburn Abbey

A1(M)

A41

Whipsnade Zoo

Luton

Aylesbury

Tring Reservoirs

St Albans

Oxford

Oxford Botanic Gdns

A40

M40

Royal Windsor Safari Park

M4

Reading

Newbury

A4

★ *localities mentioned in text*

Flamingo Gardens and Zoological Park

It is unusual in the world of zoos for a title to do less than justice to the collection – usually the reverse is true – but Christopher Marler's gardens comprise one of the finest bird collections in the world. The basis is his 720 acre farm near Olney, Bucks., within which there are sixty acres of fox-proof breeding areas with lakes and streams. The Park is the breeding station of the British Waterfowl Association, and Christopher Marler is Vice President of this organization as well as Vice Chairman of the Federation of Zoological Gardens of Great Britain.

Though the Park started as a private and successful attempt to breed endangered species in captivity, because Marler also believes that rarities should be on show, to make people more aware of their existence, the Park was opened to the public in 1968. With 8600 species of birds in the world to choose from, a selection had to be made

89

somewhere, and so the avowed specialization is on wildfowl, flamingoes, cranes, storks and birds of prey. It sounds straightforward enough, until it is realized that there are a great many unusual birds hidden away within these groups. The zoo has all six species of flamingo, every species of goose, the rare trumpeter swan now breeds, and wild Bewick's swans visit regularly. There are several of the world's cranes, a family in grave danger of totally disappearing in this crowded world, including the rare Siberian white crane. There are kori, and little and great bustards – find those anywhere else! The great bustards here are part of the reintroduction scheme presently operating on Salisbury Plain. Birds of prey include Andean condor and lammergeier! And there are hosts of storks, spoonbills, ducks, ibises, penguins and so on, the whole amounting to one of the very best bird gardens in Britain, well worth visiting for the bird's sake alone, although there are also European bison, Bactrian camels, guanaco and vicuna, Formosan sika deer, Bennett's wallaby and Highland cattle.

Visiting: the Flamingo Gardens and Zoological Park are in the village of Weston Underwood, between Olney and the A50, and five miles from Exit 14 of the M1. The Gardens are open from Good Friday to the end of September on Wednesdays, Thursdays, Saturdays, Sundays and Bank Holidays from 14.00 to 20.00 hours. There is a small shop, but soft drinks and ice creams are the only refreshments.

Birds: all the world's flamingoes and geese, Siberian white and other cranes, swans, great and little bustards, lammergeier, Andean condor.

Mammals: European bison, guanaco, vicuna, camel.

The Lodge, Sandy

The Lodge is a nineteenth-century, Tudor-style house originally built for Robert Peel's son Arthur. It was planted with many exotic shrubs and trees (275 species of flowering plants have been recorded) and the landscaped grounds are typical of their time. In 1961 the Royal Society for the Protection of Birds purchased the house as its headquarters and immediately set to creating a pond. This has added moorhen and little grebe to the breeding list of over eighty species, and the eager eyes of the RSPB staff have built up a total list of 120 species. Within the grounds, species such as nightjar, woodcock, tree pipit and the three woodpeckers all breed, while kingfishers and wood sandpipers pass through.

Like the good bird gardeners they are, the RSPB have lashed out on nest boxes and bird feeders, and a good number of species can be seen, particularly in winter. There are many fascinating displays, including a nature discovery room, a shop, and general publicity about the aims and objectives of the Society. Both school parties and individuals are welcome.

Visiting: by permit: contact the R S P B, The Lodge, Sandy, Beds. Sandy lies just off the A1 between Biggleswade and Grafham Water.

Birds: little grebe, nightjar, tree pipit, green woodpecker, great spotted woodpecker, lesser spotted woodpecker, woodcock.

Oxford Botanic Garden

Established in 1621, the University Botanic Garden at Oxford is Britain's oldest botanic garden and occupies five acres near the city centre. It is noted not only for its pathfinding botanic work, which is intimately tied up with the University and with research, but also for its walls and the famous Danby Gate – both by Inigo Jones. In a city already so well served by fine gardens and open spaces, the Garden is still a major attraction. It has a fine collection of trees, shrubs and flowering plants and good tropical houses through which the visitor can wander. A new glasshouse range has been constructed in recent years. The Garden has an out-station on the greensand at Nuneham Courtenay (calcifuges) but access here is restricted.

Visiting: open weekdays throughout the year.
Botany: excellent collection.

Ridgeway Path

The Ridgeway extends for some eighty-five miles from Overton Hill near Avebury in Wiltshire to Ivinghoe Beacon in Buckinghamshire. For much of the way it runs along the edge of the chalk escarpment that is variously called the Marlborough Downs, the Berkshire Downs and the Chilterns. Throughout its length the Ridgeway is littered with prehistoric remains from the Bronze and Iron Ages. There are fortifications, burial mounds, villages and monuments of a quasi-religious, and often ill-understood, nature. In the west the route is open to cyclists and horse-riders as well as to walkers; beyond the Goring Gap it is for walkers only.

The Ridgeway leaves the chalk from time to time, notably in Oxfordshire, where it passes through fields and woodlands alongside the Thames. Later it joins the ancient Icknield Way, then leaves this where it has become a metalled road, and takes a more attractive route along the Chiltern escarpment. Throughout its length excellent views over the surrounding countryside succeed one another; the Vale of the White Horse, Hackpen Hill and Ivinghoe Beacon were all noted viewpoints before the Ridgeway joined them together.

Chalk landscape is noted above all for its flowers, and visitors in the early part of summer will find a wealth of species everywhere away from the noted beauty spots. Some areas, however, are too important to leave open to free access, and several have been incorporated into nature reserves. Most important of these is Aston Rowant National Nature Reserve, which covers 300 acres of the Chiltern escarpment in Oxfordshire immediately adjacent to the A40 London–Oxford road. As elsewhere the chalk downland has suffered considerably through ploughing and a lack of sheep and rabbit grazing. Here the natural succession that covers the open downland when grazing ceases can be seen in a more or less 'frozen' state. Sheep, including some primitive Soay sheep from the remote Hebrides of St Kilda, are used to maintain the traditional character of the hills and to protect the rich flora and fauna.

Access to Aston Rowant is restricted to public footpaths and to a nature trail that starts outside the Reserve Centre with the Soay sheep. The trail then follows one of the sunken ways that have been worn into the Chiltern escarpment; along here the yellow flowers are ploughman's spikenard. Continue past the badger sett and rabbit warren among the yews, and beyond the trees you may find spotted orchids in June and July. Though they are scarce there are several other of the thirty species of orchids that flower on the Chilterns. The viewpoint at the end overlooks Oxford, and nearby there may be common lizards and the chalkhill blue in July and August. Hares and kestrels are also frequently seen, and along on the right an enclosure is being used for studying the flora of anthills. Species include germander, speedwell, whitlow grass, forget-me-not and rock rose.

Turning back from the escarpment the path leads to an old flint pit where autumn sees a variety of fungi. Flowers among the woodland here include yellow archangel, sanicle, wood sorrel and, of course, bluebells. As with most woodland flowers, they bloom in early spring.

Visiting: Beacon Hill Escarpment Trail is reached via the old A40 beyond Stokenchurch; Exit 5 of the M40. Please stick to the trail and do not interfere with experiments or fences. Keep dogs on a lead – there are sheep here.

Botany: ploughman's spikenard, spotted orchid, germander, speedwell, rock rose, forget-me-not, sanicle, wood sorrel, bluebell, yellow archangel.

Insects: chalkhill blue, peacock and red admiral butterflies.

Mammals: Soay sheep, badger, fallow deer, muntjac, grey squirrel, stoat, weasel, rabbit, hare.

Birds: kestrel, skylark, goldfinch.

Just across the way from Aston Rowant lies the Chequers Reserve of the Berkshire, Buckinghamshire and Oxfordshire Naturalists' Trust (BBONT) at Great Kimble. This covers eighty-three acres of a combe called Happy Valley and an adjacent thirty-three acres of grassland along the western slope of Beacon Hill. Here is one of only three natural boxwoods in the country; the others are at Box Hill in Surrey and Boxwell in Gloucestershire. Open chalk screes hold viper's bugloss, blue fleabane, chalk eyebright and musk orchid. The grassland holds fragrant, spotted and pyramidal orchids and a good growth of cowslips.

Visiting: access is to BBONT members only, except to Chequers Knap along public rights of way from Longdown Hill or the layby at Great Kimble.

Other nearby BBONT reserves include Grange Lands at Great Kimble, where twenty-five acres of grassland protect adderstongue fern felwort, bee orchid as well as several of the species found at Chequers. Butterflies include chalkhill blue, small blue and marbled white, and there are fifty species of breeding birds, including whinchat, cirl bunting and nightingale.

Pulpit Hill is also nearby, and here a wide variety of botanical habitats in a mere twenty acres include ploughman's spikenard and narrow-lipped helleborine. A larger area is Chinnor Hill to the north, where BBONT has sixty-five acres of Chiltern escarpment overlooking the Vale of Aylesbury. This has the advantage of free public access, save for the sheep enclosures which are part of the management plan to reconvert to 'natural' downland. Here, and in the more open areas, frog orchid can still be found. There is a nature trail and a printed guide.

The Chilterns are rightly famous for their orchids, and BBONT is the custodian of two of the three British spots for military orchid, one of only four spots for monkey orchid, both British stations of the ghost orchid, and the only place outside the Cotswolds for red hellebo-rine. The areas concerned cannot be made public for obvious reasons.

Visiting: The Ridgeway can be joined from the A4 west of Marl-borough or from Avebury Circle on the A361. It is crossed in many places by major roads and there are many 'formal' car parks allowing access. One of the best approaches for BBONT reserves is to leave the M40 at Exit 5.

Botany: Chiltern gentian, early gentian, wild candytuft, pasque flower, field fleawort, purple milk-vetch, coralroot, herb Paris, Solomon's seal, columbine, yellow birdsnest, marsh orchid, fragrant orchid, bee orchid, pyramidal orchid, spotted orchid, butterwort, narrow-lipped helleborine, marsh helleborine, viper's bugloss, blue fleabane, chalk eyebright, ploughman's spikenard.

Butterflies: purple emperor, black hairstreak, wood white, marbled white, chalkhill blue, small blue, Adonis blue.

Royal Windsor Safari Park

When the Smart family of circus fame went into the safari business it was inevitable that they would do so with style. At Windsor, only twenty-two miles from London, they have assembled one of the largest collections of large and impressive animals to be found in the country. They have the usual drive-through system in which lions, tigers and baboons can be seen from the safety of one's own car, and the effect is almost natural, save only that some of the tigers are overweight and the lions just will not stop breeding. Baboons climb all over the cars, and there are enough cars on a summer Sunday to cause either traffic jams or frustration at not being allowed to stop.

There are cheetahs, white rhinos, elephants, giraffes, sealions, pelicans and a waterfowl collection, all set in 150 acres of grass and woodland. There are kiddies' rides, boating lakes, a 'Wild-West Ford' and of course licensed restaurants and bars; in fact almost everything that you could want if you were not looking for a day in the country. However, go out of season and all of these empty facilities really do become attractive and the collection of 'star' animal material is really very impressive.

The Dolphinarium is a major attraction, and it is particularly difficult to see killer whales anywhere other than in these places. The fact that they perform tricks in no way makes these magnificent creatures less appealing – in fact the reverse is true.

Visiting: leave the M4 at Exit 6 and proceed to Windsor. On the south side of the town take the B3022 to the well-signposted Royal Windsor Safari Park. Admission is by carload, or on foot (a real bargain), but there are extras for dolphin shows, the reptile house and the monkey and macaw aviary.

Mammals: lion, tiger, cheetah, white rhinoceros, giraffe, Indian elephant, baboon, killer whale, dolphin.

Therfield Heath

This outstanding area of chalk downland in north Hertfordshire is a local nature reserve of the Hertfordshire County Council, open to the public at all times. While flowers are the main interest, the Heath is also of archaeological importance, with the only long barrow in the county. Outstanding are the pasque flowers, which are magnificent in April, and five species of orchid. There are also spotted cat's-ear and bastard toadflax, as well as an excellent community of other chalk-loving species. Best for all of these is the south-facing slope of Church Hill. To the north at Pen Hills there are abundant butterfly food plants, including horseshoe vetch, beloved of the chalkhill blue.

Visiting: there is a car park near the Pavilion at the Royston end of the Heath. Access by foot from the A505 and the Therfield Road.

Botany: orchids, pasque flower, spotted cat's-ear, bastard toadflax.

Insects: butterflies, including chalkhill blue.

Tring Reservoirs

Tring Reservoirs were built between 1802 and 1839 to service the Grand Junction Canal (now the Grand Union) where it cut through the high chalk escarpment of the Chiltern Hills. A series of locks up and down over Tring Summit were filled by pumping water from these four reservoirs, enabling water to flow downhill in either direction with the passing of a barge. An elaborate network of channels and sluices connects the waters, which have become less important with the decline of inland waterways.

Constructed on marshy ground, the four basins quickly built up a

95

significant place in ornithology. It was here that the first colonizing little ringed plovers nested in 1938. Today their banks and the surrounding areas of woodland are a National Nature Reserve specifically established to protect birds. Winter brings large flocks of wildfowl, including the graceful goosander, while in spring and summer great crested grebe and grey heron breed among the reeds. A flock of semi-wild greylag geese spend the summer months here, and the surrounding marshes and woodlands are alive with warblers.

The four pools – Wilstone, situated away from the others, and

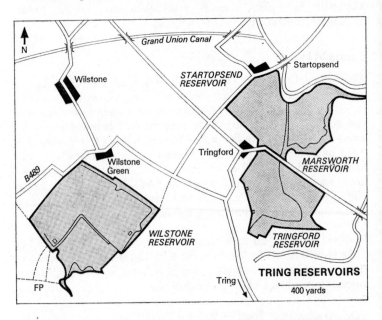

Marsworth, Startopsend and Tringford – are a major bird-watching site and a centre of interest and attraction throughout the year. Passage migrants often include a number of rarities, and waders in particular are numerous and often exotic. Black tern, osprey and little gull have all been seen in autumn with some degree of regularity.

In comparison, other branches of natural history are poorly served. The edible dormouse was introduced to Tring Park seventy years ago, and there may also be the occasional mink, but both are elusive. The remnants of a marshland flora can still be found, including fen and meadow orchids, as well as the rare orange foxtail and mudwort.

Yellow flags, water figwort and amphibious bistort may be easily seen from the north-west bank of Wilstone.

With the exception of Tringford, the reservoirs have a remarkable reputation among anglers. Coarse fishing is allowed every day in season except Sundays, and there are ten-pound bream, three-pound roach and up to twenty-eight-pounds pike to be taken.

Access is by footpath and via the nature trail that winds between the three contiguous reservoirs. The waters lie north of Tring and are reached via the B489 or B488. Wilstone can be explored along its northern banks from the village of Wilstone Green. The nature trail starts at Startops End village and runs alongside the Grand Union Canal before cutting along the embankment between Startops End and Marsworth to the junction with Tringford. It follows the west bank of that water to the pumping station. There is a nicely produced nature trail guide which concentrates (unusually) on birds rather than flowers.

Visiting: Tring lies on the A41 where it crosses the Chilterns between Aylesbury and Hemel Hempstead: the reservoirs lie to the north between the B488 and B489. The nature trail, which is the best approach for the three main reservoirs, starts at Startops End village, but Tringford and the road to New Mill is excellent for branching out in all directions. Approach Wilstone from Wilstone Green.

Birds: great crested grebe, little grebe, grey heron, teal, wigeon, shoveler, pochard, tufted duck, goosander, greylag goose, reed warbler, waders and terns.

Botany: fen orchid, meadow orchid, bog pimpernel, yellow flag, water figwort, amphibious bistort, broad-leaved ragwort, round-fruited rush, orange foxtail, mudwort.

Whipsnade Park Zoo

Covering over 500 acres of rolling Bedfordshire countryside, Whipsnade is the well-known nursery and safety collection of the Zoological Society of London. But it is also an attraction in its own right, housing over two thousand animals in large 'natural' enclosures. As a result of this revoluntionary (in 1931) zoo concept, the animals live at Whipsnade in such ideal surroundings that they breed freely. The Zoo is rightly proud of its achievements in this vital area of conservation: Père David's deer thrive here and animals have been exported back to their native China. It was the first zoo to breed warthog and the first

D

in Britain to breed white-tailed deer, snow leopard, moose and white rhinoceros. It was also the first in Britain to breed cheetah, a notoriously difficult species, but one of crucial importance because of the catastrophic decline of this beautiful plains cat in the wild. The white rhino too was on the verge of extinction when Whipsnade became the first breeding centre outside Africa. Today the Umfolozi Railway runs through an enclosure that holds a thriving herd of this, the largest rhino in the world. The North American bison breeds on the downs, musk ox in the grassy meadows, and the Thomson's gazelles have grown thicker coats to cope with the English winter.

One of the features of Whipsnade is the way in which quite disparate species are grouped together in communal pens. Birds, in particular, roam freely among the antelopes and deer, and Manchurian cranes can be found alongside hog deer and nilgai. Perhaps the most remarkable testimony to the success of this beautiful zoo is that over eighty per cent of the mammals on show were born in the Park itself.

For those who have not experienced the herds of animals that inhabit the plains of Africa and the forests of India, Whipsnade is the next best thing. While the safari parks supply an overlarge population of dramatic species like lions and tigers, Whipsnade is nearer the truth. Predators are few and hidden away; the more numerous and obvious game on which they depend get pride of place in this lovely zoo. There are the usual cafeteria, restaurant and bar facilities.

Visiting: Whipsnade is open every day of the year except Christmas Day and can be reached by leaving the M1 at junctions 9 or 11. It lies just west of the A5 between Dunstable and Markyate and is well signposted. Visitors can tour the Zoo in their own cars, or take the Zoo Motor Train in summer. It is not cheap, but that seems no deterrent.

Mammals: one of the best collections of breeding mammals in the world, mostly seen wandering freely in large 'natural' paddocks.

Birds: a good collection of the largest species that mix well with the game animals.

Woburn Abbey

Should there be anyone left in Britain who has not visited a safari park, Woburn Abbey is included in an attempt to show them what they are in for. When the British aristocracy emerged from the period of post-war austerity they were suddenly faced with the need to earn a living for the first time in many generations. It was a task that was to prove too much for many, but the thirteenth Duke of Bedford quickly rid himself of any hangups he might have had about commerce and threw his home open to the newly-mobile populace. Though the home was the major attraction, the Duke soon found that the Deer Park, and particularly the herd of Père David's deer, a species saved from extinction by his grandfather, the eleventh Duke, had an appeal all of its own. Being both a commercial animal and a born showman, the Duke quickly formed an alliance with Jimmy Chipperfield, of circus family fame, and was one of the first in the safari-drive-through-zoo-park business.

To those who love the countryside the Deer Park is still a restful place of peace and serenity and, because of the eleventh Duke's Père David associations, a place of pilgrimage. As for the rest, there are enclosures that can be driven through that are so full that the normally solitary tiger forms prides, while the lions seem intent on breeding themselves out of house and home. Unfortunately (lions apart) most of the animals to be seen have been captured for display, and there is little attempt at being self-sufficient in supplying needs for stock by successful husbandry. No doubt seeing wild animals in this way is good for the urbanized youngsters of the South and Midlands, but to participate in the queues of cars can hardly constitute a day in the country.

Visiting: Woburn lies between the A50 and the M1 near Exits 12 and 13. The nearest town is Leighton Buzzard. There are restaurants, lots to do and see, but it is not cheap.

Mammals: Père David's deer, all the usual big stars including wandering lions, tigers, camel, eland, wildebeest, zebra, black rhinoceros, olive baboon, Canadian black bear and hippopotamus.

Birds: ostrich and not much else.

Rabbits

99

London and the South-East

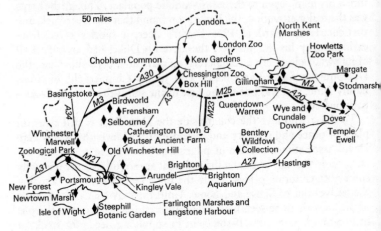

♦ localities mentioned in text

Arundel Wildfowl Refuge

The Arundel Refuge, three-quarters of a mile north of the West Sussex town, is the newest of the Wildfowl Trust's grounds and boasts the usual collection of wildfowl from all corners of the earth. Extending to some fifty-five acres, the marshy pools were already attractive to wild birds before the Trust arrived. Now the collection and feeding routines, and particularly the improvements and extension of the area of open water, makes the area even more attractive. Though still being developed at the time of writing, there will eventually be a considerable Visitor Centre that will include shop, lecture theatre, refreshment room, interpretative centre and a large viewing gallery all overlooking Swan Lake.

One significant difference from other Trust grounds is the special place of seaduck, species that requires an inexhaustible supply of clean, fast-flowing water. Here, it is hoped, the chalk springs will meet the requirements of these birds. Eventually over a thousand wildfowl will be on show, with more wild birds adding to the spectacle.

Visiting: the Arundel Refuge is open every day of the year except

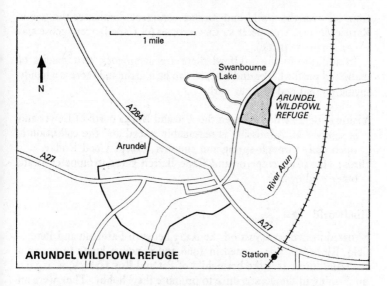

ARUNDEL WILDFOWL REFUGE

Christmas Day. It is well signposted from Arundel, which is on the A27 due east of Chichester and due north of Littlehampton and is well served by rail.

Birds: excellent wildfowl collection with seaduck a speciality. Wild wigeon, teal, pochard, shoveler, kingfisher, snipe, bearded tit.

Other: Arundel Castle nearby.

Bentley Wildfowl Collection

Ornamental wildfowl have been kept for generations, though it was only quite recently that such collections have been opened to the public and thus gained the revenue by which they could be built up to the extremely high standards of today. The Bentley Collection is the creation of Gerald and Mary Askew, and openly based on the inspiration of Sir Peter's Scott's Slimbridge. Starting in 1962 it has been continuously expanded, and is now one of the principal collections in Britain.

Of the 147 species of swans, geese and duck in the world, no less than 110 can be seen at Bentley. Mostly they roam at will through the twenty-five acres of grounds, but there are pens for specific birds, each with its own piece of water, as well as larger ponds and islands where a mixture of birds live side by side. The collection is drawn from all over the world and no one continent dominates the scene. Rarities include trumpeter swan, cereopsis (or Cape Barren) goose and Hawaiian goose (néné).

In addition to the wildfowl there are flamingoes, two species of crane and peafowl. Tea and biscuits can be bought and there is a handy picnic ground and free car park.

Visiting: Bentley lies between the A26 and B2192 north of Lewes and is signposted. Admission is reasonably priced and the collection is open daily through spring and summer, except Good Friday.

Birds: Hawaiian, emperor and Cape Barren geese, trumpeter swan, other wildfowl.

Birdworld 🐦 ♿

Situated in five acres just off the A325 between Farnham and Peters-field, Birdworld was opened in 1968 and is now a home to nearly a thousand birds. It is the brainchild of Pat and Roy Harvey, who gave up farming in Gloucestershire to promote their hobby. They were an immediate success, and the grounds are now visited by thousands of people every year.

Birdworld is situated right next to Alice Holt Forest, and many of its free-flying macaws evidently find the trees an acceptable substitute for their native South American jungles. They do, however, return to feed and roost in the comfort and safety of the grounds. Birdworld is rightly proud of its trees, and the owners take great delight in point-ing out the more interesting varieties. There are quite a number of other species that visitors can mix with, including cranes and a good collection of inquisitive geese. Many of these species breed within the grounds and thus add to the stock continuously. One of the most interesting features from the visiting ornithologist's angle are the uncaged crested seriemas, a fast-walking bird from South America. It is strange the way that birds that are invariably poorly housed and ignored in most zoos can suddenly take on stardom given the right circumstances.

The collection has eight species of pheasants, three of touracos, a couple of vultures and eagles, a pair of the world's heaviest flying birds, the Kori bustard, some very talkative mynahs and a cockatoo. The grounds are well laid out, with ponds and paddocks for various species, a café and shop and a good network of paths that wheelchairs can negotiate.

Visiting: Birdworld is well signposted from the end of the Farnham bypass and lies just north of the A325 at Holt Pound. It is open throughout the year, and a bus service stops virtually outside. Tel. Bentley (Hants.) 2140.

Box Hill ⚘ ♿

Perhaps the most popular 'day in the country' for the people of south-west London since public transport brought it within reach. Millions of feet have climbed the steep slope upward from Burford Bridge on the A24, the Leatherhead–Dorking road, and between them they have carved a deep chalk scar along the very crest of the North Downs. At the top awaits one of the very finest of Wealden views southward over the interlocking hill ranges, south-westward over slumbering Dorking to Leith Hill, 965 feet high, with its 35-foot tower to make the 1000 feet. Before the top a precipitous footpath drops away among the box trees to the River Mole below which can be crossed by stepping stones and is a pleasant place to picnic and catch minnows and stone loach.

Box Hill is not all hard work and hard walking: a turning off the B road between Mickleham and Burford Bridge leads in alpine fashion zigzag up the hill face over well grassed chalk slopes where bee and other orchids can be found in June. Just a little way off the first zig is Juniper Hall, now used by the Field Studies Council as a centre for the children of London's schools. So what was once a breath of Sunday country air for the people of Battersea and Tooting is now a rather more formalized outing for their children and grandchildren.

The North Downs Footpath will eventually pass this way, perhaps climbing the hill or conceivably following the easier low route of the old Pilgrim's Way that skirts along the chalk escarpment at this point on its medieval way between Winchester and Canterbury. On the west side of the River Mole the National Trust (who own Box Hill and its surrounds) also own the remains of the twelfth-century West Humble Chapel, which lies on the Pilgrim's Way.

Visiting: A24 to Burford Bridge between Leatherhead and Dorking.
Botany: orchids on the less frequented chalk slopes.
Other: Wealden views.

Brighton Aquarium

Established in 1869 at the height of Brighton's popularity, the

Aquarium was designed in the ornate Italian style of the time and, though frequently modernized, still retains an air of times gone by. Today, pride of place goes inevitably to the performing dolphins in their huge modern indoor pool, but they are well handled, immensely entertaining and a major attraction. Sealions perform as well, and together these two animals bring in the visitors. There are seals and turtles too.

Yet behind the façade of publicity and entertainment the Aquarium houses one of the best collections of predominantly marine fish and other creatures to be found anywhere in the country. Many are familiar and can be purchased outside together with chips, but others are semi-exotic and seldom seen on the fishmonger's slab. It is a fascinating glimpse into the underwater world that most of us still see only in films or at places like this.

Visiting: the Aquarium is on the sea front at the heart of Brighton.
  Plentiful public transport.
Mammals: dolphins, seals, sealions.
Fish: excellent collection, principally marine.
Other: little pubs in 'The Lanes': some serve outdoors in summer.

Catherington Down and Butser Ancient Farm

Situated on the east side of the unclassified Lovedean–Clanfield road north of Portsmouth, this thirty-acre reserve of the Hampshire County Council, administered by the Hampshire and Isle of Wight Naturalists' Trust, is a fine example of downland that has been ploughed only once in recent years. As a result it has a good chalk flora on open downland with small belts of woodland at the top and bottom of the slopes. Many typical flowers are present, but there is also round-headed rampion, which is remarkably abundant for so rare a plant. Orchids are not numerous, though fragrant and spotted are regular, and frog orchid and autumn lady's tresses rare. Autumn is a fine time to visit, with the blues of bellflower, small scabious and later felwort giving a splendid effect. Chalkland butterflies and moths are a further source of interest.

To the north, just off the A3, lies Butser Hill, well known as a site of prehistoric settlement. Here the Butser Ancient Farm Research Project is busily putting archaeological theories to the practical test. They have Soay sheep and a cross-bred race of cattle that exhibit many of the qualities of their prehistoric ancestors. They are planting (by hand of course) old strains of cereals such as Emmer and Speit, two primitive strains of wheat that have approximately twice the protein content of modern bread wheat, and have reconstructed various buildings and field systems of the time. No doubt the scheme is of great scientific interest, but it is also an absorbing way of spending a day in the country.

Visiting: take the main A3 from Portsmouth and turn left on minor roads to Lovedean. Thence northward toward Clanfield, with Catherington Down reserve a mile or so long on the left. Ref. 690142. There is no restriction on access. Three footpaths cross the reserve. For Butser Ancient Farm proceed to Rogate House, Rogate, off the A3.
Botany: bellflower, small scabious, felwort.
Insects: butterflies of the chalk.
Other: prehistoric working farm.

Chessington Zoo

Chessington lies in the outer suburbs of South London, in the Green Belt but with much development nevertheless. The Zoo was first opened in 1931 and continued to operate right through the war. It has always considered itself an entertainment centre, with circus, kiddies' playground, etc., from its earliest days; and in this it was ahead of its time. Visitor centres are 1970s not 1930s, and even the safari parks are only ten years old. Here a good collection is maintained in predominantly modernized conditions. There are stars like lions and tigers, polar bears and orang-utans, leopards and sealions, but there are many lesser creatures too. A good collection of monkeys includes Assamese macaque, crab-eating monkey, three species of capuchin and two of spider monkeys. A pair of gorillas and a pair of orang-utans are kept more in hope than in belief that they will breed, and unfortunately there are many other 'singles' in the collection.

There are good numbers of antelope and deer, a tapir, elephant, a goodly number of bears and a good collection of the usual zoo-kept birds – for instance, scarlet ibis, white pelican, several pheasants, a waterfowl collection, some free-flying macaws, birds of prey, rock-hopper penguins and three species of cranes. There is an aquarium and a collection of reptiles recently rehoused.

The circus, fairground, boating pool and even Jacobean banquets at Burnt Stub Mansion do not over-detract from this nice zoo so near to London.

Visiting: admission is very reasonable, but the circus, Pets' Corner and aquarium are all extras, though cheap. The Zoo (not the circus, which is summer only) is open throughout the year. It is easily reached by rail from London to Chessington South, and combined rail-entrance tickets are available. By road it lies on the A243 between Chessington and Leatherhead. There is a cafeteria, two licensed restaurants and two bars.

Mammals: lion, tiger, leopard, polar bear, gorilla, orang-utan, Assamese macaque, Brazilian tapir.

Birds: macaws flying free, scarlet ibis, pheasants, birds of prey and vultures.

Chobham Common

The 380 acres of Chobham Common were acquired by Surrey County Council in 1968 and have been maintained as a nature reserve ever since. Though situated right in the heart of the rich commuter belt, only some twenty miles south-west of London, this area of heathland has always been close to the heart of London naturalists. Indeed it is a little special, and the County Council is to be congratulated both on having acquired it and on opening up so many permissive tracks to the public. The underlying sand has created a heath landscape that exhibits a typical community of plant life. Heather, purple moor grass, bristle bent and in some places cotton grass are all to be found. Here and there sundew, marsh gentian and marsh clubmoss grow – all within an essentially suburban area. Even more staggering are the birds, which form as representative a collection of heathland species as you will find for miles. Nightjar, whitethroat, willow warbler, yellowhammer, skylark and perhaps still the declining woodlark may all be sought. There are, of course, badgers and foxes and many small mammals.

Visiting: Chobham Common is situated to the north of the B386 and between that road and the Staines and Wokingham Line Railway. Several public footpaths transect the area and many more permissive tracks have been opened to public access.

Birds: a more or less complete heathland fauna.

Botany: sundew, marsh gentian.

Farlington Marshes and Langstone Harbour

Langstone Harbour is one of the most important wetlands on the

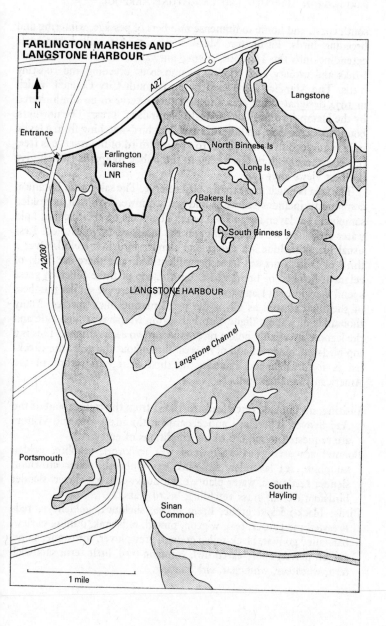

FARLINGTON MARSHES AND
LANGSTONE HARBOUR

N

A27

Langstone

Entrance

Farlington
Marshes
LNR

North Binness Is

Long Is

A2030

Bakers Is

South Binness Is

LANGSTONE HARBOUR

Langstone Channel

Portsmouth

South
Hayling

Sinan
Common

1 mile

south coast, and home to immense numbers of passage, wintering and breeding birds. Farlington Marshes consist of a walled peninsula extending into the Harbour, giving unrivalled views over the mud banks and estuary and a home to numerous breeding and roosting birds. The Marshes are owned by Portsmouth City Council, which in 1974 designated the area a local nature reserve to be administered by the Hampshire and Isle of Wight Naturalists' Trust. The northern boundary is the A27, and there is excellent bird-watching from a layby near the A2030 flyover. Access to about a third of the reserve is free, but elsewhere visitors must keep to the public footpaths (which give the best views anyway).

The area is much more than a bird reserve. The salt marsh botanical community includes sea aster and sea wormwood as well as golden samphire, sea lavender and sea pink. The pools on the marshes hold water crowfoot, water plantain and the localized fat duckweed. Less usual plants include sea clover and slender birdsfoot trefoil. Over a third of British grasses have been identified, and there are beds of eelgrass, beloved of brent geese. Up to 4000 of these Siberian geese spend the winter in Langstone Harbour, and there are similar numbers of shelduck as well as all of the usual marine duck species. Many thousands of waders flight onto Farlington Marshes at high tide and the lagoons invariably hold a rare wader or two each autumn. This is a top bird-watching site and of interest throughout the year: the check-list is formidable and includes the first European record of the American Franklin's gull.

Visiting: an unmade track leads eastward from the roundabout at the A27 flyover. There are noticeboards at the main gate and visitors are requested to adhere to the conditions of entry.

Botany: sea aster, sea wormwood, sea milkwort, seablite, golden samphire, sea lavender, sea pink, sea clubrush, water crowfoot, slender reedmace, water plantain, fat duckweed, sea clover, slender birdsfoot trefoil, grass vetchling, beard grass.

Birds: black-necked grebe, brent goose, shelduck, goldeneye, red-breasted merganser, teal, wigeon, pintail, redshank, dunlin, curlew, bar-tailed godwit, black-tailed godwit, grey plover, turnstone, snipe, golden plover, short-eared owl, common tern, little tern, sandwich tern, wheatear, whinchat, cirl bunting.

Frensham

The dry sandy heathlands of south-western Surrey are both attractive and agriculturally unproductive. Some, like the Devil's Jumps and Punchbowl, are famous beauty spots run over by thousands of people every summer Sunday. Others, like Hankley Common, are remarkably unfrequented, lonely places where heather, sand and sky combine to produce a wilderness right in the very heart of the commuter belt.

This is an area of strange contrasts. At Frensham Great Pond sailing, water-skiing and all those other noisy outdoor pursuits convert a rather attractive water into sheer bedlam. But walk away eastward up the sand ridge and soon the heather and birches insulate you from the world. At the top you can look down onto Frensham Little Pond where birds nest deep in the reedbeds and where botanists seek out the elusive plants of oakwood and heath side by side. Much of the area has been planted with conifers since the war, but these only serve to insulate areas of heather and old Scot's pines from disturbance. As a result the extremely rare hobby can sometimes be seen sweeping overhead. Reed and sedge warblers croak away at the lake's edge, and willow warblers and nightingales sing from the scrub.

Much of the area around the Little Pond is of open access, though the plantations are private property. It is possible to walk eastward through to the Tilford–Hindhead road and then cross over between houses to Hankley Common, where skylarks and the occasional deer are the only companions. To the east lies Thursley Common, offering a wider choice of habitats and a far richer fauna and flora. This is a noted winter haunt of great grey shrike and a breeding place for snipe and redshank.

To the north, the road that connects Frensham and Tilford north of the Pond area has the interesting Old Kiln Museum, housing the Jackson collection of farm implements and machinery of the past that includes a complete wheelwright's shop in working order. It is open during the summer on weekends and Wednesday afternoons. On a Sunday continue to Tilford to sample the ale at the Barley Mow while watching the cricketers trying to beat the ball over the two medieval bridges that guard the green.

Visiting: a good map and a sense of direction after reaching Farnham or Hindhead.

Birds: great crested grebe, little grebe, teal, tufted duck, buzzard, hobby, sparrowhawk, stonechat, nightjar, reed warbler, sedge warbler, willow warbler, lesser whitethroat, nightingale, redstart, goldcrest.

Botany: dry heathland flowers.

Other: Barley Mow at Tilford for summer cricket.

Howletts Zoo Park

The brainchild of John Aspinall, professional gambler turned zoo-keeper-conservationist, Howletts is a remarkable extension of one man's ideas. Aspinall is, in fact, a remarkable man. His ideas are not always popular and his philosophy of wildlife conservation is frequently attacked by the 'establishment'. Nevertheless he is successful. Putting money to use for conservation should always be encouraged, and at Howletts Aspinall has certainly created a new attraction in showing animals. His 'friendships' with his animals have been filmed for television and written about in mass circulation magazines – if he did nothing else he would have brought welcome attention to the cause of conservation. He has, however, managed to achieve much more than that. By gathering endangered mammals to his zoo he has established breeding groups, and if all the tigers in India suddenly disappeared there can be no doubt that John Aspinall would be able to keep the species alive at Howletts. There is, however, a considerable problem in reintroducing zoo-bred animals to the wild and monitoring their successful adaptation to a free existence – a problem that remains to be solved. Howletts has a surplus population of tigers and is now busily supplying other zoos, which is good news for the wild population. There is also a breeding group of Siberian tigers, the only one in Britain.

If the tiger is the star of the show then there are many co-stars. An attempt is being made to breed Indian elephants. Most zoos do not keep males, simply because they are periodically so awkward and indeed dangerous. Though tamed in Asia and put to work, all domesticated elephants are taken from the wild – a continuous drain on an already endangered population. If Howletts can build up a successful breeding herd, then it may show the way to others in Asia. The emphasis on Asian wildlife is not accidental. The only gaur in Britain resides at Howletts, and a search for a mate is being made. There are breeding chital and nilgai, hog deer and sambar.

The African animals include cheetah, roan, black rhino and, of course, gorilla. At Howletts they vie with the tigers for star billing.

The colony numbers over a dozen animals, and the first birth was in 1975. There is some reason to hope that the highly-endangered wild population might be augmented by captive-bred gorillas in the long term. Howletts also has breeding chimpanzees, and other primates including woolly monkeys. There are African wild dogs, snow leopards, leopards, wolves, clouded leopards – in fact one of the finest collections of animal stars to be found in the country. No doubt it is this 'star' quality that brings in the customers.

Visiting: leave Canterbury on the A2 Dover road and turn left at Bekesbourne. Howletts is well signposted. It is open throughout the summer from late May to the end of October. Usual facilities include a cafeteria.

Mammals: gorilla, tiger, snow leopard, chimpanzee, African elephant, Indian elephant, roan, nilgai, sambar, chital, black rhino, cheetah, Brazilian tapir.

Kew Gardens

First opened to the public in 1841, Kew Gardens extends to some 320 acres including the lake and pond. It is a remarkable institution and a must for anyone interested in the countryside. Among the fabulous collection of plants the trees are perhaps outstanding. From all over the world they have come, offering the visitor the opportunity to gain an impression of a foreign land that he is never likely to see, as well as to 'mug up' the names of trees that he ought to know anyway. Nowhere perhaps is this sense of 'foreign-ness' so apparent as in the heated houses, all glass and Victoriana. Hide away in a dank corner and with a little imagination the smell of the tropics will waft you away to some dark jungle the other side of the world. For the gardener Kew is a delight. It offers inspiration (see it here, try and buy it elsewhere) and satisfaction in just being somewhere quite beautiful.

Kew is a favourite day out for Londoners. The admission price – one new penny! – is one of the great bargains, and there are pleasant glades for picnics, etc. Staggeringly enough, the 'Living Collection' consists of no less than 25,000 individual species of plants. Many of these can be found in the various 'Houses'. There are, for instance, an Australian house, a filmy fern house and a Himalayan house as well as the more obscure tropical aroid house, succulent house and the magnificent palm house and (at the end of 1978 – closed) temperate house. There are general, reference and wood museums, a refreshment pavilion and a bookstall. There is, of course, a research staff and herbarium collection available to the serious researcher.

Just by the way, hawfinch and mandarin duck are regular.

Visiting: Kew lies on the south bank of the Thames and can be entered via the gates in Kew Green and Kew Road on the south side of Kew Bridge. From central London leave via Holland Park to the Chiswick Flyover. Buy the handy map on arrival to seek out the areas that interest you.

Botany: 25,000 species to choose from; excellent heated houses.

Birds: hawfinch, mandarin duck.

Other: charming riverside pubs.

Kingley Vale

Kingley Vale has been described as the finest yew forest in Europe. The area is a National Nature Reserve covering 351 acres and rising to Bow Hill at 670 feet. It lies to the north-west of Chichester and consists of chalk downland and mixed forest as well as the yew grove, some of whose trees are five hundred years old. The steeper slopes of the valley are typical grassland, sheltering a variety of attractive flowers including bee and purple orchids, hawkbit, eyebright, thyme and rock rose. Other plant communities are equally attractive. Birds are not outstanding, though there are nightingales, blackcaps and grasshopper warblers in summer. Both fallow and roe deer are found, though seeing them is never easy.

There is a nature trail and a useful quiz-guide that children will find attractive.

Visiting: the southern part of the reserve is of unrestricted access. Take the B2178 from Chichester to West Stoke. The car park is on the right beyond the village and a footpath leads northward to the small Reserve Centre. Follow the nature trail.

Botany: bee orchid, early purple orchid, hawkbit, eyebright, thyme, rock rose, stitchwort, red bartsia, hedge bedstraw, wild parsnip, squinancywort, stonecrop, lady's bedstraw, hoary plantain, hairy violet, salad burnet, St John's wort, dog violet.

Birds: nightingale, blackcap, chiffchaff, grasshopper warbler, marsh tit.

Mammals: fallow deer, roe deer, badger.

Insects: chalkhill and common blue butterflies.

Other: Devils' Humps, Bronze Age burial mounds some 3500 years old and very well preserved.

London Zoo 🐿️ 🐦 ♿

A day among 'wild' animals is as refreshing as a day spent among the hills and peat bogs, and there is no better place to enjoy them than the two grounds of the Zoological Society of London. London Zoo is one of the oldest, most famous, and best in the world. It covers thirty-six acres and is home to some 6800 diverse animals of 1450 species including 200 kinds of mammals, 500 kinds of birds, 200 kinds of reptiles, 42 kinds of amphibians, 270 kinds of fishes and over 100 kinds of invertebrates. It was responsible for bringing the words 'zoo' and 'jumbo' into everyday use. Opened in 1828, there are still three of the original buildings standing, though they do not house animals in the original form. All of the rest is modern, being modernized, or about to be. The result is some of the most imaginative displays of animals to be seen anywhere.

The collection, particularly of mammals, is remarkably complete and includes only one of a handful of pairs of giant pandas outside China; 'Ching-Ching' and 'Chia-Chia' arrived in 1974 and immediately became one of the prime attractions. But in spite of their star quality they are just the highlight in what is one of the best presented wildlife shows in the world. The Moonlight World on the lower floor of the Charles Clore Pavilion simulates nocturnal conditions during the day, so that we can see the host of mammals that normally remain hidden under a cloak of darkness. Loris, echidna, potto, bushbabies – all can be seen to advantage. The bird house echoes to strange tropical calls (particularly bellbirds) and the new display of primates enables these fascinating relatives of ours to be seen in something approaching their natural state.

There are collections of antelope and deer, horses and cattle, rhinos and elephants, lions and tigers, an excellent aquarium, a walk-through aviary, camels, otters, flamingoes, a good collection of birds of prey, goats and ibex, reptiles including snakes and crocodiles and, of course, an excellent children's zoo, educational exhibits, two cafeterias, a restaurant and a fine library and restaurant for the use of members and their guests. Regent's Park is 'next door' and the Regent's Canal passes through the grounds – both are 'semi-country' in the heart of London.

The London Zoo is an admirable and enjoyable place, but it is not cheap. The overheads in maintaining such a large collection under the ideal conditions in which you and I, the public, want to see them are high, and rebuilding and rehousing are expensive. But the Zoo is well worth supporting for its own sake, as well as being a splendid place for a 'day in the country'.

Visiting: the Zoo is open every day of the year except Christmas Day. It lies in the north-east corner of Regent's Park and is within walking distance of Camden Town underground station. Buses numbers 3, 53, 74, 74A stop close by. The Zoo publishes various guides and brochures, with times of feeding, that help you to plan your day to get as much as possible for your money.

Mammals: one of the most comprehensive collections in the world, including a pair of giant pandas.

Birds: good collection covering most of the major groups of the world's avifauna.

Other: Ye Knights of St John, Queen's Terrace, St John's Wood – almost a country pub.

Marwell Zoological Park

If Marwell sticks to its avowed intentions then it will be a welcome addition to the zoos of Britain, but while it claims to be something quite new, it is in reality a Whipsnade-like park in which animals enjoy large enclosures and in which people can either motor or walk the $2\frac{1}{4}$ miles round. There are no safari-type gimmicks, and the collection is a remarkably good one for such a young zoo. No doubt it will grow and become more comprehensive and representative; also doubtless its aim of breeding rare species will be put more fully to the test. At present it has herds of scimitar-horned oryx and Przewalski's horse, but these are well-established in captivity. More important are herds of onager and kulan, the wild asses which are under such threats in the wild, as well as various rare subspecies of zebra.

The Zoo is divided into four major parts according to continent. The largest area is devoted to Africa and houses one of the better collections of antelopes to be found in Britain; species in the Eurasian Zone include tiger plus an assortment of Asiatic odds and ends. Someone really must get down to building up viable herds of swamp deer (barasingha) and blackbuck before these splendid animals finally disappear from the wild. Marwell's other aims are well fulfilled and, as it progresses, it could become a zoo of considerable international importance. To do so it will have to specialize and build up herds of animals that its already established relationships with foreign zoos can then most readily benefit.

A final aim has been to maintain the beauty and feeling of the Hampshire countryside, and the Treetops restaurant gives unsurpassed views over this lovely corner of the county.

Visiting: Marwell is signposted from the A33 Winchester bypass. Take the A333 Portsmouth road and watch for signs on the left after its junction with the A3051.

Mammals: onager, kulan, scimitar-horned oryx, Przewalski's horse, Hartmann's mountain zebra, swamp deer, blackbuck, Sumatran tiger.

Birds: small part of the collection.

New Forest

Despite its appropriation as a Royal Forest in the eleventh century, the New Forest remains largely common land and the largest tract of unsown, semi-natural vegetation in lowland Britain. Over 48,000 acres of heath and woodland are of free access and another 20,000 acres are enclosed. The whole area has been shaped by man and, in particular, by his animals and their grazing and browsing. The soil is largely infertile sands and clays lying in the Hampshire Basin, and the sparse vegetation and grazing make the Forest one of the most important wildlife sites in Britain.

Though the New Forest ponies are the most obvious form of indigenous life, there are in fact red, fallow and roe deer as well as muntjac. There are badgers, and it was in the New Forest that moviemaker Eric Ashby filmed his marvellous badger and deer films. Birds are very important, and the Forest is the headquarters of the Dartford warbler in Britain as well as one of the strongholds of that rare and elusive falcon, the hobby. Buzzards are common and sparrowhawks as numerous as anywhere. There are still some red-backed shrikes, stonechats, crossbills, nightjars and the freshly colonizing firecrests, which were first found breeding in Britain here nearly twenty years ago. Additionally there are birds here that bird-watchers tend to go rather quiet about when mentioned.

The flora of the Forest is exceptionally rich, and the valley bogs are unique in Britain, and even decidedly rare in western Europe. Marsh gentian and bog orchid are two rare species, and the wild gladiolus occurs nowhere else in the country but along the Forest edges. Heath and marsh orchids are common.

Among the lesser creatures found in the Forest that are rare or scarce elsewhere, sand lizard and smooth snake are important. Here and there scorpions can be found – almost the only reliable place in England – but they are very rare and unlikely to prove a menace. The large marsh grasshopper, one of the largest of our grasshoppers, is seldom found elsewhere, and the New Forest cicada is never found anywhere else.

Many visitors to the New Forest find wildlife a disappointment, but with such large areas to explore and such varied landscape luck or hard work are necessary. Nevertheless in the New Forest it is quite possible to walk for miles without seeing another person, a remarkable attraction in lowland England. Some areas worth special attention are:

1 Beaulieu Heath, especially in the north between Beaulieu and Dibden.
2 Beaulieu Road, on the Lyndhurst–Beaulieu road the B3056 north of the railway.
3 Bolderwood Walk, along the minor road between Lyndhurst and the A31.
4 Wilverly Walk, off the A35 north or south of Holmsley Station.
5 Braemore on the A338 along the Hampshire Avon, which has retained its Tudor style and has a Saxon church and a medieval mizmaze.

Visiting: much of the area is of direct open access from the main A31 and A35. It can be walked along well-marked paths, and many of the woods can be entered, some even driven through. There is good accommodation in a number of Forest villages and camping is allowed by prior permit and at restricted sites: notices lead to permit offices. At all times visitors should respect the Country Code and be particularly careful with fires. Do not pick flowers – for all you know they might be the last of their kind in the country.

Mammals: red deer, fallow deer, roe deer, muntjac, fox, badger.
Birds: hobby, Dartford warbler, stonechat, crossbill, firecrest, red-backed shrike, curlew, snipe, woodlark, wood warbler, redstart, nightjar, nightingale, sparrowhawk, buzzard.
Botany: heather, gorse, marsh gentian, bog orchid, wild gladiolus.
Reptiles: sand lizard, smooth snake.
Insects: silver-studded blue butterfly, fritillaries, emperor hawk moth, bee hawk moth, large marsh grasshopper, New Forest cicada.

Newtown Marsh

Newtown lies on the Solent coast of the Isle of Wight between Cowes and Yarmouth. It is the major intertidal zone of the island and rich in birds, plants and other wildlife. The main marsh was formerly wet grazing, but breaches of the sea wall in 1954 allowed the area to revert to the tidal zone. Together with the Newtown River this now forms the major habitat for wildfowl and waders, which congregate in good numbers during passage periods and in winter. Adjacent areas of farmland and woodland are included in the 800-acre local nature reserve.

Perhaps the most attractive feature of Newtown is its size; it is small enough to enable most of its wildlife to be viewed without too much difficulty. Though permits can be obtained for a small fee, the average visitor need not depart from the rights of way which have been set out as a quite excellent nature trail.

Along the trail, which starts at an observation post where species of fauna and flora can be studied in advance, most of the specialities can be seen. At the start, for instance, a long-established nest of wild bees is picked out in an old oak. Attention is drawn to the marsh wolf spider, a strange creature that is submerged by the tides twice each day. The flora of the saltings include sea aster and sea lavender, long-leaved scurvy grass, once used by sailors as a source of Vitamin C, and the hybrid cordgrass that originated in nearby Southampton Water and which now threatens so many of our estuaries. The shingle spits support horned poppy and sea holly.

The route leads beside Clamerkin Lake, still used as a commercial oyster fishery and the site of Britain's first clam fishery. Onward through the Town Copse, a National Trust property, there are interesting plants which include the guelder rose, wood spurge, stinking iris and butcher's broom. Butterflies include white admiral, purple hairstreak and speckled wood, while the orange-tip occurs along the verges. Through Walter's Copse watch for red squirrel and for twayblade, tutsan, betony and saw-wort.

Birds are plentiful and warblers abound in summer. There is even a spot to wait and listen for the nightingale, and cuckoo and green woodpeckers should be heard if not seen. The marshes themselves hold waders, and spotted redshank is regular along with greenshank, ruff, good flocks of black-tailed godwit in winter, snipe and dunlin. Some 170 species of birds have been recorded, of which seventy have bred. This can be compared with the 300 species of plants that can be found.

The Old Town Hall is worth a visit at the end, for the basement contains a summer exhibition of Pleistocene mammalian remains found in the reserve.

Visiting: there is no public transport. Visitors should drive through the village High Street (marked 'No Through Road') to the end and park. There are notices on the footpath to the Quay. A leaflet is available.

Birds: cormorant, teal, wigeon, pintail, shelduck, brent goose, Canada goose, oystercatcher, ringed plover, golden plover, snipe, curlew, black-tailed godwit, redshank, spotted redshank, greenshank, dunlin, ruff, common tern, little tern, kingfisher, marsh tit, long-tailed tit, nightingale, willow warbler.

Botany: sea purslane, sea aster, sea lavender, long-leaved scurvy grass, sea arrowgrass, sea plantain, Townsend's cordgrass, guelder rose, wood spurge, stinking iris, butcher's broom, horned poppy, sea holly.

Insects: speckled wood, meadow brown, white admiral, purple hair streak, orange-tip, painted lady, comma, gatekeeper and wall butterflies.

Mammals: red squirrel.

North Kent Marshes

Between the urban conglomeration and motorways of the Medway Towns and the River Thames to the north lies a backwater of mud banks and marshes that have changed little since the days of Dickens. While London extends ever outward, and the country around it becomes an ever more ordered and tidy dormitory for its commuters, the marshes that border the Thames between Cliffe and Allhallows retain a breath of true countryside.

Along the river an embankment runs the length of the loneliest walk within thirty miles of London. Here you will meet few others – the occasional bird-watcher, the less occasional gun. On one side, mud banks alive with trips of shorebirds, with the river and the ever-present big ships beyond; on the other, ditches with kingfishers, and meadows with sheep and lapwings. Here primroses still grow among the hedgerows and poppies among the cereals. In winter the harsh easterly winds can chill a shelterless soul in minutes. Then the wild white-fronted geese honk across the skies while shelduck dabble away over the open flat by courtesy of the Thames Conservancy, which has cleaned up their river in a ten-year dash for ecological purity.

The quickest approach to the marshes is at Allhallows, where a caravan site and a rash of cafés and pubs with jukeboxes is a reminder that urban 'civilization' is not far away. From here a well-worn path leads northward to the sea wall: turn right for Yantlett Creek, where marsh birds fly against a backdrop of the Isle of Grain refinery, and left for the long walk to Lower Hope Point via St Mary's and Egypt Bays.

At the foot of St Mary's a track leads inland among the sheep walks to Swigshole, Decoy Farm and Northward Hill, the bird reserve where grey herons nest under the watchful eye of the Royal Society for the Protection of Birds. There is a nature trail, and the warden can be contacted at Swigshole Cottage, High Halstow, Rochester ME3 8SR. Visit in summer, when the herons are in the treetops.

Continuing westward along the sea wall there are the Cooling Marshes, scene of *Great Expectations*: indeed the village church still has graves that Dickens wrote about. The open spaces have hares in spring and big skies throughout the year.

Visiting: to Cliffe on B2000 from Rochester, or A228 to Stoke and minor roads to Allhallows.
Birds: white-fronted goose, shelduck, wigeon, teal all winter; grey heron in summer.

Queendown Warren

Though it covers only eighteen acres of chalk downland and has access only by two rights of way, this is a popular open space where picnics are a favourite summer pastime. It is, in fact, a local nature reserve of the Swale District Council administered by the Kent Trust for Nature Conservation, and a leaflet is available giving details of the flora. This is a dry valley heavily grazed by rabbits, and the short turf holds a wealth of chalk plants. No less than twelve orchids can be found, including early spider, bee and fly, with man and green-winged near the lower part of the slope. There are also milkwort, thyme, autumn lady's tresses and meadow sage. There is an area of woodland where traveller's joy (old man's beard), lords and ladies and dog mercury grow. Both common and chalkhill blue butterflies are found. Just over the entrance stile there is a toadstood 'Fairy Ring' fifteen yards in diameter, indicating an age of several hundreds of years.

Visiting: leave the M2 on the A249 Maidstone road and turn right for Stockbury. Minor roads lead to the Reserve, which is entered from the north next to Potter's Wood, where there is parking space.

Botany: early spider orchid, bee orchid, fly orchid, man orchid, green-winged orchid, milkwort, autumn lady's tresses, meadow sage, traveller's joy, dog's mercury.

Selborne

A small, rather nondescript village in northern Hampshire that rests its claim to fame on being the home of Gilbert White, the founder of modern British natural history. His book *The Natural History of Selborne* has passed through so many editions that its sales must be bettered only by the modern genus of field guides. It is still an essential read and companion to those who would get the best out of this typical piece of rural England. Gilbert White's home is now the Wakes Museum, open to the public. Behind it lies the beech hanger with its famous zigzag path created by Gilbert and his brother. The woods still echo to the same bird calls as in his day, though we now know that swallows do not spend their winters in the bottoms of ponds – a view current in White's time. There is a Selborne Nature Trail created by the Alton Natural History Society that leads up the path to the hanger for flowers, deer (if lucky) and birds.

Visiting: Selborne lies on the B3006 south of Alton. Visit the Wakes Museum, the Church and the hanger.

Birds: wood warbler, willow warbler, great spotted woodpecker, marsh tit, rook.

Botany: good collection of chalk woodland species.

Other: Gilbert White associations.

South Downs Way

Opened in 1972, this was Britain's first Long Distance Bridleway. From Eastbourne it stretches westward as far as Harting in Hampshire, with plans to extend to Winchester. As the name implies, you can ride a horse the whole way, or walk if you prefer. Alternatively you can break journey at a number of points where the pathway dips down to road or river level, or walk between two such points over the open Downs.

From Eastbourne, for instance, the path leads southward along the cliff edge to Beachy Head, where there are stupendous views over the Channel below. Continue on to Birling Gap, where there is a pub to set you up for the Seven Sisters Country Park in an Area of Outstanding Natural Beauty. Here the path follows the switchback nature of the cliffs and hollows of this fine chalk landscape. Here too there are typical chalkland plant communities rich in species. By the meandering Cuckmere River the path turns inland to Exceat, where Wheelers have an excellent fish restaurant at the bridge. The river here is well reeded, and sedge and reed warblers croak from their fastnesses. The main A259 leads back to Eastbourne, or you can continue northward to Alfriston before climbing back up to the Downs and follow the northern escarpment to Firle Beacon. Throughout this section and onward to the Ouse the views are open over predominantly ploughed land. The small birds are meadow pipits, the large ones lapwings. The wild flowers are few, but the odd humps and bumps indicate a human tenancy that extends back thousands of years to Neolithic times. Leaving the Way at the River Ouse, the A275 leads to Lewes or Newhaven.

Almost every viewpoint along the Way was a fortress in some far distant time. Chanctonbury Ring, east of the A24 Worthing road, is perhaps the best example. Even the strong growth of mature trees cannot hide its fortification foundations. This is the section of South Downs that is for everyman. A path leads southward from the A283 up a wooded defile to the open Downs above. It is a fine walk, and Chanctonbury lies a mile or so away to the west. For even easier downland access take the minor road to Worthing southward out of Steyning. Ploughed downland stretches away in each direction and the South Downs Way can be joined eastward or westward.

After Chanctonbury the Downs are more overgrown with scrub and less dramatic from above and below. Those who continue toward Harting are rewarded by branching off southward on the A286 Midhurst–Chichester road to Singleton where half a mile south of the village is the Weald and Downland Open Air Museum Country Park. Here there is a lake, historic buildings housing a museum, and woods and meadowland.

Whether you dip in or walk the whole way, the South Downs Way is a fine area for botanizing, for archaeology and for superb scenery.

Visiting: see leaflet published by HMSO for the Countryside Commission.

Botany: excellent flowers of the chalk in unploughed areas.

Steephill Botanic Garden

The Steephill Botanic Garden was established only in 1970, on the site of the defunct Royal National Hospital. In the face of pressures to turn the site to a multitude of other uses, it is a testimony to the local authorities that they settled on a botanic garden. At the time the garden was an overgrown wilderness, but several botanic features survived, including a huge *Cypressus macrocarpa* planted in 1897 by Princess Henry of Battenberg. As clearance progressed each vacant spot was planted, so that the overall pattern present in most botanic gardens is lacking. However, this does not detract from its appeal.

Because of its remarkable position and the underlying geology, Steephill has a remarkable opportunity to develop a fascinating collection. Already this development has been rapid. There is a 'pop' rose garden whose lushness appeals to the non-botanist, as well as many attractive plants of more specialist interest. Outstanding, perhaps, is the fact that many plants more familiar in mainland greenhouses can survive in the open in this mild climate, and that others grow in such lush abandon. When the Gardens are brought into some semblance of order this site will become one of the best of its kind in the country. Meanwhile it is a fine and beautifully tended garden.

Visiting: Steephill is 1½ miles west of Ventnor on the A3055 road.

Botany: lush subtropical growth on a highly accommodating soil.

Stodmarsh

Created by mining subsidence in the valley of the Great Stour northeast of Canterbury, Stodmarsh was declared a National Nature Reserve in 1968 to protect the community of breeding birds. The interesting western end of the marsh is still in the hands of the National Coal Board. Though considerable areas of open water remain, by far the largest part of Stodmarsh is covered by the common reed, *Phragmites communis*. Here the rare birds for which the area has long been famous can be found. They include bittern, bearded tit and the two colonizing warblers Cetti's and Savi's. The strident notes of the former are unmistakable, while the reeling of Savi's warbler can only be confused with that of the grasshopper warbler, which has a different pitch. Harriers are regularly present during passage periods and there is always an early spring influx of garganey. Indeed this is probably the most regular place to see this attractive little migrant duck. Winter brings many northern duck, and waders are always a feature.

The interesting plants of the area include great spearwort and great water dock, and there is a small area of dittander.

Access is allowed free of restraint along the Lampen Wall, which leads from Stodmarsh to Grove Ferry via the marsh and along the banks of the Stour. This is an excellent walk, full of interest the whole way.

Visiting: park carefully in Stodmarsh and take the lane past the Red Lion out to the Reserve and the Lampen Wall. The best areas for birds lie between the start of the Wall and the River Stour. Continue to Grove Ferry.

Botany: great spearwort, great bladderwort, marsh stitchwort, bog-bean, great water dock, blunt flowered rush, frogbit, water drop-wort, hornwort, hairy buttercup, marsh arrow grass, marestail, sea club-rush, dittander.

Birds: bittern, bearded tit, Savi's warbler, Cetti's warbler, sedge warbler, reed warbler, garganey, harriers, wigeon, teal, ruff, waders.

Temple Ewell

This local Nature Reserve covers fifty-three acres of chalk downland just north of Dover, and is of primary interest to botanists in search of specialities of the chalk. Though there have been considerable inroads by tor grass and by gorse, the continued grazing rights have preserved much of the open landscape that we have grown to think of as typical of the Downs, and many flowers can still be found. Orchids include scented, burnt-tip and early spider as well as autumn lady's tresses later in the year. Other specialities include chalk milkwort, dyer's greenweed, yellow-wort and dropwort. Along with the flowers a variety of butterflies occur, including both chalkhill and common blue and marbled white. Great green grasshoppers occur and among them are the similar, though much rarer, warbiter bush crickets. Birds are generally plentiful, though there are no great rarities or unusual species.

Visiting: leave the A2 between Lydden and Temple Ewell north of

Dover, on a track running north-west on the south side of the railway bridge that crosses the road. In 300 yards there is parking space. A footpath leads to the Reserve.

Botany: Burnt-tip orchid, early spider orchid, scented orchid, autumn lady's tresses, dyer's greenweed, chalk milkwort, dropwort, yellow-wort.

Insects: chalkhill blue butterfly, common blue butterfly, marbled white butterfly, great green grasshopper, warbiter bush cricket.

Old Winchester Hill

Though it apparently has no historical associations with the city of Winchester, over fifteen miles to the west, nevertheless Old Winchester Hill is an ancient site with Iron Age connections. It lies immediately east of the A32 between Alton and Fareham and has been a National Nature Reserve since 1954.

The Hill is part of the South Downs and was fortified to dominate the Meon Valley, which it overlooks. Its natural history importance stems from its downland chalk geology and from the major factors that have destroyed so much of the Downs during the last thirty years. Ploughing and the lack of grazing by a declining rabbit population have both taken their toll, and it is likely that the typical fauna and flora will survive only in areas like Old Winchester Hill, where they are carefully maintained. From most of the reserve scrub is eradicated, and the cropped grass of the traditional downland landscape is maintained by a rotational system of grazing within enclosures. This is one of the few National Nature Reserves where the visitor may wander at will, but the excellent nature trail is recommended.

Though Mesolithic and Neolithic remains have been discovered, the most impressive remains are those built at the time of the second Iron Age invasion from the Continent in 250 BC. The fort dominates the southern part of the reserve.

The chalk slopes are excellent for plants, and no less than fourteen different species of orchids can be found. These include fragrant, spotted and autumn lady's tresses. Cowslips, now so rare, are found in spring, and the aromatic thyme and marjoram are common. Lady's bedstraw, kidney and horseshoe vetch, and Carline and stemless thistles are also found. The beech and ash woods were planted about 1800 and enchanter's nightshade and dog's mercury can be found on the forest floor.

Mammals are scarce, though badger, fox, rabbit, hare and grey squirrel – or at least signs of their presence – can all be found. Though ninety species of birds have been observed there is nothing special. Butterflies are more important. Chalkhill and common blues, meadow brown, small skipper, small heath, speckled wood, as well as the migrant clouded yellow, are all found. In spring there are brimstones and small tortoiseshells and in early summer green hairstreak and Duke of Burgundy fritillaries can be seen, and there are some good moths.

Visiting: turn eastward on a minor road at Warnford on the A32. The nature trail is well signposted on the right. Take the longer version, which includes visits to a badger sett and a butterfly-rich combe.

Botany: cowslip, violet, thyme, marjoram, restharrow, rampion, fragrant orchid, wild parsnip, Carline thistle, stemless thistle, lady's bedstraw, kidney vetch, horseshoe vetch, early purple orchid, spotted orchid, twayblade, autumn lady's tresses, felwort, enchanter's night-shade, dog's mercury.

Insects: green hairstreak, Duke of Burgundy fritillary, clouded yellow, chalkhill blue, common blue, meadow brown, small skipper, small heath, speckled wood, green-veined white, small tortoiseshell, and brimstone butterflies.

Mammals: badger, fox, grey squirrel.

Birds: yellowhammer, turtle dove, stock dove, treecreeper, green woodpecker, willow warbler, chiffchaff, kestrel.

Wye and Crundale Downs

This National Nature Reserve covers 250 acres of the easternmost part of the chalk. Almost due east of Ashford in Kent, it encompasses the steep scarp of the North Downs and allows public access over a considerable area to the Devil's Kneadingtrough, a deep chalk gully, with excellent views to the south over Romney Marsh and the Channel, and occasionally to France. Further exploration of the reserve is facilitated by a good nature trail that leads down the scarp and then traverses into Pickersdane Scrubs, an area of ash and hazel coppice with whitebeam and yew. The birds and mammals are no more than one would expect, with willow warbler, blackcap, whitethroat and nightingale, fox, badger, weasel and the occasional fallow deer. In contrast the flora is particularly rich, and a considerable attraction to botanists, who will be pushed to find some species elsewhere in Britain. No doubt this is in no small measure due to the reserve's

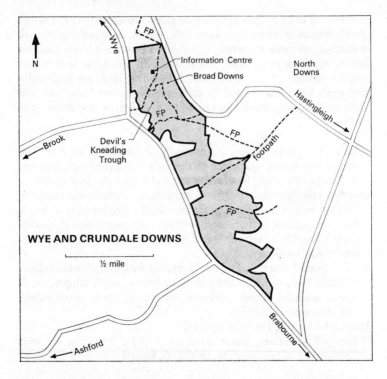

proximity to the Continent. Orchids, for instance, number no less than seventeen species. There is a small information centre on the north-west side of Broad Down, the area available to the public, which is open most weekends during the summer.

Even on the open downland there are interesting flowers to be found. Wild thyme, salad burnet, rock rose and stemless thistle mix with early purple, common spotted and pyramidal orchids. Among the thick tor grass species such as knapweed, marjoram and St John's wort manage to survive. Where the grass is grazed there is birdsfoot trefoil. Among the experimental fields where a staggered system of cutting is operated you may find fragrant and pyramidal orchids as well as marbled white butterflies. The coppiced areas hold wild strawberries, ground ivy and hemp agrimony as well as woodpeckers, nuthatches and grey squirrel.

Visiting: leave Ashford eastward on the A20 and turn left into the village of Willesborough. Continue through Hinxhill toward Hastingleigh. Broad Down is easily found.

Birds: nightingale, great spotted woodpecker, willow warbler, blackcap, whitethroat.

Mammals: badger, fox, weasel.

Botany: pyramidal orchid, spotted orchid, birdsfoot trefoil, marjoram, St John's wort.

Dartford warbler

East Anglia

★ *localities mentioned in text*

EAST ANGLIA

50 miles

Banham Zoo and Woolly Monkey Sanctuary

Banham Zoo is a comparatively small affair, but with an enviable reputation. It has always specialized in monkeys, and has one of the finest collections of these species to be found in the country. Though the collection is varied there is considerable emphasis placed on natural colonies, with the result that Banham has achieved a considerable degree of breeding success. There are spider monkeys, the howlers whose calls echo through the surrounding countryside, vervets, gibbons, langurs and the strange crab-eating macaques. There is also a chimpanzee colony, which is inevitably a major attraction, and the twenty-odd woolly monkeys. The latter form a breeding group, one of only two in Britain and half a dozen in Europe, and very difficult to keep, let alone breed. The boldly-marked black and white colobus monkey, which leaps from tree to tree in the forests of Ethiopia and West Africa, can be seen and there are also the only red colobus monkeys in Europe. For a zoo of only twenty acres this is indeed a remarkable collection, and Banham is worth visiting for the monkeys alone.

There are, however, other attractions, including porcupines, coypus, pelicans, penguins, flamingoes, egrets, sealions, several unusual birds of prey including the delicious Pallas' fish eagle, hummingbirds, parrots and a museum of bygone country crafts. The fact that there are no lions, tigers or elephants can only help to concentrate attention on these equally interesting though less spectacular animals.

Visiting: the Zoo is open throughout the year and lies on the B1113, eighteen miles south-west of Norwich. There is the usual shop and cafeteria. Tel. Quidenham 476.

Mammals: woolly monkey, red colobus monkey, black and white colobus monkey, vervet monkey, lar gibbon, spectacled langur, grey langur, black ape, crab-eating macaque, chimpanzee, wallabies, porcupines, deer, sealions.

Birds: varied assortment, including birds of prey and owls.

Benacre to Sizewell

(See map under Havergate Island, page 138.)

The north-east corner of Suffolk offers not so much a day in the country as a whole holiday full of days. The underlying geology, in part at least, accounts for the variety of the landscape, but man's history shows as well. Huge empty and mostly decaying churches testify to more prosperous days, and the thick reed marshes (intentionally flooded in 1940) to the fear of invasion during the last war. There are coverts where pheasants breed and heaths where stone curlews and red-backed shrikes cling tenaciously to one of their final British strongholds.

This corner of Suffolk is becoming a virtually continuous strip of nature reserves, with birds as the most important object. But there are plentiful rights of way and it is possible to walk for miles and miles in and out of the sanctuaries. Southwold is the natural centre, and the

River Blyth to the south of the town is the only break in the otherwise continuous beach walk from Benacre Ness to Sizewell.

This is a long, hard day, but varied and rich. The coastal broads of Benacre, Covehithe and Easton are well reeded homes of waterbirds and after six miles of beach the excellent Adnams Ales of Southwold come as a welcome relief. Continuing southward there is a rowboat ferry across the Blyth to Walberswick (crowded in summer and said to be haunted), where the Anchor Hotel is an alternative base. The marshes here are part of the Walberswick National Nature Reserve and maps show footpaths and other access details. Hosts of shorebirds frequent the pools in spring and autumn, and the bittern may be heard in early spring booming from the reedbeds. The beach itself is one of the finest hunting grounds for amber and other semi-precious stones, and the flowers are worth a journey on their own account.

Dunwich, one of the rotten boroughs that elected two members of Parliament until the Reform Act of 1832, has disappeared into the sea so many times, the bells of the sixteen drowned churches are said to be heard on stormy nights. Do not dig in the cliffs: they regularly collapse and kill people and, besides, it disturbs the sand martins.

Southward past the old Coastguard Cottages the beautiful Minsmere Bird Reserve extends inland to Eastbridge. Hides along the inner bank are open to the public and give excellent views over feeding pools where avocets and other waders feed and rest. Here there are Sandwich, common and little terns, though these latter still try to nest on the beach itself. Ask the bird-watchers who swarm along here to help you pick out the different species – they are quite human when spoken to politely. Permits to penetrate the reserve in advance only from the Royal Society for the Protection of Birds.

On to the south lies Sizewell with its diabolical monument to nuclear power: when you reach here you know you have come to the very end of the road and that it is time to return to everyday life.

Birds: avocet, marsh harrier, bittern, bearded tit, redshank, common
    tern, Sandwich tern, little tern, passage shorebirds.
Botany: reedbeds, shore salt plant community, orchids in woods.
Other: amber, cornelian and other semi-precious stones along the
    beach.

Breckland

This once vast sandy wasteland in East Anglia has been changed out of all recognition over the past hundred years. Where once a few sheep and shepherds roamed the lonely wastes, now over half of the Brecks have been turned into forestry plantations. Another wilderness has been converted to the service of man. Originally heather and gorse dominated the landscape, broken here and there by belts of old Scots pine. The area held a unique fauna and flora that once included the great bustard. Now only isolated pockets remain, and the bustard has disappeared for ever.

Fortunately some areas have been retained, usually by conservation bodies. There are National Nature Reserves at Cavenham, Thetford and Weeting Heaths, the RSPB has reserves at Horn and Weather Heaths, and the Norfolk Naturalists' Trust has East Wretham Heath. Some of these reserves are, for various reasons, closed to the public, but Cavenham Heath is generally accessible along the River Lark, and East Wretham has a hide overlooking the interesting water of Langmere, and a nature trail. Because of the facilities it offers, a visit to East Wretham is recommended for most purposes. Here there is a good chance of seeing the native red squirrel and both red and roe deer are possibilities. Stone curlews frequent the sandy wastes, although, as elsewhere, they are as likely to be found on ploughed fields as anywhere. Crossbills frequent the pines and there is still just a chance of the fast-declining woodlark. Botanists will enjoy searching out the rarer heathland plants, though the decline of the rabbit has, as elsewhere, led to considerable growth of scrub.

Visiting: the whole of Breckland between Mildenhall, Bury St Edmunds and Methwold is worth exploring, though visitors usually start at Thetford or Brandon. East Wretham Heath lies four miles north of Thetford on the A1075. Visitors should contact the Warden at East Wretham Heath Nature Reserve, Thetford, Norfolk, IP24 1RU. Tel. Great Hockham 339. The office lies at the northeast corner of the reserve. There is a small charge for entry and use of the Langmere hide. The Furze Hills at Hildersham offer an isolated area which is well known botanically for typical Breckland plants.

Botany: shepherd's cress, maiden pink, biting stonecrop, hoary cinquefoil, spring vetch, Spanish catchfly.

Birds: gadwall, shoveler, Canada goose, snipe, redshank, stone curlew, crossbill, woodlark, willow tit, whinchat, redstart.

Other: Grime's Graves at Brandon is a Neolithic flint mine.

Breydon Water

Breydon Water is the estuary of the River Yare and the boundary between Suffolk and Norfolk. It is also effectively the estuary of the whole Norfolk Broads system as well as of the River Waveney, which for most of its length is the actual boundary between the two counties. Though its exit to the sea lies southward beyond Gorleston, the estuary is fronted by the great holiday agglomeration of Great Yarmouth, and it is this Borough in association with the Norfolk County Council that owns and administers the reserve.

The estuary, which is about a mile wide and four and a half miles long, empties out at low tide to reveal the enormous mudbanks that are then thronged with birds throughout the year. If the quietest time is midsummer then at every other season there are thousands of waders and wildfowl present. Today, after almost a hundred years of active protection, it is easy to see why Breydon Water had such a hold on the minds of those nineteenth-century path-finding protectionists. Wildfowl, including small flocks of wild geese of several species, are numerous throughout the winter, especially in the new year. Most species of wader on the British list have popped in from time to time and there are good concentrations of the more common species in season. Rarities like avocet and spoonbill are regular and bitterns invariably turn up and may breed from time to time. Short-eared owls are legend here, and hen harriers visit regularly every winter. There are many small birds, including bearded tit at some times of the year.

With such a huge holiday population Great Yarmouth is to be congratulated on establishing this significant reserve on its doorstep. Let's hope that the trippers enjoy it for what it is.

Visiting: access is restricted to the walls along both north and south banks of the estuary. Both sides of Breydon are easily reached from Yarmouth; the south by crossing the Yare by the Haven Bridge and following the river bank on the right; the north by crossing the River Bure by Vauxhall Bridge, turning first left and following the river wall as it bears right at Vauxhall Railway Station.

Birds: white-fronted goose, bean goose, shelduck, wigeon, pintail, goldeneye, cormorant, bar-tailed godwit, dunlin, redshank, avocet, bittern, bearded tit.

Cambridge Botanic Garden ✿ ♿

The Cambridge University Botanic Garden was founded in 1760 in the centre of Cambridge on a five-acre plot on Free School Lane. In 1831 a larger site of forty acres was acquired some three-quarters of a mile south, and it is this area (developed in two distinct halves) that is the present home of the collection. At first only the western half was laid out; later, in the present century, the eastern half was developed as well.

As with all such institutions the Garden's purposes are a mixture of research, education and amenity. There is a long tradition of research (early genetic work for example), and it is now a fully-fledged educational institution offering a variety of courses in botany and gardening. It is, however, so near the city centre that it inevitably acts as a park for local people.

The nineteenth-century Garden was laid out by John Stevens Henslow, then professor of botany, and consists of a fine collection of trees native to Europe, though because of the light calcareous soils of the area and its 'continental'-type climate, conifers do not grow well. A walk around the outer path leads one naturally through the various groups of trees, though being now some 130 years old, many are mature while others are in decline. Systematic replanting has maintained the representative quality of the collection.

There is a stream and lake, and the natural chalk spring feeders did not dry up until the remarkable drought of 1976. Trees and shrubs dependent on water flourish, and visitors should note the parasitic (on willow) *Lathraea clandestina* with its large purple flowers. This is an idyllic spot and nearby the Water Garden holds a fine collection of native wetland flowers. There are specialist collections of tulips and cranesbills and of European saxifrages.

The twentieth-century Garden was originally developed in 1925, but from 1950 onward the research collections were established, followed by the development of representative collections of native British plants on an ecological basis. Of particular interest are the artificial limestone beds and the juniper natural variation collection. There is even a scented garden with a special seat for the blind.

The Winter Garden is a fine concept, consisting as it does of plants that are at their best between November and April. And since 1974 the Gardens have had a contract with the Nature Conservancy to build up a collection of the rarer plants of East Anglia.

No garden would be complete without its glasshouses, and over the years Cambridge University has established a full and attractive range of such exhibits. There is a temperate house, a cool fern house, a stove house, a palm house and aquarium with a central 'lantern' reaching 43 feet in height, an orchid house, tropical fern house and so on. This is a fine garden and worthy of a visit.

Visiting: open free all through the year on weekdays (except Christmas Day and Boxing Day) and on an experimental basis on Sunday afternoons between May and September inclusive. There are entrances in Trumpington Road, Bateman Street and Hills Road. There is a car park in Brookside and a nice little guidebook.

Botany: first-rate collection in fine surroundings.

Other: small but interesting aquarium.

Colchester Zoo

Based on Stanway Hall, Colchester Zoo is a zoo with its heart in the right place. Its large grounds enable animals to be kept in good conditions, in light and airy paddocks rather than cramped cages, and as a result a large number have bred. In fact there is no greater compliment to the zoo manager than having his charges breed themselves out of house and home.

Where possible, animals can be seen against something like a natural background. Brown bears and the white rhinoceros enjoy the freedom of large paddocks, and zebra look almost natural, though against a backdrop of English trees and shrubs. Others, for obvious reasons, must be more carefully confined. Lions and tigers, puma and cheetah, leopard and caracal are kept well caged, but not over-confined. Colchester boasts a black panther (really a black mutant of the common leopard), an unusual animal that cannot apparently be reproduced in captivity. Smaller predators include leopard cat, lynx and genet. There is a modern 'Moonlight World' where mongoose, bushbaby, kinkajou, armadillo and chinchilla are on display during the day (their night).

Primates include orang-utan, and there are squirrel and spider monkeys. There is an aquarium with many tropical and larger fish and a good collection of reptiles. Birds are well represented, and apart from the usual flamingoes and penguins there are condor, caracara, bateleur eagle, macaws, parrots, trumpeters, owls, waterfowl and crowned pigeons.

Visiting: the Zoo is easily reached on the B1022 between Colchester
and Tiptree. Entrance fees are a bargain and include all the exhibits
including aquarium, Moonlight World and reptile house. There is
also free car parking. The Zoo is open throughout the year and there
are adequate cafeterias.
Mammals: tiger, lion, black panther, cheetah, caracal, bushbaby,
armadillo, zebra, black and brown bears.
Birds: caracara, condor, trumpeters.

Devil's Dyke

The Cambridgeshire Devil's Dyke runs across the heathlands south of
Newmarket between Reach and Ditton Green, and extends for seven
miles. Though one of the most impressive monuments of its kind, and
despite extensive excavation in 1973, the exact purpose of this earth-
work remains a mystery. It dates from some time between AD 350 and
700, and may well be a defence of the Anglians against the Mercians
to the west. It is a splendid walk, and scheduled by the Nature
Conservancy as a Site of Special Scientific Interest.

Part of the Dyke is leased to the Cambridgeshire and Isle of Ely
Naturalists' Trust as a nature reserve, mainly for its botanical interest.
The geology is chalk and several unusual plants can be found. Indeed
the Trust (CAMBIENT) has adopted one such, the pasque flower, as
its emblem. At the Dullingham Road, bloody cranesbill is plentiful.
Wild thyme is common and the bastard toadflax rare.

Visiting: to east and west from the A11 south of Newmarket.
Botany: excellent chalk flora with pasque flower and bloody cranesbill.
Other: perhaps the most northern spot in Britain for sand lizard.

Fingringhoe Wick

All along the Essex coast, marshes and creeks, mud flats and sand
banks stretch virtually without interruption. Deep estuaries carve into
the landscape and small areas of saltings become estuarine islands.
From Southend in the south to Harwich in the north the bird-watching
is excellent. Some place names here are, for many, virtually synony-
mous with bird-watching: Foulness, impenetrable military fortress
and almost London's third airport; Dengie Flats; Bradwell, site of a
bird observatory; the Blackwater estuary; Tollesbury marshes;
Mersea, a strange mixture of birds and sailing with, inland, the

magnificent Abberton Reservoir; the Naze at Walton, a prime bird place and one of the less difficult to visit; and the Stour, shared with Suffolk and one of the best spots of all.

Much of this vast coastline is, for one reason or another, difficult to visit. Lookout places require long walks, or permission from land-owners, or the blessing of the Ministry of Defence. The Essex Naturalists' Trust administers several good places along the coast, but only members can visit if visiting is allowed at all. There is one exception – the delightful 125 acres of Fingringhoe Wick on the west bank of the River Colne only four miles south of Colchester. Based on some old gravel workings the reserve is part of the Colne Estuary SSSI (Site of Special Scientific Interest) and an important area for breeding, wintering and migrating birds. The vegetation is varied and includes horsetails, spiked water milfoil and celery-leaved buttercup. Over the sea wall there are sea thrift, sea aster, sea purslane and sea plantain.

But the major attraction of Fingringhoe is its development as an educational and interpretive centre and the headquarters of the Essex Naturalists' Trust. The reserve and the centre are open to the public five days per week (not Sundays or Mondays) and attract many visitors. There are displays, several well-sited bird hides and a full-time warden. A bunkhouse provides accommodation for four enthusiasts at a time, and a well laid out nature trail picks out the more interesting features of the reserve.

Visiting: contact the Warden, Arch Hall, Fingringhoe, Colchester, for a free permit (donation expected). The Wick is reached via the B1025 southward from Colchester and then on minor roads to the village of Fingringhoe. Turn southward at the crossroads (Church) to the reserve.

Birds: little grebe, tufted duck, mallard, wigeon, teal, redshank, common sandpiper, curlew, ruff, wood sandpiper, twite.

Botany: reedmace, spiked water milfoil, celery-leaved buttercup, sea lavender, thrift, sea aster, sea purslane, glasswort, sea plantain.

Grafham Water

Once the largest man-made water in England (nearby Rutland Water has now taken over that mantle), Grafham is an outstanding and surprisingly beautiful area. It offers recreational facilities on a remarkably large scale to both trout fishermen and sailors, and a refuge to thousands of birds at different times of the year. By and large the three different groups get along well enough side by side, but occasional difficulties arise between anglers and bird-watchers, which is unnecessary and a pity. Frankly, Grafham is large enough to cater for all.

The lake lies in Bedfordshire, just west of the A1 at Buckden. It is easily approached from north and south, though it is the latter side that holds the angling and sailing headquarters, which are well signposted with large car parks. The western, 'shallow' end of the reservoir is a nature reserve administered by the Bedfordshire and Huntingdonshire Naturalists' Trust with a land area of 370 acres. Here among the shallows truly vast agglomerations of birds occur, including thousands of gulls and duck in winter. At passage periods, in spring and autumn, virtually anything can turn up, and waders and terns are faithful visitors. Black terns in particular are regular here, resplendent in their full nuptial plumage in mid-May (try the 12th of that month) or in larger numbers throughout the autumn. A public right of way runs along the southern edge of the reserve and another on the north shore between Hill Farm and Savages Creek. There is a hide available to members free and to the public for a small fee on Sundays between October and March.

If you fancy trout fishing, a permit and rowing boat can be obtained from the Angling Centre and drifted down to the reserve boundaries any time between mid-April and October. The trout run big here.

Visiting: access at several well signposted parking areas including fishing centre, off A1 at Buckden.

Birds: Bewick's swan, pintail, wigeon, teal, common tern, black tern, common sandpiper.

Havergate Island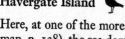

Here, at one of the more remote parts of the lonely Suffolk coast (see map, p. 138), the sea dominates the land and has, by creating a shingle bar, diverted the mouth of the River Alde almost ten miles southward. Instead of emerging into the North Sea at Slaughden the river now turns southward along the coast between grazing marshes and the sweep of Orford Ness to emerge at Shingle Street. The main roads pass well inland and even minor roads are few. In summer people come to play on the Deben to the south, but the Ore estuary (as the Alde becomes) is a peaceful lovely place. After the last war the graceful avocet was found breeding on a large flooded island in the estuary,

Havergate Island, and to the north at Minsmere. Thirty years later these are still the only places in the country where this pied wader with the upward curving bill breeds regularly.

Havergate is a reserve of the Royal Society for the Protection of Birds, and now boasts some hundred pairs of avocets every year. By systems of sluices and dykes virtually the whole island has been turned into a marsh, and visitors can watch the birds at close quarters from well constructed and strategically sited hides. As well as avocets there is a ternery and many waders pass through in spring and autumn. There are short-eared owls breeding and a harrier is frequently present.

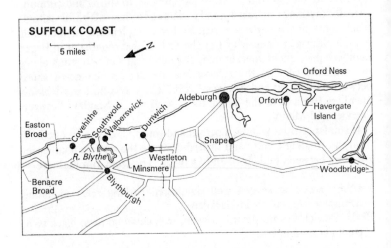

Havergate is reached by a pleasant twenty- to thirty-minute boat trip down the narrow estuary, leaving from Orford Quay, the small, attractive town frequented by small boat enthusiasts in summer. With its eighteen-sided Castle Keep and old world charm, Orford is worth an hour or two itself.

Visiting: write to the RSPB for details of the current season's arrangements for issuing permits which are very reasonably priced. The reserve is open to members and non-members alike.

Birds: avocet, common tern, short-eared owl, waders on passage.

Botany: some emergent salt-marsh plants flourish around the edges of the pools.

Kilverstone New World Wildlife Park

Kilverstone, near Thetford in Norfolk, boasts a remarkably representative collection of animals that, in the main, have their origins in the Americas. At a time when zoos are progressively breaking away from the wide spectrum of animal stars, and beginning to specialize, it was perhaps inevitable that someone would choose the remarkably rich New World areas of North, South and Central America. At Kilverstone this specialization has worked, and within a small area all of the large and more obvious mammals and birds can be seen. The elusive jaguar of South America, a predator seldom seen in the wild and only just beginning to be seriously studied, is on view along with the puma or mountain lion of further north. There are bobcats, Arctic foxes and the extraordinarily long-legged maned wolf of the pampas, which looks more like a fox on stilts than a wolf.

There are good colonies of the smaller mammals, including those ground squirrels romantically named 'prairie dogs' by the early pioneer settlers of North America, and a fair collection of South American monkeys including the woolly monkey and the tiny titi monkey. The two-toed sloth is an unlikely animal star, but there are also Brazilian tapirs, capybaras, skunks, agoutis, and a collection of birds that includes quite a few neotropical specialities like oropendolas, guans and king vultures which are not on display in too many zoos.

Kilverstone is a fine little zoo and one that deserves to be visited. Do not forget the Nocturnal House where night is turned to day.

Visiting: watch for signs two miles north of Thetford on the A11. Usual facilities include cafeteria.

Mammals: jaguar, puma, bison, maned wolf, prairie dog, capuchin monkey, spider monkey, squirrel monkey, woolly monkey, titi monkey, skunk, agouti, guanaco, alpaca, llama, capybara, collared peccary, Brazilian tapir, two-toed sloth.

Birds: oropendolas, guans, toucans, flamingoes, military macaw, Quaker parakeet.

Mickfield Meadow

A 4½-acre reserve of the Society for the Promotion of Nature Reserves administered by the Suffolk Trust for Nature Conservation, lying east of the main Norwich-to-Ipswich road. It consists of nothing more than an undrained field, where the dominant plant is meadowsweet with a selection of others including wild angelica, pepper saxifrage and yellow meadow vetchling. However, its prime attraction and the reason why the SPNR has owned it for over forty years is the presence of the fritillary *Fritillaria meleagris*. Over the years birds have destroyed much of the population, but a conservation programme is in hand to allow the seedlings to mature rather than be destroyed.

Visiting: free access at all times. Leave the A140 to Mickfield north of the A1120 junction. The reserve is one mile north of the village on the Wetherup Street road and lies to the east adjacent to a watercourse. Best time April–May.
Botany: *Fritillaria meleagris*.

Norfolk Broads

The low-lying land east of Norwich is drained by a network of rivers, and spotted here and there with large lakes – the Broads. Though they look so natural, they were originally created by man; in fact they are ancient, worked-out peat diggings. Looked at on a map they form strange shapes, and it is the huge length of their shorelines and the general inaccessibility of their banks that has turned these intricate waterways into one of the most important areas for wildlife in Britain.

A week on the Broads on a hired craft is a popular traditional holiday for town and city dwellers from both London and the Midlands. With little danger the inexperienced set out to explore the Bure, the Ant and the Thurne. Horning, Acle, Potter Heigham, Wroxham – the names have almost the same familiar ring as Southend, Blackpool and Torquay. Yet these masses of would-be mariners hardly touch the Broads at all. The reedbeds and sedges keep them at bay and the willow carrs and alders block their way. A few coots, mallards and Canada geese may get disturbed, but masses of people enjoy themselves alongside.

The Broads are noted as a home, in many cases the last home, of many rare animals and plants. Marsh harriers may still breed occasionally, the rarest of British birds of prey. Bearded tits and bitterns hide away among the dense reed beds, and in a couple of places the splendid swallowtail butterfly can be found feeding on milk parsley and confined to where this plant can grow. There are otters still, but the uninitiated might well confuse them with the far more numerous coypus. Introduced for their fur (nutria), these South American rodents are increasing again following the population slump caused by the severe winter of 1962–3. Many plants that are rare in most of Britain are quite common in some parts of the Broads. Royal fern, marsh fern, greater spearwort, cowbane, water parsnip, marsh pea, water soldier, frogbit and bladderwort can all be found.

To the angler the Broads mean pike, and big pike at that. No doubt somewhere tucked away among the backwaters is the monster that will break the British record. Naturally there are plenty of other coarse fish as well, and fishing is cheap and freely available.

Almost every stretch of water is worth a day's investigation, but three major nature reserves owned by three distinct bodies are worth particular attention.

Bure Marshes National Nature Reserve

This area of over 1000 acres lies in the Bure Valley between Ranworth and Wroxham. The surface is typical fen with four large open waters, the most important of which are Hoveton Great Broad and Ranworth Broad. It is in the open fen areas that milk parsley grows and swallow-tail butterflies are found. Adults can be seen in June and, in some seasons, in late August. Plants include bladderwort, frogbit, water soldier (rare) and the deadly cowbane, marsh fern, royal fern and water parsnip.

A typical Broadland bird community includes bearded tit, water rail, reed and sedge warblers, woodcock and duck. There are several heronries and the largest inland roost of cormorants is at Ranworth Broad. Here too common terns have been persuaded to nest on specially constructed rafts. Otters and coypu are present most of the year.

Access is virtually impossible due to the character of the terrain, but the Nature Conservancy has established a nature trail at Hoveton Great Broad where a half-mile-long path winds through fen and woodland, and where there is also an observation hide. In places logs are laid over eight feet of liquid mud, so take care and do not leave the walkway at any point. The nature trail is open from May to September every day except Saturday, though on Sundays only in the afternoon. It starts on the north bank of the River Bure just upstream of the entrance to Salhouse Broad. This is two and a half miles from Wroxham and visitors can moor their boats free of charge. There is no access by land. Boats can be hired at Horning or Wroxham. Along the trail there are spots for royal fern and the swallowtail butterfly.

Hickling Broad National Nature Reserve

Hickling is owned and leased by the Norfolk Naturalists' Trust, the

first of the County Naturalists' Trusts and the pioneer of the movement. Hickling has always been considered a fabulous place for birds,
and the enlightened attitude of the Norfolk NT ensures that this jewel
is seen by as many interested people as possible. The reserve covers
1204 acres of Broad, woodland, fen and surrounding land. Huge areas
are thickly covered with reeds and it is these that provide a home (and
a major stronghold) for bearded tit and bittern. Marsh harriers are
now quite sporadic here, and the Montagu's harriers that once cruised
over the reed tops are a thing of the past. There is a good collection of
wildfowl, including garganey and gadwall, and an outstanding assortment of passage waders, doubtless due to these excellent feeding
grounds' proximity to the east coast. While black-tailed godwit and
ruff are regular there is also a scattering of black terns, ospreys and
spoonbills.

There are swallowtail butterflies in June and this Broad, together
with nearby Horsey, is the species' stronghold in this country.
Botanically the reserve is similar to the Bure Marshes, but with a
greater preponderance of semi-brackish species.

The reserve is open from April through October every day except
Tuesday. The 'Water Trail' is a half-day with transportation by boat
and visits to seven hides. There is also a half-day without boat and
visiting fewer hides at roughly half price. Bookings (and details) from
the Warden, Stubb Road, Hickling, Norwich NR12 0BW; Tel.
Hickling 276. Unsold permits can be purchased from the Warden
between 09.00 and 09.30 hours. The Warden's House and Office are
reached by following Stubb Road from the Greyhound Inn, Hickling
Green. Take the third turning on the right at a small crossroads.
Hickling lies east of the A149 north of Yarmouth.

Horsey Mere

The Mere lies east of Hickling Broad and just a short distance from
the coast, and is owned by the National Trust. Its 120 acres together
with the surrounding Hall, grounds, farmlands and marrams amount
to 2300 acres in all. The Mere is a famous bird haunt, but it is also
noted for rare plants and insects including, of course, the swallowtail
butterfly. The huge reedbeds hold numbers of bearded tits, bitterns
and water rails, though the harriers that once counted Horsey as a
major stronghold now only pass through. Winter wildfowl are impressive, and garganey arrive in spring. Autumn waders can be very good.
There is access to the Mere by boat, but otherwise access is restricted.

The drainage windmill is usually open free during the summer. Horsey Hall is definitely not open to the public.

Visiting: as described under each section.

Birds: grey heron, bittern, wigeon, shoveler, pochard, garganey, gadwall, goldeneye, pintail, mute swan, Bewick's swan, Canada goose, greylag goose, marsh harrier, black tern, common tern, water rail, black-tailed godwit, ruff, greenshank, redshank, wood sandpiper, green sandpiper, spotted redshank, short-eared owl, bearded tit, sedge warbler, reed warbler.

Insects: swallowtail butterfly.

Botany: royal fern, marsh fern, greater spearwort, cowbane, water parsnip, marsh pea, water soldier, frogbit, bladderwort.

Norfolk Wildlife Park

The Norfolk Wildlife Park was created at Great Witchingham by Philip Wayre, and is now home to the largest single collection of European mammals and birds in the world. This in itself is a considerable achievement, but the Park is also a net producer of wildlife, and its admirable breeding record is studded with outstanding achievements. These include the first European otters to be bred in captivity in Britain since 1881, the first European lynx for over thirty years and the first European beavers, ibex and brown hare to be bred in captivity in Britain. The seven species of deer to be found wild in Britain are on view, and there are European bison, brown bear, seals, wolf, Barbary ape, badger, moufflon and so on.

Philip Wayre is Chairman of the Conservation and Breeding Committee of the Federation of Zoological Gardens of Great Britain and is ensuring that the Norfolk Wildlife Park does its bit by breeding the extremely rare eagle owl. Over sixty owls have been bred since 1960, and over twenty have been sent abroad to help with reintroduction schemes in their natural environment.

The Park is also the home of the Pheasant Trust and houses the largest collection of rare and beautiful pheasants in the world. Breeding these birds has proved highly successful, and in Swinhoe's pheasant, a very rare and highly threatened bird from the island of Taiwan, the work of the Trust has been instrumental in safeguarding the species. The even rarer mikado pheasant, only a few hundred individuals of which survive in the wild, is another species which the Trust hopes to benefit. At present exactly half of the sixteen rarest pheasants in the world are being bred at Great Witchingham, which is worth visiting on that account alone.

Refreshments, lunches, a gift shop and free car parking complete the usual facilities in this quite excellent zoo-collection where a day in the countryside means just that.

Visiting: the Park lies just north of the A1067 between Norwich and Fakenham. Watch for signposts to Great Witchingham and then for the Park. Reasonable entrance fees. Tel. Gt Witchingham 274.

Mammals: European otter, bison, lynx, beaver, ibex, wolf, red deer, roe deer, fallow deer, sika deer, muntjac, reindeer, Chinese water deer, grey seal, common seal, Barbary ape, moufflon.

Birds: cranes, flamingoes, herons, eagle owl, pheasants (best collection in the world).

North Norfolk Coast

From Holme in the west to Salthouse in the east the coastline of north Norfolk is one of the wilder and most interesting parts of lowland Britain. There are beautiful beaches but, protected behind a barrier of intertidal mud, they have not been developed as other British coastlines. Here and there a small village has become a resort of boat enthusiasts or a caravan site attempts to hide discretely in a field, but the main occupations are still agriculture and the sea, with tourism at best a poor third.

Above all this is a bird-watcher's coast, and reserves follow one after another. In the east are the marshes at Cley, where the Norfolk Naturalists' Trust have one of the country's finest bird marshes – an all-year-round resort of bird-watchers galore. Next is Blakeney Point, run by the National Trust, a fine breeding site for terns and an admirable education centre in the hands of its warden Ted Eales. Next westward is the National Nature Reserve at Holkham, near Wells, where the mudflats and the birds they attract can be viewed and where the pines behind the beach are ideal for picnics and watching small bird migrants. Scolt Head is separated from the mainland by a marshy channel and is a huge dune system of interest to botanists as well as ornithologists. Further west still, the Royal Society for the Protection of Birds has a reserve at Titchwell, where careful manipulation of water levels has turned a 1963 flood disaster into a fine reserve of varied bird-rich habitats. At the end, on the corner of the Wash,

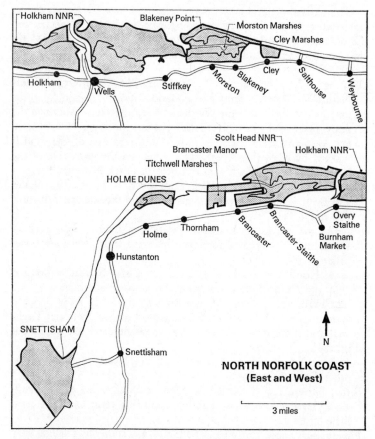

**NORTH NORFOLK COAST
(East and West)**

N

3 miles

lies Holme, another reserve of the Norfolk Naturalists' Trust. Here a reed-fringed lagoon attracts many marshside water birds.

Throughout the area nature is of paramount importance and even the villages, with their flint houses and rust-coloured tiles, fit into our image of the country life. The local people have fine accents and a countryman's sense of humour. There are huge walls enclosing the meadows and walking them can (thank heaven) still be a lonely business: try the eastern bank out of Overy Staithe, or walk the beach from Cley Harbour to Blakeney Point. Accommodation is plentiful and it is a pity to stay for a day when there is so much to see. Those short on summer time should visit Blakeney Point as a priority.

The birds along this coast are remarkably varied, often rare, always interesting. Check lists, encompassing over two hundred species, can be obtained at local shops, with marsh harrier, bittern, bearded tit, black-tailed godwit and ruff the summer stars.

Visiting: Cley: permits available from The Secretary, Norfolk Naturalists' Trust, 4 The Close, Norwich NOR 16P. Unsold permits may be obtained from the Warden at Cley after 10.00 hours on the day concerned if you wish to take a chance. Much can be seen from the A149 and from the 'East Bank' which lies east of Cley and is marked by a small car park. The marsh on the right-side of the East Bank is Arnold's Marsh and belongs to the National Trust.
Blakeney Point: reached by boat from Morston Quay: contact Eales and Bean. There is a refreshment room and the warden will show you round the terneries.
Holkham: public footpaths facilitate exploration. Car park at Holkham Pines reached directly northward from Wells Harbour: brent geese in winter.
Scolt Head: reached by boat from Brancaster Staithe signposted from the A149. Beware disturbing the terns in summer.
Titchwell: access from the east sea wall from the A149 between Brancaster and Titchwell, or from the west sea wall between Titchwell and Thornham. There is a summer hide on the beach but otherwise no access.
Holme: follow signposts from A149 north-east of Hunstanton; other details as at Cley.
Birds: bittern, marsh harrier, bearded tit, black-tailed godwit, ruff, duck, brent goose, snow bunting, sandwich tern, common tern, little tern.
Botany: rich marshland flora at Salthouse and dune flora at Blakeney and Scolt Head. Excellent Scots pines at Holkham with associated fungi in autumn. At Holme, sea buckthorn is spectacular in fruit in September, though its growth is reducing areas for rarer species such as marsh helleborine.
Other: rich deposits of mud and sand alive with intertidal creatures if you dig fast enough. Many excellent pubs: bird-watchers crowd into The George at Cley, sailors into several good inns at Blakeney and everyone into the small White Horse at Brancaster.

Otter Trust

Established in the 1970s by the distinguished naturalist Philip Wayre, the Otter Trust has the aim of presenting the otter's case for conservation to the public, acting as a clearing house for information and actively trying to conserve these highly threatened animals. In Britain the European otter is now an endangered species, generations of legal and illegal hunting having brought the population down to the level of a few hundred. Now the species is fully protected, but the otter remains a rare sight on our rivers. With the aid of the Trust its recovery will be considerably speeded up.

Elsewhere in the world otters – and there are a large number of different species in this cosmopolitan family – are suffering from the same pressures. Here too the Trust seeks to help by establishing healthy breeding stocks which can supply zoos and wildlife parks with the animals they need thus taking pressure off wild populations.

Otters are superb swimmers and remarkably appealing mammals in general. The Trust offers views of the best single collection in the country with a variety of otters from many lands.

Visiting: take the A143 westward for a couple of miles from Bungay: inquiries, The Otter Trust, River Farm, Earsham, Bungay, Norfolk. Mammals: otters.

Ouse Washes

In that vast flat landscape, famous to schoolboys as the home of Hereward the Wake and as the place where King John lost his baggage, the sky stretches 360 degrees with not so much as a hill to break it. It is artificial scenery, a land that man has dragged from the marshy wastes that once made it the largest wasteland in all of lowland Britain. Its landmarks are ditches and banks with crude names like Middle Level Drain and Nene Outfall Cut, Emneth Hungate and Friday Bridge. These are instant eighteenth-century names, not names that evolved along with the place itself. So man created the Fens, and although there are many who do not like what he has done here, fishermen intent on thirty-pound pike from a drain do, and so do bird-watchers for, as a byproduct of draining these tangled fens, the engineers had to create fail-safe overflows where they could put excess water when the rains of winter brought more water than their narrow cuts could deal with.

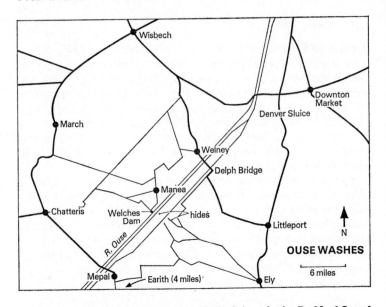

The largest and most important of all of these is the Bedford Level or, as it is known now, the Ouse Washes. From Earith to Denver stretches a fenland overflow a mile wide by twenty miles long. Every late winter the sluices are opened at Earith and excess water is allowed to run over the grassy meadows. At such times the splashes instantly come alive with birds, including the most important concentration of wild Bewick's swans from Siberia to be found in Britain. There are duck here too – pintail and shoveler, mallard and teal. Late winter bird-watching is magnificent, but as the waters subside and the wild-fowl leave two specialities move in to breed. Both require damp meadows that have been recently under water and both are very rare: the black-tailed godwit and the gregarious ruff.

So important had these wet pastures become that by the late 1960s three conservation organizations were actively engaged in their acquisition. By 1975 the three were by far the largest landowners in the area. The Royal Society for the Protection of Birds owns a central section: access by signposts from Welches Dam where there is a car park and a footpath to public hides or from Purls Bridge to the north. No permits required, but do walk below the banks to minimize disturbance. The Cambridge and Isle of Ely Naturalists' Trust also has hides in this stretch.

The Wildfowl Trust owns a section north of Delph Bridge, itself one of the finest vantage points for seeing birds in winter, which holds huge numbers of wildfowl. There is a hyper-modern observatory and a network of more traditional (and draughty) hides. Floodlights pick out the Bewick's swans after dark as well as the sixty other species numbering perhaps over 40,000 birds that may be seen.

The hosts of birds and immense richness of this area can only be appreciated by those who are prepared to give the big fenland skies a chance to show their best at daybreak or dusk. Then the effect as you walk one of their lonely embankments can be a truly moving countryside experience. The actual Washes are open for botanical studies from 1 July–30 September each year.

Visiting: the Washes lie north and south of Welney, which is on the A1101 south of Wisbech. The Wildfowl Trust Observatory is open every day, except Christmas Day, from 10.00 to 17.00 hours and all visitors should report to the Warden at Pintail House, which is 1¼ miles north-east of the Suspension Bridge opposite Welney and 200 yards south of the footbridge which gives access to the Reserve. There is some accommodation – contact the Warden, Tel. Ely 860711.

Birds: Bewick's and whooper swans, pintail, shoveler, gadwall, teal, golden plover, all in winter; in summer, black-tailed godwit and ruff along with redshank and snipe.

Botany: osier beds still cut commercially and many water-loving plants such as yellow flag, frogbit, fringed water-lily, greater water parsnip. Total of 260 flowering plants.

Peakirk Wildfowl Refuge

The collection of wildfowl at Peakirk near Peterborough was created as a safety stand-by for the main Wildfowl Trust collection at Slimbridge in Gloucestershire. With so many birds crowded together, disease is an ever-present risk, and though every conceivable precaution against epidemics is taken the idea of a reserve collection was common sense. Over the years Peakirk has developed into a collection that deserves to be known in its own right. There are now over 600 individual ducks, geese and swans of over eighty different species housed in fine, natural-looking surroundings. The Hawaiian goose, the Trust's greatest success story, wanders at will through the grounds and there are flamingoes as well.

The usual Wildfowl Trust gift shop, exhibition and refreshment rooms are available, and admission prices are really a bargain. As elsewhere, the grounds are open throughout the year except Christmas Day.

Nearby is the Borough Fen Decoy, an old commercial duck decoy that is still worked regularly and which now provides up to 2000 dabbling duck a year to be ringed. Strange as it might seem, no one has yet invented a better method of catching duck, and so this medieval technique persists today. As absolutely nil disturbance is essential, the decoy is open to visitors for only two days in late May or early June – details from the Warden, Tel. Peterborough 252271.

The Welney Wildfowl Refuge lies to the east at Welney (see Ouse Washes) and there is much to be said for visiting the two areas on the same day. Note, however, that Welney is essentially a winter place while Peakirk is interesting throughout the year.

Visiting: the refuge lies just off the A15 some six miles north of Peterborough, and is well signposted. There is a free car park and no prior booking is necessary, except for large parties. The A1 passes nearby to the west.
Birds: duck, geese, swans and flamingoes plus collared doves galore.

Rex Graham Nature Reserve

Named after a botanist-conservationist, the Rex Graham Nature Reserve is unique in being open for only $4\frac{1}{2}$ hours each year. At this time, usually the first Saturday in June, visitors can walk the board-walk erected with the aid of the World Wildlife Fund within feet of a whole bed of the rare military orchid. There is no other attraction and no other times to get in to see them. If a day in the country needs to be different then this is surely it – try finding them elsewhere.

This tiny reserve is owned by the Suffolk Trust for Nature Conservation. The site was discovered in 1955 by Mrs M. Southwell and is now recognized as a Site of Special Scientific Interest.

Visiting: access from the Icklingham–Barton Mills road, the A1101. Details should be sought from the Trust at St Peter's House, Cutler Street, Ipswich IP1 1UU, enclosing a s.a.e. and, if you feel so moved, why not a small donation? Access to see the military orchids is free, but a small charge is made for photography.
Botany: military orchid, twayblade, ploughman's spikenard.

Roydon Common

Lying immediately off the A148 King's Lynn–Fakenham road, Roydon Common is on the greensand and has a very low rainfall. As a result it is of exceptional interest to botanists, because these circumstances combine to produce a growth of ling on the drier parts, often with the parasitic dodder, while the wetter parts have a fine peat bog flora. Here bog asphodel, bog myrtle and cranberry can be found, and there are three distinct species of sundew.

Visiting: open access off the A148 near Roydon.
Botany: dodder, bog asphodel, bog myrtle, cranberry, sphagnum moss, sundews.

Wicken Fen

After the Dissolution the estates of Thorney and Whittlesey were given to the Earl of Bedford, and it was the fourth Earl who was given the right by Royal Charter to drain the Fenlands. Together with his 'Adventurers' (thus Adventurers' Fen) he employed the great Dutch engineer Vermuyden to divert the rivers and turn swamp-ridden sedges into summer grazing. The result was a dismal failure at first, but eventually new rivers were cut and wind (later steam and diesel) pumps drained the vast marshlands. Because of drainage the land shrank and became liable to reflooding. The one sizeable wetland section remaining is Wicken Fen north of Newmarket. As a direct result of the almost universal drainage, the Fen stands higher than its surroundings, and its character can only be maintained artificially.

Today Wicken Fen, together with its neighbouring Adventurers' Fen, covers 730 acres and is the property of the National Trust. It is heavily overgrown with bushes, sedges and reeds and together with cleared areas, including an artificial pool (the Mere), is a fair sample of what the Fens must have been before drainage.

The area is rich in life and a magnet for botanists, entomologists and ornithologists. The Fen is best known as the haunt of rare butterflies, but there are orchids and unusual birds as well. Many of the latter can be viewed on the Mere from the comfort of a tower hide. A labelled collection of the wild plants of the Fens grows by the Education Centre.

Visiting: Wicken is reached from the A10 at Stretham by turning eastward between Cambridge and Ely on the B1085. At the western edge of the village turn southward where a signpost reads 'Wicken Fen'. The Warden's House is on the left and visitors should sign the book and pay a deposit and small fee for the key to the observation tower. There is also a small upkeep charge. The Warden's House is closed on Thursdays.

Botany: orchids, marsh hog's fennel, and many other fenland plants in profusion.

Birds: great crested grebe, long-eared owl, grasshopper warbler.

Insects: swallowtail butterfly.

Avocet

East Midlands

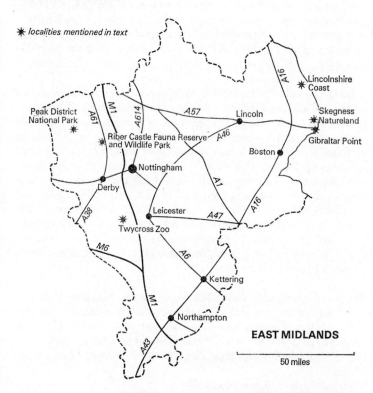

*localities mentioned in text

EAST MIDLANDS

50 miles

Gibraltar Point and Skegness Natureland

Situated at the northern corner of the Wash, Gibraltar Point Bird Observatory and Field Research Station has an enviable reputation in the field of education and public relations. Throughout the year courses as varied as marine ecology and bird ringing are taking place, and there are school visits during term-time weekdays that bring children out into the countryside to learn for themselves.

Gibraltar Point is interesting from a variety of angles, and the simple facts of its geographical existence are quite fascinating. The mudbanks, saltings, dunes and 'real land' all depend on a complex inter-relationship of the forces of the sea. The colonization of plants and the vast feeding grounds for birds that open up at every low tide are part of the same balance of forces. Every spring and autumn bird-watchers are attracted by the migrant waders and seabirds, and often vast numbers of waders congregate here in winter. Occasionally a rare land bird may appear, but it is the varied shorebirds that are the main attraction. To those who prefer to understand the countryside they walk, Gibraltar Point is an ideal spot, with plenty of information and explanatory displays.

Just a few miles to the north is Skegness Natureland Marine Zoo, a director of which is former TV zoo man George Cansdale. The idea of filtering sea water through the beach before pumping it into specially created tanks where a representative collection of marine life can be exhibited is superb. So we have sealions from California (the universal zoo sealion), the two British seals, jackass penguins and some rather good fish tanks where tropical and British fish may be seen. Some of these are marine, but many are not. There are also Chinese geese and the usual waterfowl collection, hummingbirds and tanagers in the Floral Palace, a pet's corner, some Chilean flamingoes and a tropical house with an assortment of creatures from all over the place. Though a nice place to visit this is not (unfortunately) the British answer to Florida's Marineland.

Visiting: Natureland is situated on North Parade, Skegness. It is open throughout the year and offers refreshments in summer. Gibraltar Point is free of access, but visitors should report to the Field Centre on arrival. There are overnight facilities for serious students.

Birds: knot, dunlin, oystercatcher, bar-tailed godwit, terns, Arctic skua.

Mammals: grey seal, common seal.

Botany: very interesting colonizing flora with some unusual species.

Insects: excellent spot to watch migrant butterflies in lase summer.

Lincolnshire Coast

Tetney lies on the east coast five miles south of Grimsby and consists of grazing marshes intersected by dykes and creeks and separated from the sea by a seawall. The shallow saltmarsh and the intertidal area beyond extend for up to a mile at low tide with a continuing growth of annual glasswort and sea purslane pushing out over the sandy banks. Here the Royal Society for the Protection of Birds established a reserve of 120 acres in 1975 mainly to protect the excellent population of the little tern, now Britain's rarest seabird. There are other breeding birds as well, including ringed plover, oystercatcher and short-eared owl. However, during migration seasons shorebirds and terns are numerous and varied and there is always something of interest to be seen.

At the time of writing plans are not sufficiently advanced to allow visiting on an official basis, but good birding (and botanizing) can be had from the right of way along the seawall. Contact the Society for details of visiting arrangements when the reserve is opened to visitors.

Further to the south lies the area of Saltfleetby-Theddlethorpe Dunes, which consists of nearly five miles of coastline owned or leased by the Nature Conservancy, the Lincolnshire Trust for Nature Conservation and Lindsey County Council. This fine area is of considerable interest, with the older dunes, dating from at least the fourteenth century, showing a quite distinct plant community from the more recent ones. There is a freshwater marsh as well as a good salt marsh and, of course, an open shoreline. Though the area is good for passage waders as well as birds such as short-eared owl and harriers, the botanist will find a good variety of flowering plants. Among others there are pyramidal, bee and marsh orchids, autumnal hawkbit, birdsfoot trefoil, common century, viper's bugloss, fairy flax, yellow flag, kingcup, lesser spearwort, bog pimpernel and skullcap. Butterflies include green hairstreak, and this is the only locality in the county for natterjack toad.

Visiting: Saltfleetby-Theddlethorpe is of open access (but beware RAF bombing offshore) from the coastal A1031 at Seaview, Rimac, Sea Lane, Brickyard and Crook Bank. There is parking space at each access point. For Tetney there is open access along the seawall, but contact RSPB.

Botany: pyramidal orchid, bee orchid, marsh orchid, birdsfoot trefoil. viper's bugloss, lesser spearwort, bog pimpernel, annual glasswort, sea purslane.

Birds: little tern, common tern, ringed plover, oystercatcher, short-eared owl, harriers, waders on the shore in season.

Other: natterjack toad.

Peak District National Park

Though it is a decidedly upland area, the Peak District is one of the most populous of our National Parks. It includes the high massif of The Peak, reaching 2088 feet at Kinder Scout, and Bleaklow Hill further to the north at 2061 feet, but much of the Park consists of gently rolling country with densely settled (in a rural sense) valleys and many market towns. At its heart but excluded from it lies Buxton, and the Park extends from Lack and Ashbourne in the south to beyond Crowden in the north.

A glance at a map suffices to show the strategic significance of the Park as a breath of air to the industrial cities of the region. To the south-west lie Stoke and the potteries, to the west the conurbation of Manchester, to the east Sheffield, and to the south Derby and Nottingham. Yet despite such a huge potential population intake, the District retains its rural charm and agricultural economy. Above all it is the hills, with their strange 'Edges', stone outcrops beloved of athletic rock climbers, that dominate the scenery and provide the major attractions. At Castleton, north of Buxton, Peveril Castle rises in ruins above the village. Underneath is Peak Cavern, reached along a wooded stream. Here the famous caves and the flowing water that created them can be visited without potholing equipment. Nearby is Treak Cliff Cavern, the only place in the world where Blue John stone is quarried, to be turned into ornaments.

Immediately west of Buxton is the delightful Goyt Valley, running down to the reservoirs in the valley floor. This beauty spot is so popular that it has been made a no-traffic zone at weekends. A walk down (or up) the valley passes from gritstone moorland through deciduous woodland to farmland. The valley is rich in bird-life and flowers.

In the south, Dovedale is another noted beauty spot set in the limestone district north of Ashbourne. The stream is lined by fine ash woods alive with small birds in spring and summer. Part of the valley belongs to the National Trust and there is a convenient car park off the A515. Lathkill Dale south of Bakewell is another typical wooded Peak District valley, and has the advantage of being less frequented than Dovedale.

The Pennine Way starts at Edale just south of The Peak and slogs upward to Kinder Scout as a prelude to what is to follow.

Visiting: the area is crisscrossed with roads, and access to the valleys is generally straightforward.
Birds: moorland species with excellent woodland birds in the valleys.
Botany: wide range of flowering plants.

Riber Castle Fauna Reserve and Wildlife Park

The idea of specializing in a representative collection of European animals with the intention of breeding to return to the wild is not new. But this effective Park is doing very well in its attempt to cope with the difficulties involved in breeding, say, polecats; so much so that these animals have been reintroduced in the Lake District, where they had long been extinct. Its ongoing plans for whooper swan and European quail are perhaps less likely to succeed. The Park has lynx and pine marten as well, and will be doing a considerable service to conservation when these animals are bred in sufficient quantity to release.

Among a good collection of animals, mention must be made of reindeer, beaver, wild cat, otters, European genet, Arctic fox and porcupine. Equally interesting is the collection of rare breeds of domestic stock, many of which were on the verge of disappearing altogether. The varieties of sheep, for instance, were formerly very large, but modern husbandry has turned out a 'universal sheep' to replace many of them. The same applies to cattle, goats, pigs, poultry and so on. The Park is ensuring that many of these forms will now survive – economic or not.

There is also a collection of models of prehistoric animals (some life-sized) as well as a model railway, a car museum and a farm cart collection.

Visiting: leave the A6 at Matlock eastward to Tansley then turn right (southward) on Alders Lane to Riber Castle. Beware the apparent short-cut via Starkholmes Road – it includes a 1 in 4 hill and some fraught hairpins. Large car park, reasonable entrance fees, nice countryside.
Mammals: lynx, pine marten, polecat, reindeer.
Birds: golden eagle, flamingoes and waterfowl, storks and cranes.

Twycross Zoo

Situated roughly equidistant between the Midlands conurbation and Derby, Twycross Zoo is a model of what can be achieved within the confines of fifty acres. It is also a true breath of air for the large cities that surround it, and shows wild animals to advantage. The stated aim of the Zoo is 'to educate and interest the public in wild animals and to breed those species in danger of extinction'. As a result it has one of the finest collections of primates, including the great lowland gorilla, orang-utan, chimpanzee and a wealth of monkeys, including the only group of proboscis monkeys in the country. Breeding is well established in the colobus, De Grazza, langur and capuchin monkeys and white-handed gibbon. While these are the conservation stars, visitors naturally swarm to see lion, tiger, cheetah and leopard.

Those other large and appealing animals – elephant, camel, giraffe – can be seen, and most of the exhibits are housed in large enclosures where they have room to move about at will. Many birds are housed in a walk-through aviary and there are flamingoes and waterfowl in large pools. Special performances include the ever-popular Chimps' Tea Party and Elephant Bathtime. The enclosures are well laid out and there are good facilities for eating and refreshments.

Visiting: the Zoo lies on the A444 Nuneaton to Burton-upon-Trent road just north of Twycross. It has large car parks and is set in open countryside. Moderate entrance fees.

Mammals: lowland gorilla, orang-utan, breeding monkeys including proboscis and capuchin monkeys.

Birds: good collection including tropical species.

Hare

Heart of England

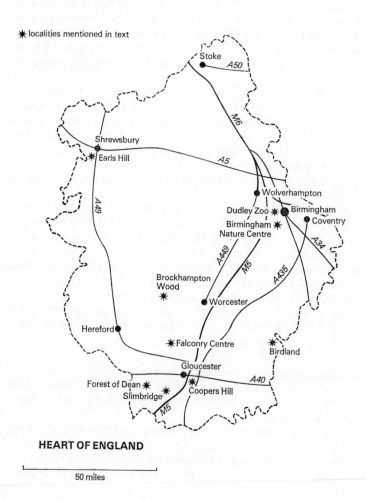

* localities mentioned in text

Stoke
A50

M6

Shrewsbury
* Earls Hill

A5

A49

Wolverhampton
Dudley Zoo * * Birmingham
Birmingham * Coventry
Nature Centre
A34

A449
M5
A435

Brockhampton
Wood
*
Worcester

Hereford

* Falconry Centre

Birdland
*

Gloucester
Forest of Dean *
Slimbridge * * Coopers Hill
M5
A40

HEART OF ENGLAND

50 miles

Birdland 🐦 ♿

Covering a mere three acres of the pretty Cotswold village of Bourton-on-the-Water, Birdland has an enviable reputation. Throughout the summer visitors come by the thousand to see Len Hill's magnificent collection of birds, set in one of Britain's most attractive settings. Neatly trimmed lawns border the trout stream and the stone houses have that typical Cotswold charm. As the visitor approaches he is quite liable to get a free view as a flight of macaws skim swiftly overhead. Indeed so many of Birdland's inmates are free-flying that there is a free bird show for the taking by just walking around the village itself.

Len Hill really got free-flying collections going, and his success has enabled him to indulge his passion for birds both captive and wild. He owns two small islands in the Falklands, Grand Jason and Steeple Jason, which have huge populations of seabirds including three species of penguins, steamer ducks and black-browed albatrosses. Zoos and conservation 'must walk hand in hand' says the guidebook, and many of Birdland's inhabitants have been born there to prove the point.

If the free-flying macaws and parrots are the stars of the Zoo show, the more discerning visitor will be watching for Lear's macaw and drawn to the tropical houses where hummingbirds fly around as you pass. Small cages house touracos of various species, hornbills, including the magnificent great Indian hornbill, and many smaller species whose names must be searched out on the cages themselves. Then there are the penguins, viewable through a glass-sided pool.

There is an excellent education centre featuring a modern lecture hall and a huge Peter Scott mural, a shop and good facilities for dining nearby. A visit is essential.

Visiting: Bourton-on-the-Water is on the A429 where it crosses the River Windrush. Birdland is easy to find from the village centre, though parking is a problem on summer Sundays. Admission is reasonably priced.

Birds: hyacinth macaw, red and gold macaw, green-winged macaw, Lear's macaw, purple-capped lory, lorikeet, great palm cockatoo, flamingoes, penguins, great Indian hornbill, Jacobean hummingbird, coquet hummingbird, sunbittern, bee-eaters, Victoria crowned pigeon.

Birmingham Nature Centre

The Nature Centre is another new and go-ahead idea developed by the progressive Birmingham Corporation. It was opened in 1975 on the site previously occupied by an old zoo, and into its four and a half acres the designers have managed to cram one of the most sensible and enlightening wildlife exhibits in Britain, complemented by museum material and educational back-up. The collections include fox, badger and small mammals; fish; reptiles and amphibians; and, of course, British birds (there are also schemes to attract wild birds). The Centre has an exhibit built around live bees, and a unique walk-through living butterfly collection. The tiny grounds show the variety of British habitats, and there is a farm collection which includes old breeds of domestic stock as well as antique machinery. Entrance is free.

Visiting: address Cannon Hill Park, Pershore Road, Birmingham, which is in the Edgbaston district opposite the BBC's Pebble Mill. Tel. Birmingham 472-7775. It is open all year round except Tuesdays and is easily reached by bus.
Botany: recreations of major British habitat types.
Birds: collection of various species.
Mammals: badger, fox, etc.
Other: walk-through butterfly collection.

Brockhampton Wood

Lying roughly halfway between Hereford and Worcester, this fine woodland area is a property of the National Trust. It has extensive plantations of larch and Douglas fir, with some old beeches and both pedunculate and sessile oakwoods. There are also stands of the exotic wellingtonia and giant redwood. Birds are plentiful, with buzzard, raven, woodcock and abundant warblers and other summer visitors. There is also a small lake that supports little grebe among other aquatic bird species. The fine nature trail takes about an hour, or a little longer if the lake is included.

Visiting: the Wood lies off the A44 some two miles east of Bromyard. The National Trust runs a car park, and guides are available for the nature trail there or at the local post office.
Botany: good variety of woodland flowers, stitchwort, dog's mercury, self-heal.

F

Birds: buzzard, raven, woodcock, pied flycatcher, redstart, wood warbler, willow warbler, little grebe, moorhen.

Cooper's Hill

Lying in the Cotswolds east of Gloucester on the A46, this area is a fine example of limestone beechwood. Some 137 acres are included in a nature reserve of Gloucestershire County Council, though this is only a part of a larger area scheduled as a Site of Special Scientific

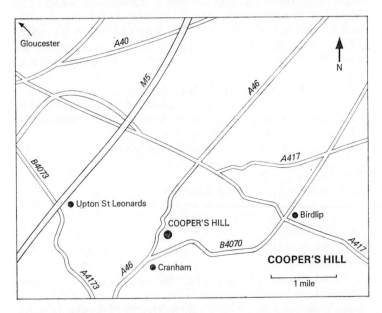

Interest. Though occupied since at least the Iron Age, there is little trace of early settlement left to see today. The Romans too found Cooper's Hill an advantageous place, and medieval times have bequeathed the traditional habit of rolling cheeses from the 'Maypole' site every Whit Monday. The Hill also offers a fine panorama over the surrounding countryside from the Malvern Hills to the Black Mountains of Wales.

Apart from the obvious signs of human activity which are pointed out by the nature trail guide, there is considerable botanical and ornithological interest. Golden saxifrage, wood sanicle, violet and yellow archangel can be seen, and birds include willow warbler, chaffinch, chiffchaff, yellowhammer and others. The whole takes about an hour and a half to walk, but make a day of it to enjoy the views.

Visiting: car park on the A46 north of Cranham about five miles south-east of Gloucester.
Botany: golden saxifrage, yellow archangel, wood sanicle.
Birds: varied beechwood species.

Dudley Zoo

Situated in the heart of the Black Country, Dudley is an old market town with a character of its own. Nearby is the old Dudley Castle and around the Castle are the forty acres of Dudley Zoo. Though a private zoo that only just survived in 1977, Dudley has a remarkable reputation for breeding rare and often difficult animals, perhaps due to the large enclosures and enterprising attitude of the management. The Zoo is particularly proud of its breeding orang-utans, Arabian gazelles, tigers and polar bears. What is achieved at Dudley and at places like it must become standard at all zoos if they are to serve one of their two major purposes.

Among an impressive array of other animals a lowland gorilla takes pride of place, though chimpanzee and gibbon, together with the orang-utan, ensure that all visitors can see the five great apes at one place: the fifth ape is you yourself. Pumas and polar bears, lions and leopards, antelope, deer, giraffe, tapirs, birds, sheep and, of course, sealions are all to be found, all kept in ideal conditions and displayed to an exceedingly high standard.

As with all good zoos, the smaller creatures are not ignored, so that small birds, small mammals and reptiles are all catered for. They may not be the stars of the show, but they are an important part of being a zoo!

The special Land of the Dinosaurs exhibition re-creates the monsters that walked the earth in the Mesozoic era 65–225 million years ago. And there are also an aquarium, a pets' corner and a children's farm, all of them included in the entrance fee.

Nearby is Wren's Nest National Nature Reserve covering seventy-four acres of disused limestone quarries. There is a nature trail which starts and finishes by the Caves Inn on Wren's Hill Road, and nowhere in the country can the connection between geology and human land use be better observed. The rocks are rich in fossils and as you wander along the trail you will see specimens of a wildlife that has long since disappeared. Though many famous specimens have been found here collecting is positively discouraged. Neverthe less it is a remarkable area as the museum in James Road, 200 yards north of the town market place, testifies.

Visiting: Dudley is extremely convenient to visit. It lies near the M5/M6 junction and is easiest to reach via Exit 2 of the M5. Just follow signs to Dudley and then to the Zoo. The Zoo is open every day except Christmas Day, and admission prices are reasonable: no hidden extras.

Mammals: orang-utan, gorilla, chimpanzee, gibbon, tiger, Arabian gazelle, polar bear.

Birds: good collection.

Earls Hill

The Shropshire Conservation Trust has made a real point of encouraging the public to visit many of its reserves by establishing well-designed nature trails and publishing quite excellent leaflets that lead the visitor along them. Earls Hill is a fine example. It lies just off the A488 some seven miles south of Shrewsbury and rises through a mixture of landforms to the peak of Earls Hill at 1049 feet. Though the trail is three quarters of a mile from the road, even that walk is full of interest. There are nuthatches, treecreepers and warblers in summer, along with cowslip, lady's smock, greater stitchwort, heath speedwell, the changing forget-me-not and greater celandine, a plant whose juice was formerly used for curing warts.

The trail itself can be as long or as short as you like, with several 'escape' routes, though the climb to the top is rewarded by superb views in all directions. Overhead, buzzard, kestrel and jackdaw soar, while dippers frequent the streams and pied flycatchers the specially-erected nest boxes. Botanists will enjoy the flowers, which vary from the rare yellow stonecrop to bluebells and primroses via a dwarf variety of the dandelion. There are masses of wild garlic, difficult to ignore, and many others.

Visiting: take the A488 south-westward out of Shrewsbury and stop at the Shell filling station near Pontesford. Park at the rear of the garage. Walk eastward along the metalled road and then turn left onto a footpath to the Reserve.

Botany: shining cranesbill, greater stitchwort, greater celandine, common figwort, wild garlic, lady's smock, cowslip, heath speedwell, mouse-eared hawkweed, changing forget-me-not, biting stonecrop, wall pennywort, lesser celandine, dog's mercury, spearwort, meadowsweet, creeping buttercup, alternate-leaved golden saxifrage, heath bedstraw.

Birds: buzzard, kestrel, dipper, pied flycatcher, grasshopper warbler, green woodpecker, raven, nuthatch, treecreeper.

The Falconry Centre

Established by Philip Glasier at Newent in Gloucestershire in 1967, the centre holds a remarkably fine collection of birds of prey from many parts of the world. The emphasis is on the noble and ancient art of falconry, but a quite amazing variety of birds have been trained to come to the hand by the traditional techniques. Whereas most birds of prey exhibited in Britain are (of necessity) housed in cages each isolated from the other, at the Centre many birds can be seen in their true glory in flight. Actually birds of prey are generally rather dull in colour and tend to sit lethargically for long periods. They thus have comparatively little appeal to the non-specialist visitor. In flight, however, they are fast and dramatic, among the most exciting of all birds.

Naturally it is the traditional falconers' birds that are usually flown, and peregrine, saker and lanner can all be seen to advantage flying to the lure. But there are goshawks, eagles and even the white-breasted sea-eagle, a species that lives on fish in its native Australia.

One of the aims of the Centre is to breed birds, thus aiding the conservation movement at a time when falcons, in particular, are under great pressure. The Centre has an incubator and is successfully producing young birds to add to its stocks. Another aim is to act as an information centre for falconry, and special courses are arranged during the year.

Visiting: Newent is eleven miles from Gloucester and is open throughout the year; inquiries to The Falconry Centre, Newent, Gloucestershire.

Birds: flying falcons, peregrine, lanner, saker, goshawk, eagle owl, barn owl, white-breasted sea-eagle.

Others: falconry courses.

Forest of Dean

The Forest of Dean is a National Forest Park covering 35,000 acres of old mature woodland. It is managed by the Forestry Commission, who have done much in recent years to improve its appeal to the visitor, whether bird-watcher, botanist or rambler. The Forest is bounded to the south by the Severn and to the west by the delicious Wye Valley. Monmouth and Chepstow are the obvious starting points.

The Forest of Dean is the most complete hardwood woodland community to be found in Britain, and of obvious attraction to anyone interested in our countryside. Here deer, badger and fox, along with many less obvious mammals find their ideal niche. Birds are plentiful, with pied flycatcher something of a local speciality. The Forestry Commission has erected masses of nest boxes for this species. Buzzard, sparrowhawk, crossbill, nightjar and warblers galore can all be found, and the forest streams are a haunt of dipper.

To the botanist the very age of the Forest is of immense attraction and there are plant communities that are as perfect as any.

Visiting: There are several very good nature trails, details of which can be obtained from The Warden, Forestry Commission, Crown Office, Bank Street, Coleford, Gloucestershire GL16 8BA. Trail starting points are given by grid reference: Biblins Adventure Trail about 6 miles (SO/540153); Cannop Ponds Forest Walk, 1¼ miles (SO/608105), ¾ miles south of Cannop; Christchurch Trail, 1½ miles to 3 miles (SO/569179); Churchill Trail, 1½ miles to 2½ miles (SO/621081), ¼ mile from Parkend/Yorkley Road; Speech House Trail 1½–2½ miles begins 3 miles from Cinderford and Coleford off the B4226 (SO/620121); Symonds Yat Forest Walk is 1 mile–2½ miles long and starts at the Log Cabin Refreshment Hut near Symonds Yat Rock (SO/562160).

For those who would explore the Wye Valley there is the Wyndcliffe Nature Trail from St Arvans above Chepstow (ST/523973), which has excellent flowers and views.

Mammals: red deer, roe deer, badger, fox.

Botany: classic hardwood community with associated flowers.

Birds: buzzard, sparrowhawk, pied flycatcher, dipper, crossbill, warblers.

Insects: butterflies including brown argus, wood white and white admiral.

Slimbridge Wildfowl Trust

Home of Sir Peter Scott, its founder and Honorary Director, and of 2500 birds of 170 species, Slimbridge is the finest collection of ducks, geese and swans in the world. As the visitor wanders among the pens and pools he can see more species of wildfowl than anywhere else. The rare Hawaiian goose, or néné, whose world population was once down to the last few birds, is now one of the most common of the Trust's guests – be careful not to trip over one. Along with greylags

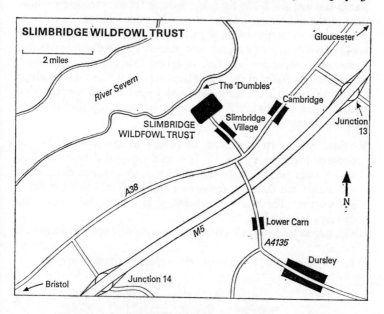

and pinkfeet, snow and Ross's geese, the nénés have the freedom of the park.

To be fair, even ducks and geese can become a bit of a bore after a couple of hours, but the Wildfowl Trust has already anticipated your needs with a collection of graceful flamingoes from various parts of the world. Among them you may find a screamer, while in the tropical house there are hummingbirds and tanagers from America. On a cold day the tropical house is particularly popular, but your binoculars and cameras will fog up instantly and can only be cleared by holding them in front of one of the electric fan heaters. Walking through this house a wonderful impression of a South American forest can be enjoyed – unfortunately it's an inaccurate one, for birds are never so common in the wild.

Slimbridge is not just a bird garden. Peter Scott chose this place primarily because of the thousands of wild white-fronted geese that spend the early part of the year on the New Grounds bordering the Severn. Up to 5000 birds have wintered here (Christmas to March) for generations, and the visitor at this time can see wild geese, often at close quarters, from one of the tower hides. Keen bird-watchers search through the flocks for hours looking for the rare lesser white-front or the red-breasted goose, often with some success.

In recent years the grounds themselves have become the winter home of wild Bewick's swans, and several hundred now grace the Rushy pool where they are fed. In spring (March) their calls are a remarkable reminder of the wild places toward which they are about to depart. Less welcome are the collared doves that find the grounds a virtual pigeon paradise, with spilt grain everywhere and nice people to feed it to them.

Visiting: Slimbridge lies north of Bristol to the west of the M5 between junctions 13 and 14. It is well signposted from the A38, which runs parallel with the motorway. Admission charges are reasonable and there are reductions on Mondays, and for children and parties. There is a restaurant, a gift shop and educational displays and exhibits.

Birds: largest wildfowl collection in the world; wild geese and Bewick's swans.

Other: Tudor Arms, Slimbridge; try a plate of elvers in spring.

Badger

Wales

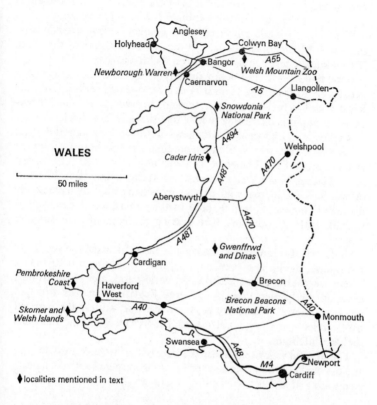

localities mentioned in text

Brecon Beacons National Park 🐦 🌿 ♿

Because they are not as high as the mountains of North Wales, and perhaps also because their name makes them sound more like hills than the all but 3000 foot peaks that they are, the Brecon Beacons are often passed by. They call back those who know them, but tempt few newcomers. The Beacons are named from their use for signal fires, for from their summits one can see across the Bristol Channel and as far as the Malvern Hills. Highest of all is Pen y Fan, just a bare 93 feet under 3000 feet. From its summit, reached via a gentle path from the main A470 at Storey Arms in not much more than an hour, the sheer face falls an awe-inspiring 600 feet before it gradually levels out.

Layers of rock can be picked out with ease, all weathered by frost and water. This central section of the Park, some 8192 acres in all, is owned by the National Trust and there is free public access.

The National Park, which covers 519 square miles, extends from the Black Mountain in the west, through the Beacons to the Black Mountains (beware confusion) and the Welsh boundary. The drainage pattern flows north and south (mainly south) and the walker who decides to go from east to west is due for a tough ordeal. Only the River Usk has really cut a way through between Brecon and Aber-gavenny, and it is interesting to note that the only large lowland water of the region, Llangorse Lake, flows northward to join the Wye, though its feeder streams rise no more than a couple of miles from the fast maturing Usk. Llangorse is something of a gem. The largest natural lake in South Wales, its reedbeds shelter a first-class collection of wildfowl (including wild swans) in winter; and an increasingly disturbed number of breeding birds including reed warbler and yellow wagtail, both of which are here nearing the edge of their summer range.

Birds are also interesting among the mountains themselves. Here red grouse, merlin and even the occasional peregrine can be found. There are golden plover and dunlin, curlew and, along the streams, common sandpipers, dippers and grey wagtails. Botanists will find much of interest. There are trout in the Usk, and at the national nature reserve at Craig y Cilan near Taf-fechan Reservoir the cliffs shelter whitebeam.

The wooded valleys and sheep pastures of the lowlands are a delight, and the banks of the streams in spring can be carpeted with anemones, primroses and violets.

Visiting: the Park is within easy reach of the Welsh Valleys (indeed Merthyr Tydfil is just outside the boundary) and the industrial cities of South Wales. There are plenty of tracks and footpaths, and a variety of accommodation.

Birds: great crested grebe, buzzard, merlin, kestrel, red grouse, dipper, grey wagtail, common sandpiper, dunlin, golden plover, reed warbler, yellow wagtail.

Botany: interesting cross-section of plants.

Cader Idris

Cader Idris rises to less than 3000 feet and seems a lot higher. From almost every side it is approached from low ground and from the west it is only a very few miles from the sea. This isolated position never fails to create an impression of majesty on anyone who looks upon it. Indeed it often seems a very remote and hostile place. It is, in fact, not difficult to climb and the rewards on a clear day are fabulous, with views out over the sea, northward to Snowdonia over the Mawddach Estuary, and westward to the borders.

Nearly a thousand acres are a national nature reserve dedicated to the study and conservation of the Arctic-Alpine flora to be found here. There are no restrictions on access. Other attractions are mainly confined to the lower slopes, where buzzard, sparrowhawk, hosts of wood and willow warblers, grey wagtail, dipper, common sandpiper and others may be found. To the north is the excellent shallow estuary of the Mawddach, with waders and wildfowl in season, while to the south-west is the tiny Broad Water backed by some really excellent grazing marshes.

Visiting: free access over Cader Idris, which can be traversed from both north and south. Nearest towns are Dolgellau and Machynlleth to north and south respectively.
Botany: Arctic-Alpine flora.
Birds: buzzard, grey wagtail, dipper, common sandpiper, warblers.
Other: superb country walking.

Gwenffrwd and Dinas

The remote hills of central Wales have always had a pull on the lowlanders who live to the east. Now many of the reservoirs that serve the Midlands are situated among the valleys, and many Midlanders look westward for their recreation. The hills are fine without being too high, the valleys green with rich sheep pastures, and between the two are the old, lichen-strewn oak woods that cling tenaciously to the rocky and often precipitous hillsides. Together they constitute the charm of this part of Wales.

The woods themselves are richest in wildlife, for while the hills above may shelter merlin and red grouse, ring ouzel and wheatear, the woods are full of warblers and pied flycatchers, finches and redstarts. There are large badger setts among the rocky woods, and fox earths too. There may still be polecats, for this is their last British stronghold, and there are still the last red kites among the hills above Llandovery.

For long the kite was said to inhabit a remote area of 'Central

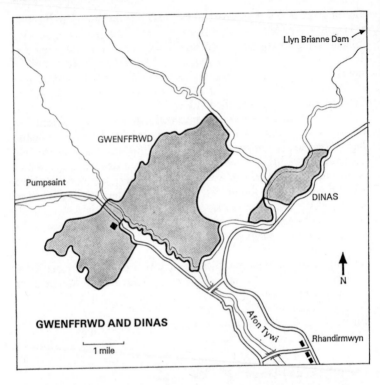

Wales', now the Royal Society for the Protection of Birds has made the Gwenffrwd and Dinas woods safe, so safe that visitors can often see this great rare bird. Though it is the major attraction there are plenty more, like the buzzards that soar on still wings over the steep valley sides, the whinchat on the hedges and the stonechats on the heaths. Curlews bubble over the moors in spring and snipe bleat on stiffly-held tails, while over all the kite hangs motionless on the rising air.

Visiting: leave Llandovery north-westward on minor roads along the upper Towy valley to Rhandir-mwyn and then turn northward to Gwenffrwd to the west and Dinas to the east. Map ref. SN/749460. Escorted tours available by contacting the Warden. Public nature trail at Dinas.

Birds: red kite, buzzard, merlin, red grouse, pied flycatcher, wood warbler, redstart, ring ouzel, wheatear.

Mammals: polecat, red fox, badger.
Botany: interesting communities on the unploughed meadows and
particularly in the old hillside woodlands.

Newborough Warren

The south-west corner of Anglesey from the Menai Straits to the Cefni
Estuary near Malltraeth is a land dominated by sand. Nearest the sea
are mobile dunes where marram grass is continually being swamped
and continually recolonizing. Further inland the dunes have been
fixed, allowing a more luxuriant growth of vegetation. Here there
are dune slacks, places between the high heaps of sand where damp
conditions allow a different flora to prosper. This is the simple
progression of a growing coastline, but Newborough has a sandy
heart that is a vast forest created by the Forestry Commission and
covering some 2000 acres. There is a huge estuary exposing large sand
banks at low tide, where hosts of migrant shorebirds gather in season.
There is a fresh marsh created by the building of a sea wall by Thomas
Telford, builder of the Menai Bridge and other miracles, in the last
century. Called 'The Cob', it is a remarkable bird-watching edifice.
And there is also a rocky promontory called Yrys Llanddwyn that juts
out into Caernarvon Bay and which is composed of Pre-Cambrian
rocks more than 600 million years old – some of the oldest in the
country.

The Newborough Warren National Nature Reserve covers the
coastal zone from Malltraeth to Abermenai Point, and surrounds
Newborough Forest on three sides. Its 1565 acres include all of the
most interesting life zones, and a number of routes lead to several
parts of the reserve. For visitors to North Wales this is a day in the
country that comes as a complete contrast to the mountains and resorts.

The flora of the reserve is rich, but the decline of rabbits and
consequent growth of scrub has turned what were once open sandy
areas into thick embryonic forests. The result has been a disaster for
flowers of open areas. The mobile dunes remain uncolonized and dune
pansy, sea spurge and sand catstail can be found. Naturally enough
the fixed dunes are richer, and plants like birdsfoot trefoil, lady's
smock, lady's bedstraw, meadow saxifrage, tormentil and marsh and
other orchids can all be found. The slacks between the dunes hold
butterwort and grass of Parnassus as well as creeping willow and
buckshorn plantain.

The salt marsh along the Cenfri is being colonized by the inevitable cord grass, though more slowly perhaps than elsewhere. Sea rush too is colonizing since it first appeared in 1956–7. Nevertheless sea aster, seablite and thrift can all be found. The rocky landscape of Yrys Llanddwyn provides niches for the spleenworts, and the grassy areas are one of the few homes of spring squill in Britain.

One cannot visit Newborough without being conscious of the birds, and each season brings its own interest. In summer there are colonies of herring gulls, cormorants and shags, oystercatchers, lapwings and curlews. The estuary invariably holds shelduck and redshank, but visitors include wild whooper swans, duck such as goldeneye and pintail, godwits, ruff and a host of dunlin and lesser waders.

Visiting: there is a nice drive through Newborough Forest south-westward from Newborough, passing the Church, that leads to a car park near the sea. Otherwise access is confined to public foot-paths leaving the major A4080 at various points between Pen-lon and the Forestry Commission Office south of Malltraeth Cob. A handy leaflet describing the reserve and access can be obtained from the car park in the summer, and there are two nature trail booklets as well. The Nature Conservancy Council, Penrhos Road, Bangor, is the address to seek permits for scientific work. Malltraeth Pool can be seen from the A4080, and there is a hide at SH/428649 overlooking Llyn Rhos Ddu.

Botany: dune pansy, sea spurge, catstail, lady's smock, meadow saxifrage, tormentil, lady's bedstraw, birdsfoot trefoil, wild thyme, marsh orchid, creeping willow, creeping bentgrass, sand sedge, jointed rush, wintergreen, butterwort, grass of Parnassus, spleen-worts, spring squill, sea aster, seablite, sea arrowgrass.

Birds: whooper swan, shelduck, goldeneye, pintail, wigeon, teal, cormorant, shag, herring gull, oystercatcher, lapwing, redshank, greenshank, wood sandpiper, green sandpiper, ruff, dunlin, curlew, black-tailed godwit, bar-tailed godwit.

Offa's Dyke Path

King Offa of Mercia constructed the Dyke that bears his name in the late eighth century to keep the Celts at bay and prevent invasion of the plains by marauding hillmen. Border towns grew up around the major forts in the Middle Ages and the Dyke then became a routeway. Today the Dyke marks the start and end of Offa's Dyke Path, and for some sixty miles the path coincides with this ancient bank and ditch.

It runs from north to south through Monmouthshire and the Welsh border country, crosses through the Shropshire Hills, an Area of Outstanding Natural Beauty, fringes the Brecon Beacons National Park and runs along the beautiful valley of the Wye.

For much of its length it is fine country walking suitable for anyone in a reasonably fit state, but the Denbigh Moors and the Black Mountains at the northern and southern ends of the trail respectively are severe tests and should not be attempted by those without experience in navigating by map and compass. Good boots, protective clothing and adequate food are essentials in these areas.

Starting from Prestatyn in the north, the path scales the Clwydian Range and continues over the moorland and hills to Llangollen (try not to arrive during the festival if you plan on overnighting). The Vale of Llangollen is crossed by way of the Pont Cysyllte aqueduct and the Path continues past Chirk Castle and coincides with lengthy parts of the original Offa's Dyke along the foothills of the Berwyn Mountains. It then drops down to the Severn flood banks and climbs the Long Mountain to Beacon Ring. The best of the ancient earthworks is then followed across Clun Forest on to Knighton and Kington. Leaving the old wall, the Path leads to Hay-on-Wye (visit the largest of British bookshops) before climbing the Black Mountains and heading off over moorland to Monmouth. The Path then drops down through the fine woods of the Wye, keeping either to the Dyke or to the bank of the river itself. Total time two to three weeks in favourable weather.

Visiting: there are plenty of roads crossing Offa's Dyke giving access to various sections of the Path. Youth Hostels are handy, though few are actually along the route itself. Clun Forest is the most typical stretch that coincides with the ancient wall.

Birds: a good cross-section of border birds including moorland, woodland and streamside species. Red grouse, pied flycatcher, wood warbler, ring ouzel, merlin, buzzard, wheatear, whinchat, redstart, dipper and common sandpiper should all be seen.

Mammals: scant.

Botany: highly varied with the landscape and underlying geology.

Other: Glyn Valley Hotel at Glynceiriog for good trout and salmon fishing.

Pembrokeshire Coast National Park

Covering 225 square miles, this is at once the smallest and arguably the most beautiful and interesting of our national parks. It is pre-dominantly coastal, but also includes the uplands of the Prescelly Mountains and the deep sea inlet of the upper Milford Haven. There are some spectacular cliffs, some fine beaches, a few quaint villages and some of the most impressive seabird colonies to be found in the North Atlantic. Additionally the Pembrokeshire Coast Path was the third long distance footpath to be opened and, in the words of the pathways' brochure: 'It runs for nearly 170 miles . . . through scenery as beautiful and impressive as any in Europe'.

The National Park is not a wilderness devoid of life. The people here are engaged in agriculture and fishing, as well as in the more recent industries of oil and tourism. But the landscape is truly and refreshingly rural. There are many days' enjoyment to be had here – walking the Coast Path in various sections for its full length, for instance, or exploring the convenient Mynydd Prescelly, where you may have sheep and very little other company. There are the birds of St Ann's Head in the south and Strumble and Dinas Heads to the north, some of the very best on the British mainland. And, of course, the fabulous seabird islands of Skokholm, Skomer and Grassholm (see next section).

This then is a fabulous day in the country for those who live near enough to enjoy it. To those who live further afield the motorway network brings even this once remote corner of the country much closer than you had imagined; a weekend is quite certainly more than just a possibility.

Botanically and geologically the area is a true feast, with the unique Tenby daffodil hidden away in a few meadows near the south coast town. There are otters, a dying breed, along the streams, as well as badgers and foxes.

Visiting: National Park: the National Park is as open as any other area of the countryside, no more and no less. In general hill farmers are tolerant of walkers, but visitors do not have special rights because of the National Park status of parts of Pembrokeshire.

Coastal Path: the path runs from St Dogmaels in the north to Amroth in the south, and is continuous apart from a ferry crossing of Milford Haven and a couple of detours to avoid military firing ranges. By and large it clings tenaciously to the coast itself. There is a Countryside Unit at Broad Haven on the coast due west of Haverfordwest, offering open-air lectures and organized walks all packed with local expertise on geology, natural history and history.

There are four information centres: County Museum, Haverford-west, Tel. 3708; Drill Hall, Main Street, Pembroke, Tel. 2148; City Hall, St David's; The Norton, Tenby, Tel. 2402. As with other long distance walks, the acorn symbol is used as a waymark.

Mammals: otter, badger, fox.

Botany: Tenby daffodil.

Birds: guillemot, razorbill, puffin, fulmar, Manx shearwater, kittiwake.

Skomer and the Welsh Islands

Of all the seabird islands that surround the coast of Britain, those off what used to be Pembrokeshire, now Dyfed, are among the most famous. Certainly they are rich in both numbers and species, and the ease with which they may be visited has made them a popular day out for both naturalist and tripper alike. Most frequently visited, and also the best for birds, is Skomer Island, the site of the first Welsh nature trail. From the sheer clifftops visitors can look down (and across – important for photographers) on one of the most spectacular assemblies of seabirds. Puffin, guillemot, razorbill, fulmar and kittiwake are present in their thousands, and it is a soulless person who is not moved by the experience. There is a unique mammal, the Skomer vole, to be searched for and a good sea-cliff flora. Day trips are easily arranged with local boatmen from Martins Haven, St David's and Milford Haven. Martins Haven is the nearest, and a boat leaves regularly at 10.30 hours each day from Whitsun to early September. A landing fee (small) is payable by non-members of the West Wales Naturalists' Trust. For enthusiasts, simple overnight accommodation is available: details from the Trust at 4, Victoria Place, Haverfordwest.

Skokholm is a smaller island with a similar collection of birds, but it is the site of a bird observatory and is really for the enthusiast bird-ringer and migration student. Accommodation is available for weekly or longer periods by arrangement with the Trust. Organized parties may be catered for, and the island offers opportunities for group study.

Grassholm is smaller still, and further out in the Atlantic. It is a flat-topped mound that has been half taken over by one of the North Atlantic's largest colonies of gannets. Though these birds can be seen on the surrounding seas a visit to the gannetry itself is a unique experience. The reserve is administered by the RSPB and landings – which are infrequent and always after mid-June – must be arranged well in advance through the Society's Welsh Office, 18 High Street, Newtown, Powys SY16 1AA.

Visiting: Skomer by local boatmen, especially out of Martins Haven
  between Whitsun and September. Skokholm for serious students.
  Grassholm by arrangment with RSPB.
Mammals: Skomer vole, rabbit.
Birds: guillemot, razorbill, puffin, kittiwake, fulmar, cormorant,
  gannet.
Botany: sea-cliff flora: thrift, rock samphire, tree mallow, and a
  surprising display of bluebells before the bracken grows up.

Snowdonia National Park

Snowdonia National Park includes the Snowdon massif, as well as the
adjacent mountains that are frequently referred to as 'North Wales'.
But it also includes a lot more besides. In the north it borders Conway
Bay at Aber near Bangor. In the south it reaches Aberdovey at the
mouth of the Dovey estuary not too far from Aberystwyth. On a map
it looks as if a quarter of Wales lies inside the Park; in reality it is
only 845 square miles, making it the second largest National Park in
Britain.

Within the Park there is a great variety of landscape, and considerable variety of fauna and flora. In altitude it encompasses Snowdon,
at 3560 feet the highest British mountain outside Scotland, while the
deep estuaries of the south coast have huge intertidal areas of sand
and mud. There is open rugged country walked by sheep and hikers,
there are deep open valleys, wooded valleys with tinkling streams, and
low bog-filled moors where meadow pipits are almost the only companions. There are cwms and lakes, forest plantations and sweet green
grazing farms.

The whole area is well populated with cars throughout the summer,
and there are caravan and camping sites, cottages to let, bed and
breakfast places, and a variety of hotels. Throughout the year serious
climbers come to test their skill on the sheer drops of the Snowdon
crags. 'Very Severes' are two a penny here, and you can watch from
the comfort of Llanberis Pass as young brightly-clad youngsters seek
to come to terms with the Joe Browns of this world. Drop down the
valley a little and seek out the choughs that soar so effortlessly among
the slate quarries. They are a rare bird now.

One constant factor in all hill districts is water, and here there always
seems to be plenty. The streams are the centres of life – our roads
follow their courses, we live in the valleys they have created and, as
far as wildlife is concerned, they are much richer than the surrounding

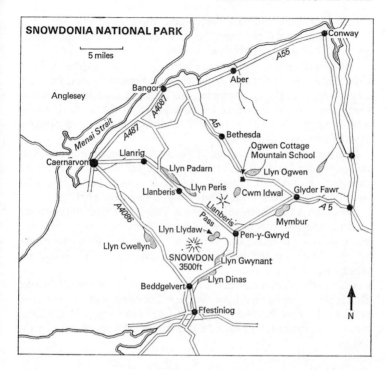

hills. Along the streams, full of small trout and the occasional salmon, grey wagtails, dippers and common sandpipers stake out their territories, while in the woods alongside there are more wood warblers than in any other part of the country. There are pied and spotted fly-catchers too, and willow warblers and redstarts. These woods are more typical of the southern part of the Park, away from Snowdonia proper, in what was once Merionethshire and is now part of Gwynedd. They are predominantly oak and hung with green trailing lichens. They grow among the rocks that hug the hillsides over which buzzards mew endlessly. In the southern part of the Park the buzzard is almost as common as in Devon, some think it more so.

High up on the open grassy moors, beyond the range of even the hardy hill cows, a revolution is taking place. Grass and heather are giving place to young conifer plantations built on a terrace structure that follows the contours. This new crop displaces the ring ouzel, the red grouse and the few merlins that remain. The young plantations

179

attract other birds to replace them – whitethroats and later great tits. Just occasionally the hen harrier nests – otherwise it is found only in Scotland, and northern Scotland at that.

The torgoch or Welsh charr (a subspecies) has been isolated at Llyn Padarn and Llyn Peris near Llanberis for ten thousand years. Recently a hydro-electric scheme eliminated this little fish from Peris, and it is found now only at Padarn and Llyn Cwellyn to the south. It reacts well to maggot bait and is said to be delicious if you fancy eating a piece of rare evolution in action.

Dominating the south is one of the most impressive mountains in Britain, Cader Idris, all dark and menacing. Its buttresses are severe enough to attract rock climbers, though it is said that anyone who overnights will awake mad, blind or a poet (see page 170).

This then is the Snowdonia National Park. Over most of the moors visitors can walk without let or hindrance, even the grazing meadows can usually be trodden, and there are well-marked footpaths everywhere. Watch for the path to 'hwyr Cyhoeddus' – it's Welsh for 'Footpath'.

Within the Park there are no less than fifteen National Nature Reserves varying in size from the huge Snowdon NNR at over 4000 acres to the tiny thirty-three acres of Coed Gorswen. Though all of these are of interest, four have created nature trails specifically for the visitor.

Coedydd Aber

Leave the A55 southward between Bangor and Conway on a minor road through Aber. Park just before the bridge as signposted. A trail leads along the Afon Rhaedr Fawr and a booklet is available. The woods here are oaks with hazel and birch near the tops. The open area near the bridge where the trail begins has wych elm, alder, ash, blackthorn and sallow. Early spring produces primrose, bluebell, wood sorrel and wood anemone, and there is navelwort to be found as well. At Nant Farmstead there is a ruined sheep dip, and as well as the Welsh mountain sheep, there are Welsh mountain ponies. At the end of the trail the falls tumble 120 feet down Creigian Rheadr Fawr, where the rocks, found nowhere else in Snowdonia, are igneous granophyre. There are several liverworts associated with the falls. Birds along the way may include buzzard, grey wagtail and dipper.

Cwm Idwal

Park at Ogwen Cottage Mountain School and follow the footpath southward up the hill to Llyn Idwal. The trail starts here and immediately crosses the outlet stream to proceed along the western bank of the lake. The reserve covers 984 acres, and it is the geology and the dependent botanical communities that are the primary interest. From Point 2, excellent glaciated scenery include the U-shaped valley of Nant Francon, hanging valleys and moraines. At the enclosures note the strong growth of heather when protected from sheep, and watch out for feral goats from here onward. The lake has trout, but birds are few; fossils can be found among the pebbles, they are 450 million years old. At Point 4 look for bogbean and marsh cinquefoil among the boggy areas around the lake. The enclosures at Point 8 are richer than those encountered earlier, and around the head of the lake there are more flowers to be found. At Point 9 there are the remains of a plant community that was common at the end of the Ice Age. Species include purple saxifrage, mountain sorrel, Alpine meadow-rue, green spleenwort and greater woodrush. Move on to the Idwal Slabs and then back along the lake shore. Flowers are a major interest all the way.

Snowdon

The Miners' Track leaves the A4086 at Pen-y-pass – the top of Llanberis Pass. It leads directly southward to Llyn Teyrn and then to Llyn Llydaw, where it ends at the lake. The ongoing path eventually leads up through Glaslyn to Snowdon Summit. Point 2 is rich in calcium and the plant growth attracts sheep to the grazing; plants include wild thyme and heath bedstraw. Point 3 is wet peat, and here cotton grass, bog asphodel and butterwort are found. Point 5 is on dolerite, and this is rich and conducive to flowers. Point 6 overlooks Llyn Teyrn (Tyrant Lake) with some trout and plants like quillwort and water lobelia. Point 7 is on peat, and looking skyward might locate chough. Otherwise it's wheatear, ring ousel and raven. At Llyn Llydaw the causeway and buildings are remains of the old copper industry.

Coedydd Maentwrog

This reserve covers 169 acres north of the Vale of Ffestiniog around Llyn Mair, and protects some of the original old oak woods in this part of the country. The nature trail can be started at Tan y Bwlch Station or from the car park near Llyn Mair. From the station from Point A to Point B the trail passes through meadows thick with primroses, violets and celandines and butterflies like meadow brown, hairstreaks and fritillaries. At Point C there is a display of nest boxes. Point D offers whooper swan and goldeneye on the lake in winter, and now you are at the car park where you may start or finish.

Cross the stream and walk northward along the eastern bank where mosses grow in profusion. The valley is beautiful, but interesting botanically after crossing the bridge to a small marsh (Point 6) where marsh thistle and meadowsweet can be found.

These nature trails only scratch the surface of this rich and varied national park. Their advantage is that, step by step, the landscape is explained; the countryside itself comes alive.

Visiting: as specified.
Mammals: polecat, fox, badger, otter, feral goat.
Birds: chough, buzzard, raven, merlin, curlew, redstart, wheatear, stonechat, whinchat, wood warbler, grey wagtail, dipper, ring ousel, red grouse, pied flycatcher.
Botany: navelwort, marsh cinquefoil, purple saxifrage, mountain sorrel, Alpine meadow-rue, green spleenwort, bog asphodel, quillwort, water lobelia, marsh thistle.
Other: Butterflies including fritillaries, hairstreaks and meadow brown; the dwarf grayling lives on the nearby cliffs of Great Ormes Head.

Welsh Mountain Zoo

This claims to be the only mountain zoo in Britain, though it is difficult to see why a hillside situation outside the bustling resort of Colwyn Bay should count as 'mountain', and it certainly is not the only 'mountain' zoo in the country. Indeed if a mountain situation and a mountain fauna are the reasonable prerequisites of a mountain zoo, then there are no such institutions in Britain.

Nevertheless this is an interesting place, with a reasonable collection of animals from a variety of lands housed in large enclosures. About half of the thirty-seven acres are developed at present, and the remainder is left natural to encourage local wildlife including fox, badger, weasel and (claimed) polecat. The usual woodland birds are present, and the whole makes a nice background for the collection.

Indian elephant, lion, puma, leopard, chimpanzee and gibbons as well as spider, woolly and capuchin monkeys are the stars of the show – though they have little to do with mountains. There are sealions, llamas, wallabies, and black and brown bears as well as many smaller mammals and birds. All this is fine, and pretty standard stuff, but the Zoo has one speciality – birds of prey. Gathered here is one of the best collections of these birds in Europe, and there are eagles, condors, vultures, falcons, hawks and buzzards all to be seen. The outstanding feature is the daily flight of trained eagles and falcons, trained that is in the methods of falconry. Here free-flying birds of prey can be seen as they would be in the wild. Suddenly a rather dull-coloured hawk sweeps into the air and impresses everyone with its power; a great piece of conservation propaganda were it not for the fact that these already scarce birds are in great demand by falconers. It is not the falconers who have made them rare, but it might be they who put the last nail in the coffin. There is a Tree Tops Safari Restaurant over-looking the lion enclosure, a zoo shop, a children's zoo and a Lookout Cafe.

Visiting: leave the A55 as it passes through Colwyn Bay on Kings Road, which is well signposted to the Zoo. Frequent buses operate from the Pier. The Zoo is open every day throughout the year: Tel. Colwyn Bay 2938.

Mammals: lion, puma, leopard, elephant, llama, sealion, wallabies, chimpanzee, spider monkey, woolly monkey, capuchin monkey, lar gibbon.

Birds: free-flying displays by eagles and falcons.

Golden Eagle

North-West England

NORTH-WEST ENGLAND

50 miles

Carlisle

A69

A595

M6

Lake District
National Park

Ravenglass

A590

Morecambe Bay
and Leighton Moss

A65

Barrow

Morecambe

South Walney

Winged World

Blackpool Zoo
and the Tower Aquarium

Blackpool

M55

A646

Preston

M61

Martin Mere

Bolton

A59

M62

Liverpool

Birkenhead

Manchester

A6

M56

Cheshire Meres

Chester

M6

Chester Zoo

A41

A49

*localities mentioned in text

Blackpool Zoo and the Tower Aquarium 🦌 🐦 ♿

Though quite distinct and separate institutions, the would-be visitor to the wildlife attractions of Blackpool should not miss either of these. The Aquarium is the older of the two by ninety-nine years, and indeed pre-dates the famous Blackpool Tower that now stands (literally) over it by twenty years. Throughout its history it has been a famed home of fish, particularly local marine species, but with more recent additions of a tropical collection and a British freshwater section. Now some 2000 fish representing over 225 species are on show – a marvellous place for anglers to brush up their identification and for students young and old to see many otherwise elusive fish.

The Zoological Gardens are one of Britain's newest zoos and form only the beginnings of a much more ambitious project. This does not mean that the Zoo is not well worth visiting right now. It was opened in 1973 and is owned by Blackpool Corporation, which no doubt saw it as another attraction to be set alongside Blackpool Tower, Blackpool Rock and the illuminations, but it is much more than that. The collection is full of quality, with lion, tiger, elephant, lowland gorilla, orang-utan, and the highly-endangered Arabian gazelle. There are camels, gazelles, antelopes, and a first-class poly-thene Bird Hall where the visitor can walk among the birds as they fly about the exotic vegetation of their large home. There are over 300 species of birds to be found – a good day out, that!

Already there have been some notable successes. The Arabian gazelles are breeding quite freely and a good herd is in the making. There is some hope that the siamang might also breed. An unusual zoo animal is the all-but-exterminated white-tailed wildebeest, with its handlebar-type horns. The species is now confined to a few South African parks and cannot be found in very many zoos. From the same general area comes Chapman's zebra, another vanishing animal, while Grevy's zebra is from further north in East Africa.

One of the features of Blackpool's Zoo is the zoogeographic approach to the layout of the enclosures. This enables a cross-section of the animals of a particular region to be seen one after another and, perhaps, contrasted with an adjacent region nearby. Thus one area of the Zoo is devoted to American species, and puma, bison, llama, tapir, peccary and monkeys can be seen. In another area the fauna of Australia is on show, with kangaroos and wallabies in a variety of different forms. There is, of course, a European section as well as a children's zoo.

Visiting: Blackpool Tower Aquarium is under the Tower – it's difficult to miss. Having paid the entry fee to the Tower the Aquarium, as well as a tiny zoo at the top, is free. The Zoological Gardens are on East Park Drive, but are signposted as you enter the town. The Corporation would not want visitors to miss it. It can be reached by bus and train and is open throughout the year. There is a licensed restaurant, a cafeteria, snack bar and shop.

Mammals: white-tailed wildebeest, Arabian gazelle, lowland gorilla, orang-utan, tiger, lion, elephant, Bactrian camel, chamois, llama, sealion, puma, plains bison, Chapman's zebra, Grevy's zebra.

Birds: walk-through polythene aviary with over 300 species.

Cheshire Meres

Lying just off the M6 at Exit 19, Rostherne and Tatton Meres are the most famous of the lowland Meres of Cheshire. They are handily situated for the inhabitants of the Manchester conurbation and are popular resorts at summer weekends. Tatton Mere is part of the 2086 acre Tatton Park estate, which was acquired by the National Trust in 1960. Its surrounding deer park and gardens are open to pedestrians through most of the year (except Mondays and Christmas Day) and the house is open at various times in summer. When it comes to opening times the National Trust is a law entirely to itself, so always check with them beforehand before visiting any of their properties. Though considerably disturbed, Tatton Mere is a good haunt of wild birds, including goodly numbers of duck in winter. Summer sees great crested grebes displaying, and there are a few wild flowers in the less frequented corners. For picnics, swimming and fishing Tatton Park is the place; for more serious bird-watching the larger lake to the north, Rostherne Mere, is better.

Rostherne Mere was declared a National Nature Reserve in 1961 and the 118-acre lake is now enclosed by some 250 acres of protective woodland and farmland. It is a deep lake and offers little food to the hordes of wildfowl to which it is a winter resort. Its main function is to protect these birds from disturbance, and access is thus limited to permit holders and to a few observation points from public highways and rights of way. Duck, particularly mallard and teal, are often present in their thousands, along with wigeon, shoveler, tufted duck and pochard. There are occasional goldeneye and goosander to be found among the throngs. Several thousands of gulls come in to roost in the winter evenings and a few great crested grebes and Canada geese breed. There is a regular migration of black terns and a total of 161 species had been recorded by 1975.

The A. W. Boyd Memorial Observatory was opened by the late James Fisher in 1962 as a testimony to the man who was primarily responsible for saving Rostherne Mere, and permits, valid for a calendar year, can be obtained from the Manchester Ornithological Society, Woodhouse Farm, Ringway, Wythenshawe, Manchester M22 5WR. These are available only to bona fide bird-watchers who live in the area and can watch regularly.

Visiting: A. W. Boyd Observatory. Also view from Manor Lane and Rostherne Churchyard off the A556; and from Dirty Lane at the north-eastern corner near the A556. The Nature Conservancy Council has produced a leaflet. The A556 joins the M6 to the M56.
Birds: great crested grebe, little grebe, mallard, teal, shoveler, wigeon, tufted duck, pochard, Canada goose, woodcock, reed warbler, hawfinch.

Chester Zoo

Though no more than a couple of miles from the city centre, Chester Zoo has an enviable reputation as a haunt of outstanding wildlife displayed in a modern and thoughtful environment. Its full name, 'The North of England Zoological Society Gardens', gives a hint that entrance fees paid here will buy a little more than the razzamatazz provided by the safari parks. The brochures and guides are so cheap and so full of information that they must have been produced by a non-commercial outfit. Nevertheless the Zoo attracts over a million visitors a year and spends almost all of its income on the animals and their greater comfort. The majority are housed in large outdoor enclosures, but with ample covered quarters for all during bad weather.

The outstanding attractions are both mountain and lowland gorillas, orang-utan, rhino, hippo, antelope of great variety, collections of waterfowl, birds of prey, the big cats and so on. There are tropical houses where flowers are as attractive as the animals they shelter, and there are even Arabian gazelles, Amur leopards and tuataras. In the nocturnal house, secretive forest animals can be seen in their own twilight world.

Most of the animals are kept in decent-sized family groupings, and because of the continuous year-round care that is lavished upon them they respond by breeding. In fact it is the open quality of the enclosures

187

plus the caring of the staff and the Society that has made Chester one of the great zoos of the world. Worth a day any time.

Visiting: the Zoo is well signposted within Chester and is situated just off the A41 Chester By-pass at Upton, to the north-west of the city. Entrance fees are not cheap, but they are good value for money, and you are contributing to a really worthwhile cause.

Mammals: mountain and lowland gorillas, orang-utan, elephant, rhino, lion, tiger, cheetah, leopard, zebra, deer, antelope, wallabies, bison.

Birds: huge variety including Andean condor, birds of prey, flamingoes, waterfowl.

Lake District National Park

The Lake District was the second National Park to be created and covering 866 square miles is still the largest of them all. It covers the vast majority of the hills and fells of the Lake District roughly westward of the Kendall-Penrith road and includes Scafell Pike, Helvellyn and Skiddaw together with seventeen of the major lakes. This is one of the backwaters of Britain, and the hills and valleys, farms and towns have changed but little over the past hundred years. The only new development has been the influx of visitors seeking the beauty and relaxation that such a fine and unspoilt area can offer. Inevitably this influx has had an effect on the very attractions that brought visitors in the first place.

Initially it was the poets (artists and writers are inevitably the first to discover attractive backwaters) Wordsworth, Coleridge and their set that put the Lake District on the tourist map. Later it was the motorcar that enabled everyman to penetrate the wilderness, and latterly the passion for boating has turned some of the larger lakes, Windermere in particular, into teeming pleasure grounds. Yet despite the masses of people who pour into the area during the summer, the fells of the Lake District remain one of the last unspoilt wilderness areas of Britain. The Pennine Hills may be more lovely, but the Lakes have a majesty and grandeur that outstrip everything else to be found this side of the Scottish border.

In geographer's terms the Lake District is an excellent example of radiant drainage. Look at a map and almost every lake and river stems from a central point – the great massif of Great Gable and Scafell Pike. This is the heart of Lakeland, and those who would penetrate the great hills would need to start from here. There are two major routes inward. In the north the road southward from Keswick along the eastern shore of Derwent Water leads to Seatoller, where a lane leads in turn, southward through Borrowdale. At the end of the road a shepherd's farm may offer a cup of tea and a cake in the parlour to the walker as he sets out along the footpath that leads up to Sty Head Pass, a wonderful spot from which Scafell can be climbed or the route across the enormous screes of Great Gable can be walked. Beyond is the loneliness of Wasdale, where the hills dip down to Wast Water. This is wonderful country and is within a day's exploration of much of the industrial north. The routes are not very long, but the terrain is tough and the explorer should not step lightly onto these fells without map, compass and the experience to use them. A companion is also essential – break a leg with a silly slip, and you may die.

Another route into this central section is via Langdale, where the Old Dungeon Ghyll Hotel has been a mecca for climbers since climbing was invented. From here famous paths lead up to the Pikes of Stickle, to Bow Fell, and over into Borrowdale itself.

The valleys are flat bottomed with green meadows full of sheep, and streams full of trout. Mostly the hillsides have been grazed clean, but here and there birch woods cling tenaciously to their toe-hold sites and willow warblers sing their sweet trills. Along the streams grey wagtails, dippers and common sandpipers can be found, and high above there are a few golden plover, ring ouzel and the occasional buzzard. In the late 1960s the golden eagle returned to breed in England for the first time this century – do not ask where!

Along the Ambleside-Keswick road there are large maturing plantations of conifers, and to the east the long sweep of Helvellyn dominates. Climb to the top and walk Striding Edge to the east, but return westward for over the other way the fells are empty and you will have them all to yourself.

If villages attract you, then Grasmere is one of the best, and a good centre for starting a tour. Ambleside is nice, but a bit busy, Windermere is full of boats and nineteenth-century hotels, and Keswick is a town. Borrowdale is delicious, with expensive hotels and cheap picturesque places for tea. There are numerous guides to the Lake District, but Wainwright's seven guides to the Lakeland Fells (available in all shops or from the publishers, The Westmorland Gazette, Kendal) are in a class of their own. To walk the area without the appropriate 'Wainwright' is to miss everything and even to take a chance on getting lost. They are unique, superb and essential – no hill walker should miss an opportunity to follow in the footsteps of the master.

As this is a National Park there are several Information Centres scattered about. They are at:

Ambleside – Old Court House, Church Street; Tel. Ambleside 3084.

Bowness – (caravan) The Glebe; Tel. Windermere 2895.

Brockhole National Park Centre – Windermere; Tel. Windermere 2231.

Keswick – Moot Hall; Tel. Moot Hall 2803.

Waterhead – (caravan) Ambleside.

Windermere – District Bank House, High Street; Tel. Windermere 2498.

The Lake District is so immense that visitors must purchase a guide and seek out what they want for themselves. Nevertheless there are some nice hill walks that can be accomplished (round trip) in a day provided you do not consider hill walking a countryside stroll.

Easedale

From Grasmere take the road to Easedale House and cross the river through nice woodland. A footpath is well marked along Sourmilk Gill to Easedale Tarn. There and back makes a nice day's walk if the weather is fine.

Stickle Tarn

Take the footpath behind the Hotel up Dungeon Ghyll in Langdale – steep at first, easier later. Keep to the left of Stickle Tarn and climb Pavey Ark if you have a head for heights. It's a good scramble, but dangerous for those with shakey knees. Cross to Pike of Stickle, enjoy the view and descend once more to Langdale. Compass, map, protective clothing, experience essential.

Sty Head

Take the B5289 through beautiful Borrowdale, all woodside streams and singing birds – watch for common buzzard. Turn left to Seathwaite (not Stonethwaite) and park at the end of the road. Walk up the valley and turn right over Stockly Bridge before climbing up to Styhead Tarn and on to Styhead Pass. A wonderful place if you are prepared for nasty weather. If not, do not take a chance.

Helvellyn

Take the A591 to the southern end of Thirlmere and then the footpath eastward from Wythburn. Follow the well-worn path to Helvellyn and then out and back along Striding Edge. You cannot miss it! If foot-loose and free, continue to Patterdale and one of the least spoilt parts of the Lakes.

Visiting: there is accommodation and food to suit all tastes in the Lake District from farm house to international luxury. The scenery is beautiful, but the wildlife pleasantly unspectacular. Go to walk, to fish or just to wonder.

Birds: buzzard, raven, sparrowhawk, dipper, grey wagtail, common sandpiper, willow warbler, pied flycatcher.

Botany: varied communities at different altitudes.

Martin Mere

Once the site of the largest stretch of inland water in England, the Wildfowl Trust acquired Martin Mere for its usual double-pronged development. Here, over the last few years, it has created a wildfowl collection that contains close to a hundred species and where the visitor can wander and watch birds in comfort. There are excellent amenities, including a shop and refreshment facilities for the day

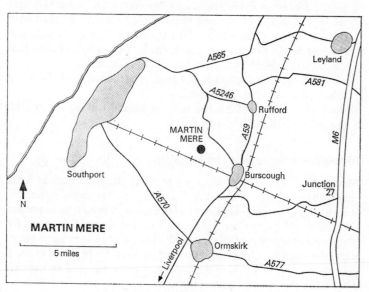

visitor as well as a lecture theatre, laboratory and classrooms for educational purposes. While all of this development attracts visitors throughout the year, it is winter, when the wild geese come, that brings the naturalist here.

For generations thousands of pink-footed geese have roosted on the open flats of the River Ribble and flighted inland to feed on the marshes of Martin Mere. The Southport Sanctuary established the foreshore itself as a National Nature Reserve and controlled access and shooting. Now the Wildfowl Trust has taken care of the other end of the pink-feet's daily commuting and opened up the sight of 15,000 wild geese to public view. At few other places this side of the Atlantic can such a wildlife spectacle be enjoyed by the ordinary public. The geese are present throughout the winter and this is the peak period for a visit.

Martin Mere is a miniature fenland composed of peat that, in many places, is up to twenty feet deep. It has been artificially drained over the years and most of the area is now turned over to arable farming. The Wildfowl Trust owns 360 acres and has excavated an eighteen-acre lake that will, it is hoped, attract breeding as well as wintering birds. Hides are well sited to view all of the wild birds in comfort.

Visiting: The grounds are open every day except Christmas Day, and are best in winter for the wild geese flocks. They are reached from the A59 north of Ormskirk, which is south-east of Southport, and the nearby M6 brings them within reach of the whole of industrial Lancashire. Follow signs from the village of Rufford.

Birds: pink-footed geese by the thousand, plus thousands of ducks and other birds; wildfowl collection.

Botany: some flowers of the peat still remain and will regenerate with the establishment of the new lake.

Morecambe Bay and Leighton Moss

Morecambe Bay is one of those places where the tide comes in faster than a man can run. It's a bleak, dangerous, lonely sort of place, but it is also one of the most important wildlife sites in Britain, so important that the Royal Society for the Protection of Birds paid £150,000 for 3600 acres of it in 1974. All they got for their money were some pretty worthless saltings, a lot of sand covered by the tides twice a day and a collection of up to a half of the 200,000 waders that feed on the rich marine life that shelters among the sand.

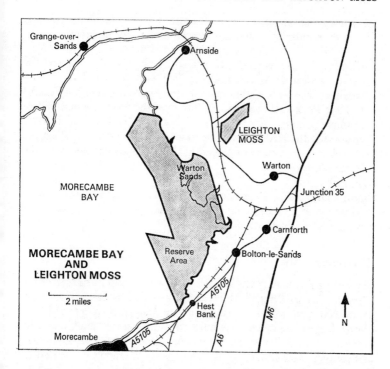

For long only the cockle fishermen and a few wildfowlers penetrated the fastnesses of Morecambe Bay; now the birds have it to themselves. In fact, as yet, there are not even any plans to open the reserve to the public, though the best roosts of birds at high tide can be seen from Hest Bank. Thousands of waders congregate there, including huge banks of knot, dunlin, oystercatcher and curlew. At various times of the year, except June and July, almost all of the shorebirds of Europe pass through.

Duck and geese are regular visitors, and those who time their visits to coincide with a rising tide (two hours before high water) are in for a staggering treat. A great variety of other birds frequent the general area, and another RSPB reserve at nearby Leighton Moss offers the chance of different birds in different surroundings. The Moss, which is adjacent to the village of Silverdale (you'll find out why when you get there), is a large reedbed and fresh marsh reserve that echoes to the sound of the bittern every spring. Harriers, duck, waders and warblers

G

are among the attractions, and there are hides to facilitate viewing. Otters are regular here, and can be seen reasonably frequently.

Visiting: Leighton Moss can be visited by permit only – contact the RSPB for details. Morecambe Bay is a vast area, and those who would see the birds well should take the A5105 north of Morecambe to Hest Bank and cross the railway over the level crossing. There is ample parking space and visitors should arrive before high water and watch the birds come in to roost. A walk northward along the shoreline from the end of Morecambe promenade will suffice on the lower tides.

Mammals: otter.

Birds: knot, dunlin, oystercatcher, curlew, redshank: and at Leighton Moss, bittern, greenshank, common sandpiper, little stint, common tern, reed warbler, bearded tit.

Ravenglass

Since 1954 Ravenglass Gullery has been a local nature reserve of the Cumbria County Council. It lies at the mouth of the River Esk on the south-west coast of Cumberland near the A595 at Ravenglass village. Here a huge dune system has built up at the estuary mouth, and its general inaccessibility has made this a favourite resort of huge numbers of breeding black-headed gulls. The colony is among the largest in Europe. Among the many thousands of birds it is often difficult to pick out the less common species, the Sandwich, Arctic, common and little terns as well as the ringed plovers, shelduck and wheatears that also breed.

The whole object of the reserve is to protect the nesting birds, and access is thus (and rightly) a secondary consideration. Nevertheless the Council have marked out trails, and visitors do pass within the gullery and experience the thrill of being inside a genuine seabird colony. Even school parties are encouraged, though limited to thirty-five people.

Visiting: permits, available in advance only, from The County Estate Surveyor and Valuer, The Castle, Carlisle CA3 8UR. Charges are nominal, but check current prices. The reserve is closed between 15 and 31 May, the peak hatching period. Serious photographers wishing to use a well-sited hide pay an extre fee. Access is from Drigg Lane to the north of Ravenglass only.

South Walney 🐦 🦅 ♿

Walney Island is a low-lying strip of land at the southern end of the Lake District off Barrow-in-Furness. The southern part is a Nature Reserve administered by the Cumbria Naturalists' Trust and is best known as the largest ground-nesting colony of lesser black-backed and herring gulls in Europe, as well as the southernmost colony of eiders in Britain. It is also the site of a recognized Bird Observatory and is a noted haunt of waders and wildfowl in winter. In fact the area is one of the major wader roosts of the huge Morecambe Bay complex, and at high tide these birds number many thousands. Being created by the sea the area is interesting in showing the colonization by successive plant communities.

Visiting: the Reserve is open daily and there is cottage accommodation to be booked in advance. Contact Mr J. H. Mitchell, 82 Plymouth Street, Walney, Barrow-in-Furness (but enclose s.a.e.).
Birds: lesser black-backed gull, herring gull, eider, oystercatcher, knot, dunlin, shelduck, wigeon, teal.
Botany: colonizing plants including silverweed, sea holly, sea campion, corn salad, sea sandwort, mouse-eared hawkweed.

Winged World 🐦 ♿

Opened only in 1966 by the Blackpool and Heysham Corporation, Winged World has quickly become one of the primary foreign bird collections in the country. It presently houses over 400 individuals of over 150 different species, all of them displayed in the most imaginative modern ways. By far the most impressive section is a huge free-flight enclosure in which visitors and birds are together to interact as they please. The principle is not new, but the results in terms of breeding birds have been remarkable. Several species have bred in captivity for the first time in Britain. In line with this bar-less approach to viewing the birds are the glass-fronted enclosures where exotics such as hummingbirds are kept in surroundings as close as possible to their natural environment. A large part of this same main building encloses a variety of waterbirds such as egrets and ibises behind a wall of darkness. The birds are illuminated while visitors watch in darkness with nothing between the two. This outstanding and imaginatively displayed collection is among the major attractions of Blackpool.

Visiting: take the B5273 south of Morecambe for a couple of miles to Heysham Head: inquiries, Winged World, Heysham Head, Heysham and Morecambe, Lancs. Tel. Heysham 52391.

Birds: superb collection from all parts of the world: hummingbirds, egrets, spoonbills, ibises, Rothschild's starling, blue-crowned motmot.

Other: adjacent children zoo.

Otter

North-East England

Bempton Cliffs

Bempton, which lies just north of Flamborough Head and Bridlington on the Yorkshire coast, has long been known as a major seabird breeding site. For a good number of years it was the only gannetry on the British mainland, but the birds stubbornly refused to increase from the handful of pairs present before the war. Finally in the 1960s they took off, and now a good population (about forty pairs) of these spectacular birds can be seen. Around them are 60,000 other cliff-nesting seabirds, and come spring and summer the cliffs are alive with their calls. The spectacle from the clifftops is exhilarating, moving and remarkable for being so freely available. There is no entry charge, no fees to pay, simply a lovely walk along the white chalk cliffs, watching the birds wheel over the sea below. Being chalk, the clifftop flowers are worthy of investigation, though at all times be wary of the drop below. Sometimes binocular botany is the better part of valour.

Visiting: **leave Bridlington northward on the B1255 to Flamborough,** turn left and then right continuing on the B1255 to the coast. Walk northward along the cliffs for miles.
Birds: gannet, guillemot, razorbill, puffin, kittiwake, fulmar, shag.
Botany: chalk-loving species.

Blacktoft Sands

This wetland reserve of the Royal Society for the Protection of Birds lies at the confluence of the Yorkshire Trent and the Yorkshire Ouse where they combine to form the Humber. The area, which was originally created by the Dutch engineer Vermuyden before he embarked on his most noteworthy British project, the draining of the Fens, is partly submerged by the tide. It also includes much 'dry' land and some huge reedbeds, and is a habitat of numerous breeding birds. The flat landscape echoes to the calls of redshank and reed and

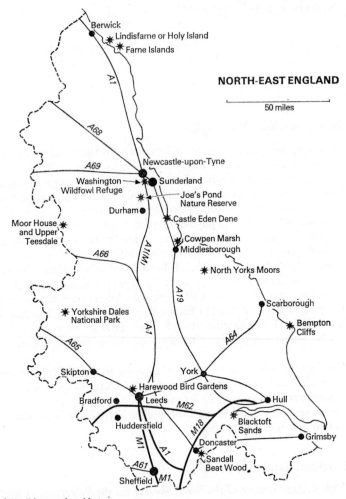

NORTH-EAST ENGLAND

50 miles

✱ localities mentioned in text

sedge warblers through the summer, but in winter it is a well-established resort of the wild geese that have found refuge in this part of the Humber for generations. In early autumn this is the most important arrival point in England for pink-footed geese, with up to 5000 regularly present. Most roost on Whitton Sands nearby. The geese also resort to Read's Island downstream, where thousands of wigeon and mallard can be found. Other birds, especially passage waders, are even more numerous, with large flocks of dunlin together with oystercatchers, redshank, etc.

As elsewhere, the RSPB is trying to create even better conditions for birds by managing the water level and by creating lagoons where birds can feed in peace and people watch without disturbance. Among the specialities they search for are bearded tit and short-eared owl.

Visiting: access free at all times along the footpath-seawall which begins opposite Ousefleet School. The Warden at Hillcrest, Whitgift, near Goole, can supply further details and advice.

Birds: bearded tit, short-eared owl, grasshopper warbler, reed warbler, tree sparrow, redshank, dunlin, oystercatcher, pink-footed goose, wigeon.

Botany: interesting colonization by 'salting' species.

Castle Eden Dene

Owned and developed as a local nature reserve by Peterlee Development Corporation, this recently created local authority is justly proud of Castle Eden Dene. Comparatively few local authorities have taken advantage of their powers to create nature reserves, and fewer still have achieved such an important contribution to wildlife and recreation. Situated in the heart of the coastal colliery land of Durham, Castle Eden Dene is the largest of the densely-wooded ravines that cut through this coast. To the north, Hawthorn Dene is a private nature reserve of the Durham County Conservation Trust, but Castle Eden is a larger and richer site. To the people of Hartlepool, Tees-side and Durham this is a true day in the country.

The Dene extends to 500 acres and stretches four miles inland. It is densely wooded with oak, ash and conifers, a small area of beech and some magnificent yews. The geology is varied, and this in turn creates a variety of soils supporting a richness of life. In spring the woods are carpeted with anemone, bluebell, wild garlic, primrose, violet, wood sorrel and lesser celandine. Summer brings a show of early purple and spotted orchids, wood cranesbill and pink campions.

Butterflies are sometimes quite numerous, including the Eden argus, a race of the brown argus. Other species regularly observed are orange tip, large skipper and common blue. Fifty-six species of birds have bred and its excellent geographical position attracts a regular variety of passage migrants. The nuthatch is here approaching its northward limit, and both treecreeper and great spotted woodpecker breed. There are goldcrests, and in winter snow buntings haunt the beach. Mammals are rather thin on the ground, but both badger and fox are regular.

Visiting: the reserve lies immediately south of Peterlee, extending from the A19 to the coast. There are access points at the A19, at A1086 in the east, and just off the B1281 in the south. Three footpaths leave the suburbs of Peterlee southward to penetrate the reserve. There are several footpaths and more (not less!) are planned to facilitate access and the enjoyment of this fine wooded valley.

Botany: wood anemone, bluebell, wild garlic, primrose, violet, wood sorrel, lesser celandine, golden saxifrage, wood avens, water avens, pink campion, wood cranesbill, meadow cranesbill, early purple orchid, fly orchid, spotted orchid, bird's-nest orchid (rare), sweet woodruff, hawkweed, burdock, toadflax, enchanter's nightshade, grass of Parnassus, hartstongue fern, great horsetail.

Birds: nuthatch, treecreeper, great spotted woodpecker, marsh tit, coal tit, long-tailed tit, tree sparrow, bullfinch, garden warbler, blackcap, goldcrest, spotted flycatcher, grey wagtail, yellow wagtail.

Insects: Castle Eden argus butterfly, green-veined white, large white, orange tip, common blue, meadow brown, small tortoiseshell, dingy skipper, large skipper.

Cleveland Way

Virtually encircling the North York Moors National Park, the Cleveland Way extends nearly 100 miles over the Cleveland Hills and North York Moors. It offers the walker some of the finest and least-used hill walking in the country, as well as a lengthy stretch of some of the best coastal scenery to be found in northern England. Adjacent to the Teesside conurbation, it is already well used in parts.

From the attractive market town of Helmsley, with its twelfth-century castle, the route strikes westward to Rievaulx Abbey, founded in 1131 but now a majestic ruin. It continues along Whitestone Cliff to pick up the scarp of Hambleton Hills leading northward to Osmotherley before climbing to Mt Grace Priory and thence on over Whorlton Moor, Carlton Moor and Cringle Moor to Hasty Bank. On across Ingleby Moor to the village of Kildale, then northward out of the valley to Captain Cook's monument on Easby Moor and on to Roseberry Topping, Cleveland's best-known monument. Across

Gisborough Moor, and the Way slowly descends to reach the coast at Saltburn.

Turning southward, the National Park is re-entered beyond Skinningrove, and the Way then heads over Boulby Cliffs to Staithes, Runswick Bay, Sandsend and Whitby. A bird's-eye view of this charming fishing town can be obtained by climbing the 199 stairs of the Church. Whitby was formerly the site of a small jet industry, and pieces of this fossilized wood can occasionally be found along the shoreline. Past Whitby Abbey the Way continues to Robin Hood's Bay, Ravenscar and Scarborough, where the path ends. This latter stretch is generally good for seabirds, but lacks the cliffs and stacks that are such a feature of the coastline further north. Indeed birds and mammals are of no great interest throughout the walk, or in the adjacent National Park come to that. Botanically there is considerable variety to be found, with areas that have not been disturbed by man for generations alongside more recent quarries and constructions. Archaeologists will find the marks of man over most of the route; some remains date back to the Bronze and Iron Age, especially around Danby and on Shooting House Moor.

Visiting: the walk is well signposted, and there are Youth Hostels at Helmsley, Saltburn, Whitby, Boggle Hole and Scarborough. There are small inns here and there and some shepherds make visitors really welcome in their homes.

Botany: good and varied flower communities including stinking hellebore.

Birds: usual moorland species with passing seabirds offshore during the latter parts of the walk.

Cowpen Marsh

Lying adjacent to Teesmouth and surrounded on virtually all sides by the teeming industrialism of Middlesbrough and Tees-side, Cowpen Marsh is really a remarkable place. First it belonged to a chemical giant, then a local enthusiast persuaded the giant to make it a reserve, and now it is a fully-fledged bird reserve of the Royal Society for the Protection of Birds. Large, open but shallow waters are surrounded by grazing marshes and, with effective wardening, the birds have prospered. Duck and waders in winter and on passage in spring and autumn are the major attractions, along with a gasp of (almost) fresh air in the overdeveloped little world of Tees-side. There are shelduck, godwits, curlew, oystercatcher, dunlin and plovers as well as the terns that frequently gather to feed in the estuary in vast numbers in August.

Visiting: there are signposts and a car park on the A178 between Middlesbrough and Hartlepool and public hides nearby from which many of the birds can be seen. The reserve is open throughout the year.

Birds: dunlin, curlew, oystercatcher, shelduck, teal, bar-tailed godwit, grey plover, golden plover, ringed plover.

Farne Islands

Thirty-odd islands constitute the Farnes, some two to five miles off the rugged Northumberland coast. These are romantic islands brimful of history, stories of the seventh-century St Cuthbert – eider duck are still called 'cuddy-ducks' to this day – and of Grace Darling's heroic deeds. St Cuthbert was, of course, a patron saint of animals, and it is the tameness of the birds and seals that still inhabit these low-slung islands that most captivate the visitor. For many, a trip to the Farnes may just be a day in the country, but their fame has stretched so far that visitors arrive from all over Europe. Mixed with the trippers there are the bird-watching enthusiasts of a continent.

Surprisingly enough, both groups, layman and devotee, come for the same purpose – to soak up the atmosphere of one of the most accessible genuine seabird colonies in Europe. Here guillemots crowd together on the offshore stacks, terns by the thousand nest over the flat grasslands and scream overhead. The enthusiast's eyes search for the rare roseate tern, others are more easily satisfied with the spectacle itself. Eiders, the most confiding of duck, will allow themselves to be stroked on the nest, and common and grey seals bask in the sun. Puffins, razorbills and cormorants all nest and can often be approached close enough for photography, and fulmars are abundant.

Visiting: only two islands, the Inner Farne and Staple, are open during the summer months. The Inner Farne, which has a nature trail, is best. Boats can be obtained at Seahouses Harbour, where landing tickets can be obtained from the Information Centre. They can also be purchased (quite easily) from the watchers (wardens) on landing. The Warden/Naturalist can be contacted in advance at The Shieling, 8 St Aidan's, Seahouses, Northumberland.

Birds: cormorant, shag, fulmar, eider, common tern, Arctic tern,

Sandwich tern, roseate tern, guillemot, razorbill, puffin, oyster-catcher, ringed plover, kittiwake.

Harewood Bird Gardens

Situated five miles north of Leeds, Harewood Park and its House have been open to the public for some years. In 1970 Lord Harewood opened the Bird Gardens and today they represent one of the best collections in this part of the country. There is a walk-through aviary, a tropical house, enclosures, and cages housing many different species. As an added attraction there is a lake in the grounds that is a noted haunt of a large flock of Canada geese together with various wild ducks in winter. There are also breeding great crested grebes.

Among the many attractions there are penguins, flamingoes, a geese and duck collection and free-flying macaws. But for those in search of the less usual species the tropical house is alive with hummingbirds from the New World and sunbirds from the Old, while the walk-through aviary houses the delightful touracos and no less than half a dozen species of mynah. There are rare pheasants, many starlings including Rothschild's, and the magnificent red-billed blue magpie, which is difficult to see in its natural habitat. A good bird library may be consulted by appointment.

Visiting: the Park and Bird Gardens are open throughout the year and there is a restaurant, snack bar, shop, etc. It is reached on the A61 roughly halfway between Leeds and Harrogate.

Birds: Andean flamingo, crowned crane, black-necked swan, macaws, Rothschild's starling, red-billed blue magpie, pheasants, humming-birds, sunbirds, plus wild Canada geese, great crested grebe and duck.

Other: grounds by Capability Brown.

Joe's Pond Nature Reserve

Deep in industrial Durham this nature reserve covers only eleven acres and is the primary creation of Joe Wilson, who leased it from the National Coal Board and has now handed it over to the Durham County Conservation Trust. It is no more than a freshwater pond carefully maintained by Joe against pollution and vandals. It is stocked with a self-maintaining population of trout and has been modified to attract a variety of birds. There are tufted duck, coot, little grebe and moorhen and many small birds in the shrubbery. The emergent vegetation is rich and varied. But what really counts is that Joe Wilson cared enough to create this little bit of nature in such hostile surroundings.

Visiting: Joe is often on the Reserve in the afternoons and evenings: otherwise contact him at home: 5 Finchdale Terrace, Woodstone Village, Fence Houses.
Birds: little grebe, tufted duck.

Lindisfarne or Holy Island

Lindisfarne lies on the Northumberland coast just south of the Scottish border. It is a considerable tourist attraction with its old cathedral and historical connections and the romance of access only at low tide. At such times a car can drive across the causeway that separates Fenham Flats to the south from Goswick Sands to the north, between the village of Beal and the island. Visitors should plan their retreat, or be prepared to await the turn of the tide. This is a fine open area with marram-clad dunes, huge open flats alive with birds and a wildness that has an atmosphere of its own. While birds are the major attraction,

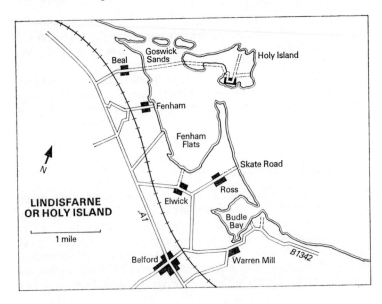

and these include brent, pink-footed and greylag geese in winter along with hordes of wildfowl and waders, there is much to interest other lovers of the countryside. In particular the dune system of the Snook shows the colonization and succession from open shore to the grassland of the dunes.

Though much of the area is a National Nature Reserve, shooting on a controlled basis is still allowed: permits from The Secretary, The Lindisfarne Wildfowl Panel, c/o The Warden, Sionside, Belford, Northumberland. Otherwise the Reserve is of free access everywhere. Visitors to Holy Island should not trespass on farmland; there are several tracks that facilitate full exploration.

Visiting: access by several minor roads directly from the A1 trunk road between Alnwick and Berwick.

Mammals: seals, hare.

Birds: hosts of passage and winter wildfowl and waders including brent goose, pink-footed goose, greylag goose, and, at times, bean goose; also all the British grebes in season.

Botany: excellent salt marsh and dune flora.

Moor House and Upper Teesdale

Moor House National Nature Reserve, covering nearly 10,000 acres, lies high in the North Pennines and is as lonely an area as any could wish for. It was once a grouse moor, and red grouse are still characteristic birds of the heather-clad hills. Much of the ground is wet, and in places the underlying peat is ten feet thick. Here the typical sounds of spring are curlew 'bubbling' and meadow pipit 'tweeting' before dropping to the ground like miniature parachutists. Botanically the area holds the normal upland plants of wet peatland. The old shooting lodge has been converted into a field station and is the centre of much experimental research.

A little way to the south lies Upper Teesdale, scene of a heated environmental conflict between the giant ICI and local conservationists in the 1960s. The plan to build a reservoir here involved the destruction of much of the unique flora, and the price paid was the establishment of this National Nature Reserve, which is so full of unusual species of an Arctic-Alpine nature that access is restricted to serious students undertaking scientific work. Apply to the Deputy Regional Officer, The Nature Conservancy, 33 Eskdale Terrace, Newcastle-upon-Tyne NE2 4DN.

At Moor House there are a number of rights of way that facilitate casual exploration, though permits are required to leave them.

Visiting: Moor House and Upper Teesdale are reached via the B6277 between Middleton-in-Teesdale and Alston taking a minor road north at Newbiggin.
Birds: curlew, lapwing, meadow pipit, wheatear.
Botany: unique flora with many species otherwise not found in Britain.

Northumberland National Park

Northumberland National Park covers 398 square miles of some of the most remote land in Britain. It lies in England, but like so much of the border country it is ignored by the Sassenachs heading northward to the more obvious beauties of Scotland, and by the Scots because of its 'Englishness'. It lies astride the Pennine Way, but along one of that path's least frequented sections; and yet it is truly a beautiful region full of interest to the outsider. It includes the area north and east of the A68 at Byrness, a mere five miles from the border, from the River Rede to include the upper reaches of the River Coquet above Harbottle. It extends south-westward to include much of the upper Tyne and Wark Forest.

Much of the landscape is bleak and boggy, but there are no great hills and much is simply sheep country. Here it is possible to walk for a day in spring and see only the occasional shepherd's cottage among the hills. There are curlew calling, wheatears flitting and the ever-present meadow pipit. Dippers and grey wagtails frequent the streams and there are wild flowers of a variety of different species. Like so much of upland Britain there is nothing special, nothing outstanding or rare; just beautiful countryside largely devoid of people save only for fellow searchers after solitude. The Romans, of course, were not seeking solitude so they built the fort at Housesteads to house a thousand soldiers and the temple of Mithras at Carrawburgh.

Visiting: use the access points of the Pennine Way (see page 207) or start walking north or south from the River Tyne above Bellingham.
Botany: good general upland botanizing.
Birds: short-eared owl, curlew, wheatear, meadow pipit.
Other: Roman connections.

North York Moors National Park

Covering 553 square miles, the North York Moors is one of the less frequented of our National Parks. If it is less spectacular than some, less open than others, it makes up for this in its immense beauty and variety of landscape. It includes a goodly chunk of the coast, with spectacular fishing villages like Staithes and Runswick, it has high moors dissected with deep beautiful valleys, it is almost encircled by the Cleveland Way (see page 200) and it has the unique attraction of the Farndale Local Nature Reserve. A recent estimate found that 56,000 people visited this valley during the brief daffodil season, for Farndale is the Vale of the Daffodils.

The colonies of wild daffodils (were they planted by medieval monks?) stretch for seven miles along the banks of the River Dove and were regularly picked by visitors until 1955. By then it was obvious that the increasingly mobile population of Tees-side was going to destroy this unique site and picking was prohibited by bye-law. Now the local nature reserve covers 2500 acres of the lower valley north of Lowna. In April and early May a one-way traffic system comes into operation and visitors may tour the fields (almost in convoys at peak weekends) to enjoy the magnificent sight of so many wild flowers. Visitors are handed a plan (yellow naturally) that will enable them to get the best out of Farndale's daffodils.

Visiting: Hutton-le-Hole, the starting point for exploring Farndale, lies north of the A170 north of Kirkbymoorside; for the National Park see Cleveland Way.
Botany: daffodils in April and early May.

Pennine Way

Opened in 1965, the Pennine Way was the first of the long-distance footpaths and, covering 250 miles, is both the longest (until the completion of the South-West Peninsula Path) and toughest of them all. Its route runs from the Peak District in Derbyshire northward along the backbone of England switching first this way then that to take in points of interest en route. Along the way it scales high peaks, visits outstanding natural scenery, uses old drove roads and miners' tracks and crosses some peat-sodden moors that only the fit and experienced should attempt. The scenery is beautiful, the landscape often remote, and there are people to be met who live a life that seems quite remarkably isolated in late twentieth-century Britain.

The Way starts at Edale in Derbyshire, immediately climbs the great inhospitable moor of Kinder Scout, and continues over uplands until it reaches the moors of the Brontë country by way of the Calder Valley. It continues to the limestone and dry stone wall area around Malham, skirts the eastern side of Malham Tarn, and climbs Fountains Fell and Pen-y-ghent. Those who wish to can stay overnight in upper Ribblesdale and take in Ingleborough with its huge limestone caves at Gaping Gill, or even the peaks of Ingleborough, Whernside and Pen-y-ghent (again!) to complete the Three Peaks in a day. An old packhorse trail leads to Wensleydale.

Onward the path leads to Tan Hill and Britain's highest inn before crossing Teesdale. The waterfall at High Force should not be missed and the Way continues to its highest point at Cross Fell (2930 feet). It then drops down to the Tyne and joins Hadrian's Wall eastward and at its best part. It passes between the high-level loughs at Broomlee, Greenlee and Grindon, best known as a winter haunt of whooper swans and as a resort of the rare and elusive bean goose in February. The Way then winds over the border moors, past the Cheviot, to finish at Kirk Yetholm in Roxburgh. This last stretch, between Byrness and Kirk Yetholm, is twenty-seven miles which must be covered in a day or with an overnight stay at a shepherd's cottage in Upper Coquetdale.

Throughout its length the Pennine Way has been planned with stopovers in mind. Youth Hostels are quite well supplied and there are a number of old inns where accommodation can be had. It's a long hard walk, and many will be content with walking even a short section of it. It also passes through some of the loneliest parts of Britain, and offers a true opportunity to think and refresh oneself. Wainwright, the guide to generations of Lakeland walkers, has produced a guidebook to the Pennine Way throughout its length.

Wildlife among the hills is generally rather scant. Meadow pipits accompany the walker all the way and wheatears and curlews are quite common. Short-eared owls haunt the younger plantations in the border country, and ring ouzel and merlin should be seen. The streams hold dipper and grey wagtail and the heather is the haunt of the native red grouse. Botanically the Pennine Way is of interest because of the variety of geological structures over which it passes. From the plant-rich limestone outcrops to the bare and uniform peat hags there is much to see, much to identify.

Visiting: the Pennine Way is dangerous and should not be attempted by anyone not experienced in finding their way with the aid of map and compass and nothing else. Walks average twelve or fifteen miles daily over heavy and rough going, and protective clothing, good boots, emergency protection and food are still not enough if suddenly you are confronted with rain or mist, snow or gale.

Birds: red grouse, meadow pipit, wheatear, curlew.

Botany: rich and varied communities on the limestone, poor collections on the peat.

Sandall Beat Wood

To most, Sandall Beat Wood is barely worth a trip, but to the people of Doncaster it is a lungful of fresh air on their doorstep. It is small, notable for the absence of rarities, but a delight all the same. The wood was planted by the Town Council in 1810 in response to the need for wood for ships to fight Napoleon. Fortunately wooden ships disappeared from the naval scene before the plantations were ready for use. Larch, oak and ash are the dominant species, with chestnut, elm and beech close behind. For the botanist such a mixed wood with such a definite date of origin is particularly interesting. A nature trail has been laid out from the entrance to the reserve in Sandall Beat Road and the visitor is guided along to the major points of interest. In late spring the rhododendron bushes are in full flower and visitors are numerous; at other times the woods may be completely empty.

In addition to the woodland there is a small fen where the succession from open water, through reed marsh to willow carr, can be seen. Here the birds of the woodland are replaced by marsh-loving species such as snipe, reed and grasshopper warblers and willow tit. In the woods themselves a good variety of birds reflects the variety of habitats. There are woodcock, great spotted woodpecker, willow warbler, blackcap, long-tailed tit, tree pipit, treecreeper, titmice and so on.

For the botanist too there is much to find, aided by the excellent checklist published by the Doncaster Museum.

Visiting: access from Doncaster via Sandall Beat Road.

Birds: woodcock, snipe, grasshopper warbler, long-eared owl, great spotted woodpecker, moorhen, goldcrest, willow tit.

Botany: purple small reed, reedmace, great reed, fungi.

Washington Wildfowl Refuge

The people of Tyneside have always been favoured by open country-side on their doorstep, so it is not perhaps surprising that Washington New Town should act as hosts to the Wildfowl Trust in their first venture in the north-east. The refuge covers 103 acres along the northern bank of the River Wear just west of Sunderland, and at present houses 800 wildfowl of eighty species. There are plans for extending this collection, particularly of American species, with Washington's obvious transatlantic connections. Thus hooded mer-

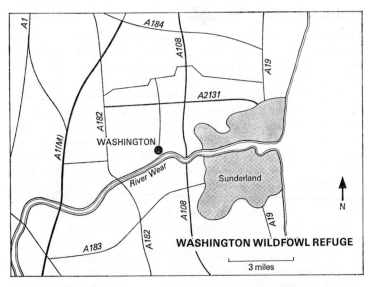

ganser, Carolina duck, black brant, emperor goose and other American species are the centrepieces of the collection. This does not mean that Washington will be free of Hawaiian geese, black swans or Laysan teal.

As is usual with the Wildfowl Trust, a large part of the refuge is given over to wild birds, and there are ponds alongside the river where waders come to feed and roost along with small numbers of wild duck. No doubt as the refuge develops the feeding and habitat management programmes of the Trust will ensure some spectacle of wild birds.

There is an exhibition building, a small gift shop, and vending machines offering hot drinks. A nature trail is planned for Hawthorn Wood in the south-west of the refuge.

Visiting: Washington lies immediately east of the A1(M) and north of the River Wear due west of Sunderland. Road construction here will change all directions for a few years, but following signs to Washington District 15 will (with tolerance during alterations) lead to the refuge, which is open every day except Christmas Day. The address is The Wildfowl Trust, Middle Barmston Farm, Pattinson, District 15, Washington, Tyne and Wear.
Birds: wildfowl collection, waders.

Yorkshire Dales National Park

The Yorkshire Dales National Park covers 680 square miles of some of the finest upland scenery in Britain. It lies in the heartland of the Pennines and is roughly bounded by the towns of Reeth in the north-east, Grassington in the south, and Kirkby Stephen in the north-west. In the south it includes the 'Three Peaks' district and the Malham area, and in the west the beautiful upper part of Dentdale with its magnificent scenery.

This is a rolling landscape with moors and wooded dales typical of the Pennines. It is a gentle land, though the peat hags and bogs of the poorly-drained tops are as bleak as any could wish. The small towns are all market places for the local sheep rearing industry, and while many sheep have the freedom of the hills others are confined by the dry-stone walls that are such a feature of the landscape.

The Pennine Way runs through the Park from Gargrave to Tan Hill, opening up the landscape to the long or short distance walker. There is no better method of exploration for those seeking a day (or more) in the superb countryside of the Yorkshire Dales. But to those who wish to branch out on their own, the appropriate Ordnance Survey map, a compass, protective clothing and some experience can lead across fells and sheep paths where the sight of another walker is cause for surprise.

To the botanist the Park offers excellent opportunities to examine a typical upland flora, and plants associated with peat proliferate. The peculiar formation known as 'Limestone Pavement' occurs in several areas, notably around Ingleborough. This is limestone that has been worn into deep fissures by weathering. A typical flora exists including several ferns and the beautiful bloody cranesbill. To the bird-watcher there are opportunities to find breeding dunlin, golden plover, red grouse, curlew and other typical upland species. To the potholer the area is full of magnificent opportunities – the very best part of England. And to the walker the Park is simply a joy.

Visiting: several well-used roads cross the area. The A684 from Sedbergh to Aysgarth (note the Falls) is the major route, but the B6259 leads northward to Kirkby Stephen and the B6255 southward to Burton in Lonsdale giving access to more remote areas. The B6479 from Settle leads to Horton-in-Ribblesdale and the B6160 from Bolton Abbey to Kettlewell and the remote Langstrothdale. In the north the B6270 runs along Swaledale.

Birds: red grouse, merlin, raven, curlew, wheatear, meadow pipit, cuckoo.

Botany: varied, but explore limestone pavements for bloody cranesbill.

Sandwich terns

South Scotland

Ben Lawers

Covering 8000 acres, Ben Lawers is owned by the National Trust for Scotland and administered as a nature reserve. The mountain of the same name is the highest in Perthshire at just under 4000 feet, and for those with the energy to climb, it offers views from the North Sea to the Atlantic with the massive Cairngorms to the north. The reserve lies immediately north of Loch Tay. From the excellent visitor centre and car park, much of the area can be explored on foot, but visitors would be well advised to follow one of the nature trails that winds its way up toward the top of the peak armed with an inexpensive little guide. Though there are birds on Ben Lawers – wheatear, dipper, red grouse and curlew – it is the remarkable flora that attracts the visitor. Even from the trail a few Alpine flowers can be seen, but the high cliffs offer protection from sheep grazing to the most significant Alpine flora to be found in these islands.

It is a strange series of coinciding factors that has created the unique flora of Ben Lawers. The same (or similar) flowers flourish only among the mountains of central Europe and in the high Arctic. Left behind by the last ice age the plants died out on most other British mountains. Here on Ben Lawers the rich minerals of weathered schist enabled them to survive. So among the cliffs, where the ubiquitous sheep cannot graze them, there are Alpine golden rod, devil's bit scabious, viviparous fescue, northern bedstraw, purple saxifrage and harebell. Other and more widespread plants that survive despite grazing are Alpine lady's mantle, Alpine meadow rue, gentians and wild thyme. Apart from such specialities Ben Lawers offers many of the other typical highland flowers, flowers that have survived the onslaught of man and sheep alike.

Visiting: leave the A827 along the shore of Loch Tay and follow signs to Ben Lawers Visitor Centre. Park (small fee), explore the centre, buy something to help the work continue and follow the nature trail to the foot of the cliffs.

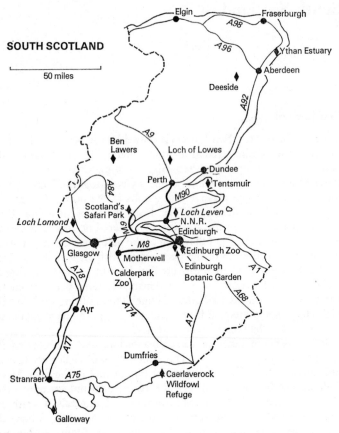

SOUTH SCOTLAND

|———————| 50 miles

♦ localities mentioned in text

Botany: the most remarkable Alpine flora in Britain.

Other: the excellent Kenmore Hotel, one of the nicest hotels in
Scotland with several miles of good salmon fishing and some
remarkably voracious small trout.

Caerlaverock

For generations Caerlaverock has attracted wildfowlers to try their
hand with the wild geese over the merse – the close-cropped grassland

on the seaward side of the sea wall. Later, bird-watchers turned the area into a place of wintery pilgrimage. Today the merse grasslands are a National Nature Reserve with access strictly limited and shooting carefully controlled, and the adjacent agricultural land, Eastpark Farm, is owned by the Wildfowl Trust. Thus the true wilderness of this fine spot on the Scottish Solway can be visited and enjoyed in comfort by thousands of people every year.

There is a small pond on which a collection of wildfowl are kept to decoy the wild birds. The system works well, and both wild swans as well as geese and duck have been attracted to land. There is a good observatory with educational displays.

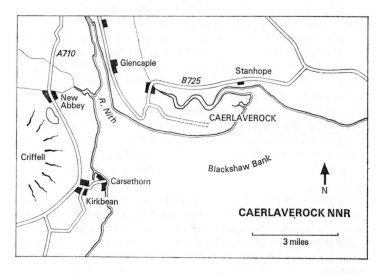

The main attraction of the area is its status as the traditional home of the Siberian barnacle geese. The birds, up to 5000 of them, arrive in early October and stay to early April. Throughout this period they are viewable every day from the numerous hides positioned at strategic intervals along the surrounding embankments, and from the Saltcot Tower (courtesy of the Nature Conservancy Council) that gives such excellent views over the merse and the Solway. Other geese are to be seen here as well as the occasional wild swan. Hen harriers are regular in winter and there are always duck and waders to be seen.

Visiting: Caerlaverock is reached from Dumfries via the B725 and from Annan via the B724. There is a reasonable admission charge with reductions for children and parties during the season, which lasts from 1 September to 15 May. Visitors are escorted by the warden starting at 11.00 and 14.00 hours daily except Christmas Day.

Birds: barnacle goose, pink-footed goose, whooper swan.

Calderpark Zoo

Calderpark Zoo is owned by the Zoological Society of Glasgow and the West of Scotland and covers forty-five acres near Uddingston on the A74, the main Glasgow–Hamilton road. From elsewhere, the junction with the A74 and M74 is the most straightforward approach.

This reasonably-priced Zoo has a commendably strong educational side to its activities, catering as it does for the youngsters of Glasgow. It offers most of the usual zoo animals including all of the big stars – elephant, white rhino, lion, tiger, leopard, cheetah, etc. It has Przewalski's horse, some black leopards, Père David's deer and a motley array of smaller attractions. Though many of the animals breed (a good thing) the *raison d'être* of the Zoo is its exploitation of the immense educational opportunities provided by a collection of wild animals. Such exploitation, in fact, compensates for the taking of animals from the wild which is still such a characteristic of *all* zoos.

There are lecture tours for primary schoolchildren and special tours for those taking 'O' level examinations. The Society publishes an excellent magazine, *Zoolife*, which is well written and illustrated, and it also provides lecturers for schools free of charge. It is refreshing to see a zoo make such a point of good and informative labelling of its exhibits.

Visiting: A74 and M74 junction, thence signposts. Uddingston Station is two miles away and buses leave both Anderston and Buchanan Bus Stations regularly. There is parking for 1500 cars. The Zoo is open throughout the year from 09.30 to 17.00 or 19.00 hours according to season.

Mammals: white rhino, elephant, camel, llama, zebra, Przewalski's horse, Père David's deer, polar bear, tiger, leopard, cheetah, porcupine, racoon, ring-tailed lemur.

Deeside

It has always proved a difficult decision for the naturalist wondering which side of the massive Cairngorms he should visit. To the north this mountain massif is bounded by the Spey Valley, well known, touristy, but full of interest none the less. To the south lies Deeside, unfrequented and with a distinctive charm all its own. Between the two, and an excellent mountain walk for the fit and well prepared, lies the Lairig Ghru, the high-level pass that cuts deep between the mountains. Further north is Glen Feshie, less austere, with pines and meadows offering the best chance of seeing both red and roe deer.

On Deeside itself there are some quite excellent wildlife areas, outstanding among which is the Balmoral Estate, part of which Her Majesty the Queen has allowed to become a Scottish Wildlife Trust Reserve. This is easily reached by a minor road leading southward along Glen Muick out of Ballater. To the west the craggy Lochnager is worth a climb from Spittal – here all the specialities of the Highlands can be found, including golden eagle, ptarmigan and blue hare.

To the north of Ballater too the hill of Morven is another fine moorland area, full of red grouse and blue hare.

Visiting: centres for exploration are Ballater and Braemar, with trips up many side roads including along the River Dee up toward Glen Feshie and Glen Muick.

Mammals: red deer, roe deer, blue hare.

Birds: golden eagle, ptarmigan, red grouse, black grouse, greenshank, golden plover.

Botany: good Alpine-type flora.

Other: Balmoral Castle.

Edinburgh Botanic Garden

The Royal Botanic Garden at Edinburgh had its origins, as did so many other gardens, in the physic or medicinal gardens of earlier times. Its origins date back to 1670, making it second only to Oxford among British botanical gardens. It has been in its present site at Inverleith since 1820. The Garden is exceptionally beautiful and attracts many visitors, though the authorities are quick to point out that its real purpose is botanical research, especially taxonomy – the classification of plants. Today the Himalayan region and south-west China are its specialities and the Herbarium, occupied since 1964, houses a remarkable $1\frac{1}{2}$ million specimens mostly from that region. It has one of the finest botanical libraries in the world.

On 25 October 1967 the exhibition houses were opened to replace a series of ancient and outdated structures and house a remarkable collection of plants in mostly systematical sequence. Thus there is a cactus house, a warm temperate aquatic house, a temperate plant house, a fern house, an orchid house and so on. Additionally there are Victorian palm houses and an exhibition hall opened in 1970.

The visitor could easily be utterly confused faced with such a superabundance, but a sound guide draws the attention to specific plants and their biology and relationships one to another, a vast improvement over the 'plastic label search for it yourself' approach to plant displays.

With their excellent guidebook, and the series of well-laid-out paths that enable much to be seen even on a short visit, the Gardens are rather like a tamed nature trail with the Tea Room and Modern Art Gallery as the ultimate reward. Though the plant houses are of interest throughout the year, the seasonal nature of flowering plants indicates a visit between April and July; earlier for azaleas, later for lilies.

Visiting: the Garden is open to the public throughout the year (except Christmas Day) and can be entered from the West Gate on Arboretum Road or the East Gate on Inverleith Row.
Botany: huge collection in beautiful surroundings.

Edinburgh Zoo

The Scottish National Zoological Park of the Royal Zoological Society of Scotland is one of Britain's senior zoos and one of the best. Its animals, which include many breeding pairs or groups, are well housed in modern, light and airy enclosures. The Zoo is situated on the north side of the main Edinburgh–Glasgow road between Murrayfield and Corstorphine. Because of its urban situation it has been appointed suitable for quarantine purposes, so it houses a floating population of other zoos' and collections' animals.

Starting at the entrance there is the Carnegie Aquarium, which houses a couple of the world's turtle species as well as numerous fishes. A series of adjacent ponds are home to sealions, waterfowl and polar bear, while the Bramton Aviaries have a good collection of pheasants. Further north there is a monkey house, penguin and seal colonies, elephant and giraffe flanking the Education Centre, and various animals such as Père David's deer, capybara, beaver, pygmy hippopotamus and a flamingo lake. In the north-east are the tiger enclosures, the lion house, a very large orang-utan enclosure and clouded leopard. There is an ape house, a tropical house and a house for nectar-eating birds. In 1939 three pairs of night herons escaped, and these birds formed the basis of the free-flying flock that feed in the local ponds and return to the Zoo each morning to roost away the daylight hours.

In the far north-west, on ground rising to Corstorphine Hill, there are Soay sheep, highland cattle and yet more tigers. This stress on tigers is due to the success of the Zoo in breeding this species. One tigress bore twenty-six cubs and brought the Zoo £10,000 from sales. If zoos are to continue to show rare animals, then, like Edinburgh, they must breed them themselves.

The Edinburgh Zoo is an admirable institution. Its educational facilities and services are as excellent as its exhibits. It has lectures, guided tours, audio-guides and project sheets, interlinked with radio and TV broadcasts. It produces a ZooEd Services brochure and the thrice-yearly *Gannet* for its junior members' society. Its guidebook, however, is full of accurate facts and marvellously useful information all presented in the manner of a report by some government committee: good text, good photos but rather lacking in design and appeal – a minor grouse!

Visiting: well signposted on the Edinburgh–Glasgow road at Murray-field, the Zoo is open throughout the year and there is a large car park. The Post House Hotel is convenient for those who want to stay.
Mammals: tiger, clouded leopard, orang-utan, polar bear.
Birds: very good and representative collection including night heron.

Galloway

For those who enjoy their Scotland, but who have become rather fed up with the tourist developments in the Highlands, there is always Galloway, a place too often rushed past on the way north. Here, west of the geese grounds of Dumfries, are moors and mountains, streams and lakes and a superb bonus in the form of outstanding estuarine habitat nearby. Three major areas attract the visitor, though there is much else besides. Wigtown Bay is a major haunt of greylag geese, joined by pink-feet in March prior to departure. There is a huge flock of summer scoter, and duck are very numerous in winter, as indeed are waders virtually throughout the year. Work the estuary on the minor road running northward from Wigtown.

Northward, immediately east of Newton Stewart, the ideal centre of exploration, rises Cairnsmore of Fleet, a superb area best explored via the B796 between Creetown and Gatehouse of Fleet. Further north still is the Galloway Forest Park on the slopes of Merrick, the highest hill in the region. Here golden eagle and red deer can be found along with other interesting birds including hen harrier. There is Loch Trool with its old oak woods as well as vast areas of spruce, larch and pine. Access is from the A714 north of Bargrennan and there are nature trails, marked walks, picnic spots, camp sites, etc.

Other attractions that may persuade the visitor to rest longer are the cliffs of the Mull of Galloway, where seabirds nest, and Scar Rocks offshore from Luce Bay, where gannets breed. At Logan south of Stranraer is the Edinburgh Botanic Garden's subtropical out-station; what are perhaps the finest tree ferns in the British Isles flourish in an extraordinarily mild climate.

Visiting: Wigtown Bay can be viewed from the A75 along the eastern shore, but is best in the west from an unclassified road north of Wigtown. Explore Cairnsmore of Fleet from the B796, but be prepared to walk for superb views from the top. The Galloway Forest Park is reached via the A714 north of Newton Stewart. The bird cliffs of the Mull of Galloway are approached on the B7041 to the lighthouse. Ask the keepers for permission to view. Scar Rocks can be approached by boat from Drummore or Port William.

Mammals: red deer, roe deer, wild goat.

Birds: golden eagle, buzzard, sparrowhawk, hen harrier, curlew, snipe, golden plover, dunlin, short-eared owl, crossbill, willow tit, greylag goose, duck.

Botany: plants of all Scottish habitats except the true Alpine.

Loch Leven

Covering nearly 4000 acres, Loch Leven is one of the richest lowland lakes in the country. It is the most famous trout lake in Scotland, with anglers virtually queuing up for the privilege of dapping a fly over its surface, and it is also the main point of arrival for huge numbers of geese that later spread through Scotland to winter. But such bare facts do not do justice to this magnificent water. Beautifully situated in a shallow depression, and virtually ringed by hills, Loch Leven is remarkably easy to get to. Cross the Forth Road Bridge near Edinburgh and a few minutes' motoring leads directly to Kinross, the major access point. From the main A90 hordes of birds can be seen, especially in autumn when the geese arrive.

Despite its size the Loch is of restricted access and visitors may approach via three points only. Best access is at Vane Farm, where the Royal Society for the Protection of Birds has its 300-acre reserve and Loch Leven Nature Centre. Vane is farmed commercially, but this does not interfere with the main activity of showing people geese. A nature trail leads from the observation post up the Benarty Hills through woodland with redstart and redpoll to the rivers above with their panoramic views over the Loch and with curlew and red grouse nearby. Several thousand geese arrive at the end of September to feed on the barley stubbles, and about 12,000 pink-footed have been counted on the Loch as a whole. Duck are often present in their thousands, and there are several hundred whooper swans in winter. Numerous duck breed on St Serf's Island, but this is out of bounds to visitors. Up to 80,000 brown trout are caught annually, with an average weight over a pound.

Visiting: access at Kinross Pier and Kirkgate Park; at Findalrie next to Vane Farm; and at Burleigh Sands two miles north-east of Kinross on the A911. There is also access to Castle Island, with its associations with Mary Queen of Scots. For the visitor intent on geese, Vane Farm is the best bet. The Centre is open throughout the year, except on Fridays, and offers excellent views of birds plus interesting natural history displays.

Birds: pink-footed goose, greylag goose, whooper swan, wigeon, pochard, tufted duck, shoveler, goldeneye, goosander, gadwall, mallard.

Other: first-class trout.

Loch Lomond

Loch Lomond has always held a special place in the minds and hearts of Scots and Sassenachs alike. Heading northward it offers a first taste of the Highlands, and to the millions who live in the Glasgow conurbation it is wilderness on the doorstep, an ideal day's run to freshen the body and spirit. Even along the resort-strewn western shore there are fields of flowers, farms and superb scenery along with camp sites, bed and breakfasts, boats and jetties, cafés and all the other industries that follow people to the countryside. In contrast the eastern shore is unspoilt. There is a road, but it does not go anywhere. Beyond Rowardennan there are only tracks, with goosander, buzzard and common sandpiper, red deer and wild goat. Loch Lomond National Nature Reserve at the mouth of the Endrick is a place where wildfowl flock in winter and where mink have become established since the 1960s. From Balmaha, a little further north, boats can be taken to Inchcailloch Island. Out of season this can be a very pleasant way to enjoy the countryside, and there is a nature trail through oakwoods full of warblers, including wood warbler. The main bird attractions are the

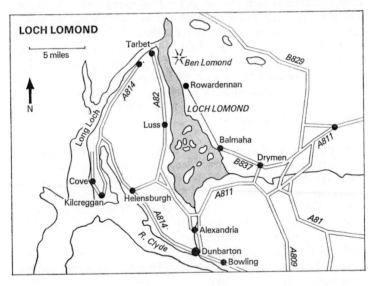

greylag geese in winter, along with wigeon, pochard, red-breasted merganser and goldeneye, and in summer the typical Highland birds. The Queen Elizabeth Forest Park beyond Balmaha has good nature trails, but this is best approached from the east via Aberfoyle, remembering to stop at David Marshall Lodge Wildlife Centre.

To the south of Loch Lomond near Balloch lies Cameron Loch Lomond Wildlife Park, opened in 1972 as a modern drive-through safari park with bears as a speciality. Four distinct varieties can be seen. Nearby is another drive-through section specializing in sub-Arctic animals such as yak, bison and various species of deer. There is a good collection of wildfowl, several species of cranes, many small mammals including otters, and an expansionist policy that will make the Park progressively more attractive.

Visiting: Loch Lomond lies east of the A82 out of Glasgow. The National Nature Reserve at Endrick is approached on the A811 toward Drymen, turning northward on a loop road west of Gartocharn.
Cameron Loch Lomond Wildlife Park is off the A82 near Balloch. It is open throughout the summer and there is a cafeteria and shop.
Mammals: grizzly bear, Himalayan black bear, Canadian black bear, bison, yak, red deer, fallow deer, muntjac, otters.
Birds: greylag goose, wigeon, pochard, tufted duck, red-breasted merganser, goldeneye.
Other: superb scenery on Glasgow's doorstep.

Loch of Lowes

Situated in Perthshire just east of Dunkeld, the Loch of Lowes is a reserve of the Scottish Wildlife Trust and is splendidly set against a woodland background. Its main attraction to the general public is the pair of ospreys that nest every summer and which, apart from the famous pair at Loch Garten in Speyside, are the only viewable ospreys in Britain. There is an information centre and observation hide, but there is much else here besides these avian stars. A good population of ducks in winter includes both goldeneye and goosander, and greylag

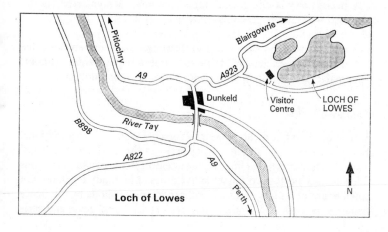

223

geese are regular in small numbers. In summer duck are also present, along with grebes and a variety of woodland birds.

Other interests are less prominent, though the keen botanist will find the ferns and fungi of interest.

Visiting: leave Dunkeld on the A923 to Blairgowrie, forking right after a couple of miles onto unclassified roads. Much can be seen from the lay-bys. Access to the information centre by following signs: The Warden, Butterstone Schoolhouse, Dunkeld, Perthshire, Tel. Dunkeld 337.
Birds: osprey, duck, geese, grebes, woodland species.
Botany: ferns, fungi.

Scotland's Safari Park

Despite its somewhat presumptuous title, this safari park offers good fare to those who enjoy the drive-through-Africa type of zoo. The animals are the usual species, with large areas devoted to lions and little else, but there is a unique cheetah drive-through enclosure and another with elephant, zebra, eland and a 'monkey jungle'. There are giraffe, camels. a dolphinarium and tigers, together with the usual pets' corner, a garden centre, refreshments, shops, etc.

It is all very commercial, of course, but nevertheless good value for the inhabitants of the Scottish Lowlands whose ambitions do not reach to the hills to north and south. The park lies to the west of Stirling at Blair Drummond and is conveniently placed on the A84. The nearest city is Glasgow, though Edinburgh is connected via the M9 motorway and is probably quicker to reach.

Visiting: by road on the A84 near Stirling. Usual car entrance fee includes all passengers, but there are minibus trips for those without.
Mammals: tiger, cheetah, lion, eland, elephant, zebra, dolphin.

Tentsmuir

Tentsmuir Point and the adjacent Morton Lochs are both National Nature Reserves in Fifeshire, lying between the Firths of Forth and Tay. Tentsmuir itself is a huge dune system stretching from the famous Eden estuary northward for some five miles. The sandy foreshore is a noted haunt of waders, terns and gulls, perhaps outshone by the richer estuaries to north and south. There are regular 'grey' geese and seals present. Morton Lochs are small, lie a mile south of Tayport and are excellent places for birds. No fewer than forty-five species breed, though winter is perhaps more appealing, with large numbers of duck, while passage periods bring many waders.

The Eden estuary, flanked in the south by the famous greens of St Andrews, is a splendid place frequented by hordes of wildfowl and waders. Being little more than a mile across at its widest point, it is eminently viewable, and a contrast to the huge Firths nearby. There are always scoter and eider present, along with many terns, and little gulls are a springtime speciality.

Visiting: approach Morton Lochs first on the B945, turning left two miles south of Tayport on a track that runs between the lochs. Much can be seen from the road, but permits can be obtained to use the hides from the Nature Conservancy Scottish Office. Continue on to Morton and Fetterdale, where forest tracks lead to Tentsmuir Point. Cars cannot enter the Reserve. For the Eden estuary, approach along the foreshore from St Andrews Golf Course, or view from the A91 at various points.

Birds: tufted duck, gadwall, shelduck, goldeneye, greylag goose, pink-footed goose, wigeon, long-tailed duck, scoter, eider, redshank, sanderling, common tern, Arctic tern.

Mammals: seals.

Ythan Estuary and Sands of Forvie

Few areas in the country can be so famed for both angling and birding as this fine little estuary north of Aberdeen on Scotland's east coast. That splendid hotel the Udny Arms not only offers the finest sea trout fishing in the country, but also publishes a guide to *Bird-Watching in the Newburgh Area*. If you want to catch summer running sea trout, fish from a boat after dark; if it's birds you're after, there is something of interest throughout the year.

The estuary is no more than a few hundred yards across, and so the waders, terns, gulls and wildfowl are all brought within easy binocular view. At high tide the birds flock to the island of Inch Creek, just north of the village of Newburgh, and they are easily viewed from the road. Redshank, oystercatcher, dunlin and curlew are invariably present, but in autumn their numbers build up and they are joined by hordes of migrants from further north: greenshank, ruff, whimbrel, spotted redshank. At this time the local breeding terns are joined by migrants

H

and huge numbers of kittiwakes. Naturally the pirates follow and a concentration of Arctic skuas regularly harass the terns and gulls. All four British skuas can sometimes be seen.

Winter sees concentrations of wildfowl including a build-up of shelducks together with wigeon, goldeneye and red-breasted merganser. Geese are regularly to be seen feeding on adjacent fields and

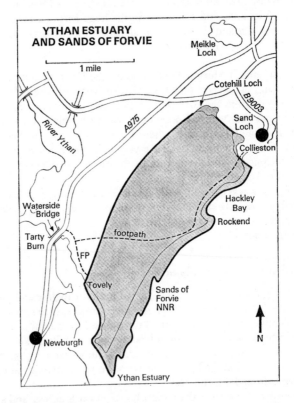

roosting on Meikle Loch across the river on the way to Peterhead. Pink-foot and greylag are the dominant species, but others occur from time to time.

Breeding terns hold their territories at the southernmost tip of the Sands of Forvie, a National Nature Reserve that covers 1774 acres between the Ythan and Collieston. For obvious reasons visiting is not allowed, save for a public footpath that leaves the Waterside Bridge via the southward track on the eastern bank, and leads to the coast at Rockend and proceeds onward to Collieston. The track is a right of way southward along the Ythan east bank as far as Tovely and the Nature Reserve boundary. Sandwich terns are the dominant breeders, but there are also numbers of common and Arctic terns, and a few little terns. Eiders nest among the dunes with – over 2000 pairs in a good year – the largest concentration in Britain. In winter they are joined by wigeon, merganser, goldeneye, scaup and scoter. Geese of several species winter, and thousands may roost on Meikle Loch.

Visiting: Newburgh is reached via the A92 from Aberdeen turning off on the A975. The base for the area, and the source of fishing permits, etc., is the Udny Arms Hotel in Newburgh – an excellent establishment with good food and wine. Most of the birds can be seen from the highway and from footpaths on the eastern shore through the Sands of Forvie.

Birds: black-headed gull, Sandwich tern, common tern, Arctic tern, little tern, kittiwake, Arctic skua, cormorant, shag, red-throated diver, eider, shelduck, wigeon, merganser, goldeneye, long-tailed duck, scaup, common scoter, velvet scoter, pink-footed goose, greylag goose, whooper swan, grey plover, knot, dunlin, oyster-catcher, redshank, turnstone, greenshank, ruff, wood sandpiper, spotted redshank, whimbrel, sedge warbler, water rail.

Salmon

Highlands and Islands

Isle of Barra

The southernmost major island of the Outer Hebrides, the Isle of
Barra is one of the most beautiful. In the west its long sand-shell
beaches are backed by the sweet grass machair (pronounced 'macha')
where fat sheep graze. Inland the hills rise green only to fall away into
the more rugged and austere country of the peat in the east. Yet it is
along this barren eastern coast that the larger part of the population
lives. This apparent contradiction is explained by the lifestyle of the
people, who live predominantly by fishing with a little subsistence
crofting thrown in for good measure.

The island was formerly owned by the clan MacNeil, and it was the
forty-fifth chief of the clan, Robert Lister MacNeil, an American
architect, who returned to restore the family seat – the castle in
Castlebay. His son is now the chief, and he returns most years from
America to holiday in the austere castle surroundings.

Barra is small enough to manage a complete walk-around in a day,
but there is more to see and explore, and even a week is insufficient
to see it all and soak up the unique atmosphere. The hills – Heavel at
1260 feet is the highest – offer superb views southward over the last
outliers of the Hebridean chain. To the east the Cuillins of Skye stand
out on a clear day. To the north lies a huge beach called the Cockle
Strand, where the island air service lands on a schedule dictated by the
tides. The alternative to air travel is Caledonian MacBrayne's steamer
out of Oban, which in summer sails into the setting sun with the
islands before it. Transportation is thin on the ground, though the
school bus may take a party out when not on official business, but there
are bicycles for hire and walking (even on the fourteen miles of road)
is a pleasure.

Birds are a major attraction, with most British seabirds seen offshore in the west. There are small breeding colonies in the north-west
at Greian Head. Immediately to the south lies Seal Bay, where a few
songs may encourage the grey and common seals that loaf on the

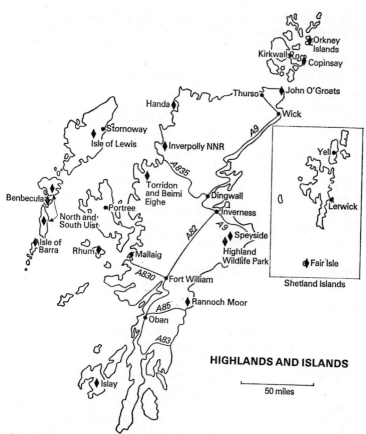

HIGHLANDS AND ISLANDS

50 miles

Shetland Islands

◆ localities mentioned in text

offshore rocks to come in close to the beach. The only other mammals of note are the rabbits, which are everywhere. For an outstanding wildlife experience the visitor must take the regular Sunday excursion from Castlebay to the island of Mingulay, where he can walk among the puffins and watch the spectacle of a massive seabird colony. At other times a charter may be arranged locally. There are buzzards on Barra, but no eagles, and small birds include wheatear, rock pipit, etc.

The island boasts over a thousand species of flowers, though it is perhaps best known for the largest banks of primroses in the country. There are also some attractive orchids.

A variety of accommodation can be obtained, from crofts to the delightful, though modern, Isle of Barra Hotel, overlooking the beach at Halaman Bay. This is a splendid place, well run and offering excellent accommodation and service. Saturday night in the bar is Gaelic (and occasionally English) singing time – and very good it is too.

The steamer service continues from Barra northward to Lochboisdale on South Uist. Aircraft land on the Cockle Strand.

Visiting: by Loganair from Glasgow with connections to other southern cities by British Airways. Or by Caledonian MacBrayne ferry from Oban via Lochaline, an experience in itself.
Botany: 1000 species including gigantic primrose beds and orchids.
Mammals: grey seal, common seal, rabbit galore.
Birds: gannet, puffin, razorbill, guillemot, black guillemot, shag, fulmar, kittiwake, great black-backed gull, buzzard, wheatear, rock pipit.
Other: history, Gaelic, atmosphere, scenery, hospitality.

Copinsay

A small dot of 210 acres surrounded by sea and with some pretty fearful cliffs is the memorial to James Fisher, first of the modern bird popularists. To James seabirds were a passion, perhaps even more so than his love of islands, and it is appropriate that his memorial should be a seabird island in the Orkneys, a place where he would have felt very much at home. From the top of the 210 feet high north-western cliffs one can look down on row upon row of guillemots and razorbills, fulmars and kittiwakes – it is a great seabird island. James Fisher was much more than a popularist, he was the man who counted the gannets of the North Atlantic, wrote the best monograph on a single species of bird ever published, *The Fulmar*, and got this author going on birds. Copinsay is a great little island, and if you get there for a day out of Newark Bay remember James Fisher.

Visiting: boat out of Newark Bay, Tel. Deerness 245.
Birds: guillemot, black guillemot, puffin, razorbill, kittiwake, fulmar, cormorant, shag, great black-backed gull, lesser black-backed gull, Arctic tern, rock dove, rock pipit.

Fair Isle

Politically part of Shetland, Fair Isle is now easily reached by regular Loganair air services from Sumburgh. Though the hard-working could explore its cliffs in a day, it would be better to overnight at the Bird Observatory and devote a couple of days or more to exploring what is an exceptionally attractive island. In few other similar-sized islands is the naturalist so well looked after and catered for. The buildings are modern, well equipped and inexpensive; but they are also crowded in autumn, when the island has a reputation for attracting the rarest of rare birds. In summer, however, you may share with only a few other fellow seekers after solitude. Armed with a packed lunch you can trek up Ward Hill and explore the western cliffs where the best seabird colonies are. Walk southward into the crofting area, or explore the cliffs around Sheep Craig, where puffins will stand and stare. Everywhere there are Arctic skuas, and great skuas as well.

Visiting: fly via Sumburgh to Fair Isle airstrip, a short walk from the Fair Isle Bird Observatory, where accommodation may be had by booking in advance.

Mammals: grey seal, common seal.

Botany: well catalogued by the Observatory.

Birds: similarly well known, but migrants might be anything. Arctic skua, great skua, puffin, razorbill, guillemot, black guillemot, kittiwake, fulmar.

Handa

Though small islands have been largely excluded from this guide, Handa, a reserve of the Royal Society for the Protection of Birds, is so attractive and so accessible that it deserves a place in any book on British wildlife. Extending in all to 766 acres, Handa is one of the primary seabird resorts along the bird-rich north-west coast, in Sutherland. Its magnificent cliffs hold all of the species that make Britain so rightly famous for its seabirds, and truly monumental numbers can be seen and photographed without risk. Guillemot, razorbill, kittiwake, shag and fulmar are all numbered by the thousand, and there are several hundred puffins and black guillemots. Both Arctic and great skuas breed, and there are Arctic terns, truly wild rock doves, eider and the occasional visiting golden eagle. The nearby mainland is rich in other species typical of the Scottish Highlands, giving the area a strong pull on those interested in birds. There is a reconditioned bothy available for overnighting to members of the RSPB – details from their Scottish Office, 17 Regent Terrace, Edinburgh EH7 5BN.

Visiting: day visitors can obtain boats at Scourie or, better still, at Tarbet to the north which is a shorter crossing. No landing permits are required, though the Society appreciates donations or, better still, membership.

Birds: razorbill, guillemot, puffin, black guillemot, fulmar, kittiwake, eider, Arctic tern, Arctic skua, great skua, rock dove, twite.

Highland Wildlife Park

Situated halfway between Aviemore and Kingussie in the beautiful Spey Valley, few zoos or wildlife collections can rival the majestic backdrop enjoyed by this excellent establishment. With 250 acres to drive through, it is the nearest thing to a real wildlife safari that most people are ever likely to enjoy – but it is a remarkably authentic experience. The major difference is that this beautiful park has made a point of specializing in Scottish wildlife as it was ten thousand years ago. There are perhaps rather more animals than at that time, but the species are more or less right.

European bison wander over the vast landscape, across streams and into the woodland. They breed freely and are approachable as well. Alongside them gallop Przewalski's horses, not truly Scottish, but representatives of the wild horses that once did extend from Britain across Eurasia to the China Sea. They delight in the huge enclosures, romp, chase, even fight, and of course breed. Red deer wander in herds, all taken from the stock of the surrounding hills. Feral goats, Soay sheep and Highland cattle are all found in the huge grounds, and among them the discerning visitor will be able to pick out wild birds breeding. Curlew and wheatear, snipe and lapwing, red and black grouse all nest in the enclosures, and some nests of wild birds near the road are signposted so that visitors can find and pick them out easily.

As well as animals in the large drive-through enclosures, there is a central section of the park where visitors can leave their cars and wander freely among the collection of animals that cannot be left to roam. Wild cat, golden eagle, snowy owl, polecat, pine marten, beaver, wolf, lynx, eagle owl, brown bear and reindeer can all be seen in close-up, but displayed in pens and cages that are large enough not to make the animals feel cramped. As a result they too breed freely.

Set in magnificent country, this is truly a splendid park and a true addition to the range of animals and variety of display methods offered to the public. It is also the only place in Britain where saiga antelope can be seen, though only one of the four imported survives.

Visiting: the park is well signposted on the A9 south of Aviemore. Entrance is by car or coachload only, and there are binoculars for hire and free kennels for visitors' dogs. Open every day from March till October. Tel. Kincraig 270.

Mammals: European bison, Przewalski's horse, red deer, Highland cattle, wild goat, Soay sheep, saiga, polecat, roe deer, lynx, reindeer, wolf, brown bear, Arctic fox, wild cat.

Birds: snowy owl, golden eagle, white-tailed eagle, capercaillie, black grouse, dotterel.

Other: Lynwilg Hotel north of Kincraig is very homely and Coylum-bridge Hotel near Aviemore is modern and excellent.

Inverpolly

Inverpolly, covering 26,827 acres, is second only to the Cairngorms Reserve in size, but second to none in wildness. Here, between the sea and the high sandstone peaks, is a true British wilderness, a place of immense diversity frequented only by those who would stalk the red deer, fish for trout and salmon, or watch wildlife. There is good access from a series of minor narrow roads, but the whole area is crisscrossed by an intricate network of streams, rivers and lakes. By and large access is unrestricted, save only in the stalking season from 15 July to 15 October, but visitors who intend to leave the roads or nature trail paths should contact the Warden in advance.

This wild country offers perhaps the best opportunities in the whole of Britain to those who seek wild cat, pine marten, otter, golden eagle, greenshank, black-throated diver and ptarmigan. There are also treats for the botanist at the base of the cliff at the Knockan nature trail where a strip of limestone is found, with moss campion, globe flower, mountain avens and yellow mountain saxifrage. Above all, this is deer country, and both red and roe occur in good numbers and are not difficult to see if you are prepared to penetrate the mountain fastnesses. The easiest route to higher ground is to climb Stac Polly from a layby on the Achiltibuie road next to Loch Lurgain. Here, on the sandstone, Alpine flowers can be found, and red deer and golden eagle are possibilities.

Bird-watchers will wish to penetrate the more remote areas of eastern Loch Sionascaig and the high peak of Cul Mor. The best way to reach this area is from Lochinver southward to Inverkirkaig and then follow the River Kirkaig eastward.

All visitors would be well advised to start at the Knockan Reserve Centre and Nature Trail, which is open six days a week during the summer. It is situated on the A835 adjacent to Lochan an Ais, where there is a convenient car park. The geological features indicate a considerable degree of folding and overlaying, and by studying the evidence here geologists were able to find the key to the understanding of the origin of mountain chains throughout the world. Plant life is interesting too, with the juxtaposition of lime-rich and lime-poor soils giving rise to a diverse flora. The inaccessible cliffs have protected the plant communities from damage.

After a viewpoint and a geological section that asserts a staggering indication of time, the trail seeks to show brown trout, greenshank, common sandpiper, water lobelia and lesser spearwort before moving upward toward the cliffs, with their spleenworts, wood sorrel and polypody. Higher still the trail encounters red grouse, golden plover and then ptarmigan and perhaps snow bunting. At Point 12, red deer may may be seen by those with binoculars. Among the heather, emperor moths may be found.

Visiting: despite its remoteness Inverpolly is not without facilities. Lochinver is a good centre, but the pleasant Inchnadamph Hotel by Loch Assynt is a favourite haunt of anglers. Cam Loch by Elphin is rich in birds and trout, and the visitor centre is just to the south. You can find the Warden, T. W. Henderson, at Knockan Cottage, Elphin, by Lairg.

Mammals: red deer, polecat.

Birds: black-throated diver, red-throated diver, grey heron, red-breasted merganser, wigeon, golden eagle, buzzard, peregrine, red grouse, golden plover, common sandpiper, greenshank, raven, hooded crow, ring ouzel, wheatear, stonechat, whinchat, twite, redpoll, snow bunting.

Botany: aspen, creeping willow, dwarf willow, crowberry, wild thyme, wood sage, Alpine bistort, wild angelica, self heal, English stonecrop, common birdsfoot trefoil, bog asphodel, heath bedstraw, speedwell,

heath spotted orchid, herb Robert, wood sorrel, Alpine lady's
mantle, green spleenwort, common spleenwort, common polypody,
yellow mountain saxifrage, golden saxifrage, autumn gentian,
mountain avens.

Other: there is a geological trail at Knockan with a special leaflet
available.

Islay

In general, the Inner Hebrides are not a great attraction to the
naturalist, which is a pity, for they contain some of the most superb
scenery in Britain. For those who want seabirds the great Outer Islands
stacks are far better, while for those seeking flowers or mammals the
mainland holds far more interest. Nevertheless the island of Islay
(pronounced 'I'll a') is an exception, and a magnificent one at that. It
is a rich land with good grazing, is large enough to support a fair-sized
town and, being open to the Atlantic, has some excellent cliffs. Unlike
the Outer Isles there are some decent-sized woods as well as substantial
moorland hills. It is this variety and lushness perhaps more than
anything else that make the island such an excellent place both for
birds and other wild life.

For the bird-watcher Islay offers a variety of interesting species.
There are good cliffs with colonies of guillemots, razorbills, puffins,
black guillemots and kittiwakes. In particular the cliffs at Portnahaven
and in the extreme west of the island hold a variety of species. There
are rock doves and choughs too, some of the last left in Scotland,
though the visitor seldom has to travel far to see these acrobatic crows
and there are often a few at the airport. Also on Islay are peregrines,
while the moors support a good population of merlins, red grouse are
found on all of the hills, and black grouse are widespread. Even hen
harriers breed in some numbers.

However, while Islay has its summer attractions, in winter it becomes one of the most significant wildfowl haunts in the country.
Up to 17,000 barnacle geese – that's about a third of the world
population – winter here. The grazing is ideally suited to their needs,
and they fly out from their two main roosts at the heads of the two sea
lochs that form a 'waist' between the eastern and western parts of
Islay, Loch Gruinart and Loch Indaal. White-fronted geese, of the
Greenland race, are also numerous, and several thousand spend the
winter here. There are also a few greylags and a host of duck and
waders to be seen off the flats at Bridgend.

235

Both native seals, the common and the grey, can be found around the coasts, and the hares are of the Irish race. There are roe deer too, one of their few strongholds in the islands, and there is also much of interest for the botanist. Though so far to the north, pale butterwort occurs here, and otherwise only in the south-west and again in Iberia. There is an excellent flora associated with the machair.

Visiting: Islay is served by steamer from West Loch Tarbert to Port Ellen, and by air from Glasgow. There is a good variety of accommodation and cars can be hired.

Mammals: common seal, grey seal, roe deer, blue hare.

Birds: chough, peregrine, merlin, barnacle goose, white-fronted goose, wigeon, guillemot, razorbill, puffin, black guillemot, shag, red grouse, black grouse, hen harrier, Arctic tern, common tern.

Botany: frog orchid, lady's bedstraw, birdsfoot trefoil, wild pansy.

John o'Groats

For reasons best sought by psychologists, thousands of visitors flock to John o'Groats every year. It is a strange pilgrimage, for there is nothing there but a small village and the usual array of tourist mementoes. The views northward over the Pentland Firth to Orkney are pleasant enough, but this is neither the northernmost nor easternmost point of Britain, though it is the 'far right hand top corner' as Land's End is the 'far left hand bottom corner'. Those who make the pilgrimage are often startled by the similarity between these two outer points of our islands. After the long drive over rough peat moors and craggy hills the green mellowness of Caithness comes as a pleasant surprise. The area enclosed by the Wick–Thurso road is by and large fine grazing land with some of the finest cliff scenery in Britain. Just out of Wick, across the airport runway, lies Noss Head, a fine seabird cliff with approachable puffins, fulmars and kittiwakes. From Duncansby Head (near John o'Groats) the cliffs stretch southward, covered with birds for mile after mile. Just stop by the coastal road and walk over the fields near Auckingill.

To the west lies Dunnet Head, actually the northernmost point of the mainland, where the cliffs are more spectacular. Ask the lighthouse keepers to let you through a 'No Entrance' gate for superb views of thousands of birds.

Away from the coast, birds are interesting too. There are short-eared owls and hen harriers as well as curlews galore and a few pairs of Arctic skuas. The large lochs may prove of interest and St John's Loch is noted for its trout.

Visiting: Wick has a well served airport and there is a variety of accommodation there and at Thurso.

Birds: gannet (offshore), razorbill, puffin, guillemot, black guillemot, kittiwake, shag, fulmar, red-throated diver, curlew, Arctic skua, great skua, short-eared owl, hen harrier.

Botany: species that prefer more fertile soils.

Other: castles here and there, including one used by the Queen Mother.

Isle of Lewis

Largest of the Outer Hebrides, the Isle of Lewis is joined by a narrow isthmus to Harris to the south, but the road is a tough climb and the two are to all intents and purposes separate. Harris is a bleak and austere place, the scene of Lord Leverhulme's attempt to industrialize island life and home of the world-famous tweed, although any tweed made in the Outer Hebrides bears the same name. Lewis in contrast is magnificent. It has vast open hills and moors where roads are non-existent and people seldom seen. There are red deer here, and much of the landscape is devoted to 'sport' in one way or another. Huge lakes dissect the region into separate mountain massifs, and rivers run their short courses to the sea. Yet despite its emptiness in the north and west this island is the centre and in parts the most densely populated area of the Outer Hebrides, and the standing stones at Callanish, second in stature only to Stonehenge, testify that man has lived here for thousands of years. Stornoway is the only sizeable town.

The rivers, especially the Grimersta River, have some of the best salmon fishing in Europe, and the red grouse attract hunters from the south. But it is the lakes with their breeding waders and divers, and the moors with greenshank, hen harrier and Arctic skua that are the main attractions. This is golden eagle country par excellence and several pairs can be seen by those with an eye for them.

Students of bird migration have found the Butt of Lewis an exciting place, particularly in autumn, when flocks of geese arrive from the north. Barnacle geese even winter along the beaches and grasslands of the west coast. The woods at Stornoway Castle, now an educational institution and of free access, were planted by Lady Leverhulme and are the only significant area of trees on the whole of the 'Long Island'.

237

As a result they have a host of birds such as blue and great tits, wood-pigeon, jay, etc., that, while common enough on the mainland, are decidedly rare out here. For the winter though a stay at Carloway, where there is the good Doune Braes Hotel, enables exploration of a fine coastline and access via motorized transport to the excellent Loch Roag area. From the road toward Gisla one can branch off southward into magnificent wild country.

Visiting: by air to Stornoway from Glasgow, and by Caledonian MacBrayne steamer to Stornoway from Ullapool. Access also to Tarbert in Harris from Uig in Skye. At present there is no steamer service from island to island up the length of the Outer Hebrides – a pity.

Botany: varied flora of sweet grassland in the west and peatland in the east. Some interesting remnants on the higher hills that escaped glaciation during the last ice age.

Mammals: red deer, grey seal, common seal.

Birds: golden eagle, red-throated diver, Arctic skua, great skua, hen harrier, buzzard, red grouse, greenshank, redshank, lapwing, barnacle goose.

Other: standing stones at Callanish, 'Black Houses', Harris tweed woven in crofters' homes, Gaelic.

Orkney Islands

A large group of islands off the north coast of Scotland, the Orkneys, like the coast of Caithness to the south, are lush and green in com-parison with the stark beauty with which we frequently associate Scotland. In particular they can be contrasted with the bleak Shetlands to the north, though each in its different way has an irresistible appeal. Though a mass of islands constitutes the group, Mainland is dominant, and it takes more than a day or two to explore it thoroughly.

Almost inevitably the visitor arrives either by air or sea at Kirkwall, a grey stone place with a few quaint corners, an old red cathedral and not much else. There are hotels, but they are much of a kind and not too kind at that. The alternative is Stromness, where the ferry from Scrabster berths, and that at least is smaller. For the general visitor Mainland offers some excellent scenery – the historic 'Churchill Walls' built between the southern islands to protect the naval base on Scapa Flow, and incidentally facilitating inter-island exploration; the Italian Chapel, a masterpiece of *trompe l'oeil* created by the Italian prisoners of war who constructed the 'Walls'; Skara Brae, a Celtic settlement of great beauty set among the dunes of the west coast, and some interesting and excavated burial chambers. The outer islands – Hoy, Westray and Papa Westray, Sanday, Stromsay, etc. – offer a sample of island life, for there are no hotels and the visitor must stay in crofts or on farms.

For the naturalist there is much else besides. The 'Moors' road between Dounby and Georth climbs high over the major hills of the island where great and Arctic skuas chase all summer. There are hen harriers here too, for this is their British headquarters, though they may also be seen at the excellent little marsh near Dounby. Here there is a good collection of waterbirds among the reeds, though Loch of Harray and Loch of Stenness to the south are generally better for duck. There is excellent trout fishing in Harray and a good fishing hotel at Mirbister.

Around the coasts there are shelduck, oystercatcher, eider, Arctic tern and redshank in good numbers. Both grey and common seals can be found. But Orkney has one truly outstanding sight – the seabird cliffs at Marwick Head. There are larger seabird colonies, and some with a greater variety of seabirds, but few are so easily watched over and give such spectacular views as these. Marwick lies on the west coast and is easily approached along narrow lanes. A monument stands high on the clifftops marking the nearest point to where Lord Kitchener was killed at sea: it is also a very convenient checkpoint for seabird watchers. Approaching across the fields, the best cliffs lie to the left, a place to sit and wonder. Marwick is a reserve of the Royal Society for the Protection of Birds, but there are no limitations on access. Enjoy the thrill of masses of seabirds and then join the RSPB to support its work.

The other great seabird site of Orkney is Papa Westray, which together with nearby Westray is the richest by number of species in Britain. No less than nineteen species breed here, but the logistics of viewing pose far more problems.

Visiting: by air to Kirkwall from Edinburgh, Inverness or Wick via Loganair or British Airways.

Mammals: grey seal, common seal.

Botany: rich and varied.

Birds: puffin, razorbill, guillemot, black guillemot, shag, fulmar, kittiwake, hen harrier, short-eared owl, great skua, Arctic skua, Arctic tern, shelduck.

Other: Kirkwall Cathedral, Skara Brae, Italian Chapel.

Rannoch Moor

Rannoch Moor, though only about eighty kilometres north of Glasgow, is one of the loneliest places in Britain. Roads and a railway skirt along its edges, but its heartland is a wilderness of moors, hills, lochs and peat bogs. To cross the Moor on foot is a considerable journey and not one to be undertaken lightly. The mileage may not be over-long, but the going is as tough as any. Here, for those who would go prepared, are red deer, with greenshank, snipe, golden plover, dunlin, black-throated diver and golden eagle. Part of the area in the north-east is a National Nature Reserve covering nearly 4000 acres. It is the only such reserve to include high-altitude (1000 feet) blanket bog, and is of considerable botanical interest. It is easily reached from the east via Rannoch Station.

In the west the main A82 crosses the edge of the Moor between Lochan na Achlaise and Loch Ba. This is an excellent area, with several typical birds on Loch Ba and the possibility of golden eagle overhead. Continuing northward the magnificent Glen Coe is a bonus of unusual quality.

Yet another good area lies to the south and is not properly part of Rannoch Moor at all. Loch Tulla can be seen from the A82, but for excellent wildlife opportunities take the A8005 to Inveroran, where the shoreline is backed by a remnant of the old Caledonian Forest of Scot's pine which once covered so much of the Highlands. Here red and roe deer may be found, along with capercaillie, and there are goosander and divers on the Loch. Waders on the marshes are an added attraction. The hills have otter and wild cat, though they are difficult to see.

Visiting: Rannoch Moor can be approached from the east on the B846 along Loch Rannoch to Rannoch Station, where the National Nature Reserve can be explored. In the west the A82 near Loch Ba is easily found, and southward the A8005 to Victoria Bridge is excellent.

Botany: bog flora.

Mammals: roe deer, red deer, wild cat, otter, fox, badger.

Birds: golden eagle, black-throated diver, goosander, greenshank, golden plover, dunlin, snipe, capercaillie, ring ouzel, wheatear.

Other: the loneliest country in Britain.

Rhum

Until 1957 Rhum, in the Inner Hebrides, was a private, forbidden island. No one could land there without permission – which was seldom granted. Even today visitors are not welcome to enjoy the Island's delights – though for different reasons. Since 1957 Rhum has been a National Nature Reserve and an open-air laboratory of the Nature Conservancy. The Island is devoted to research, and those who would stay to explore will have to convince the Conservancy that they are serious students carrying out worthwhile research. However, day visitors may land at Loch Scresort and explore a considerable area without formality. Though there is no catering there are toilets and a picnic spot. As you sail up the Loch there are cliffs with breeding seabirds to the south, and eiders and mergansers on the water itself. Red deer may be seen on the slopes of Hallival. After landing, a walk along the left bank of the Kinloch River to the waterfall at Balach Mhic Neill is worthwhile; and the Conservancy have set up a nature trail along the south side of Loch Scresort from the jetty to a deserted village. There is a booklet available from the White House.

Botanists may well be frustrated by the Alpine flowers that they cannot get to in the short time available, and bird-watchers that they cannot get among the Manx shearwaters that nest by the thousand among the mountains – the largest British colony. But there is a chance of golden eagle, peregrine and merlin, and visitors will see the shearwaters offshore in the evening. Just under 1700 red deer inhabit the island.

Visiting: by charter from Mallaig or Eigg to Loch Scresort. Free access over immediate area. Permission required elsewhere.

Mammals: red deer, grey seal, common seal, Rhum pony.

Birds: guillemot, razorbill, puffin, kittiwake, fulmar, eider, golden eagle, peregrine, merlin, Manx shearwater.

Botany: ling, bell heather, bilberry, bearberry, crowberry, little heath milkwort, lesser butterfly orchid, bog myrtle, bog asphodel, grass of Parnassus, moss campion, and various saxifrages and ferns.

Shetland

The furthest north of the British Isles, Shetland is a rugged landscape that has developed at a remarkable rate since the discovery of oil in the North Sea. New villages, construction works and a new road system have all taken their toll on the landscape, but it is not difficult to get away to isolation and peace in these wildlife-rich islands. Oil business or wildlife – there are few other reasons for coming as close to the

Arctic Circle as this. Yet Shetland has a mysterious beauty, a positive charm, that is most evident on the offshore islands of Hoy, Unst and Fetlar. Of course there are wild places on the mainland, but not with the atmosphere of these more manageable smaller places. Fetlar has always been favoured. Known as the 'Green Island' because its underlying geology makes it fertile, it can be walked and explored virtually without let or hindrance. There is a small guest house (very homely) and a number of crofts take in visitors. From them long days out on foot are rewarding. There are excellent seabird cliffs in the north of the island, where fulmars, kittiwakes, shags and puffins abound and where both seals can be seen. To get to them you must walk the shore the long way round rather than over the top of Vord Hill. This is a reserve of the Royal Society for the Protection of Birds, and the site of Britain's only snowy owls, a pair of which bred until quite recently. Odd individuals are still present, though a strong male seems to be lacking. Merlin, red-necked phalarope, whimbrel and other waders are to be seen, but do not expect anyone to say *exactly* where.

On one occasion, at a small and intentionally nameless pool, a screaming mass of Arctic terns was wheeling over a pair of otters playing in the surface. As soon as they saw they were being watched they disappeared, only to be replaced by three diminutive red-necked phalaropes that swam by within arm's length.

To the north the more austere hulk of Unst sticks out of the sea. Bird-watchers flock to Hermaness, a National Nature Reserve and, with the exception of Muckle Flugga, the most northern point of Britain. Along the way they pass pools with red-throated and black-throated divers and marshes with redshank and black-tailed godwits, all to get at some of the finest seabird cliffs in Britain. Those with nerves of steel may descend among the birds themselves and get face to face with puffin, guillemot, razorbill and gannet, but it is not to be recommended without a guide. Arctic and great skuas are numerous and there are whimbrel, golden plover and dunlin as well. Accommodation is at Baltasound, which can be reached by Loganair and by steamer from Aberdeen and Wick.

Yell is perhaps the most neglected of islands, yet in that lies its charm. There are plenty of birds, including breeding scoter, and some splendid wild country. The new ferry system connects Brough and Copister, making motorized access straightforward. The far north is worth anyone's time, especially if they wish to be alone.

Visiting: easily reached from the south by air to Sumburgh with on-ward connections via Loganair to all the other main islands. Also a regular steamer service from Aberdeen and Wick to Lerwick, the capital. Because of the oil boom Lerwick tends to be crowded, and hotel rooms are at a premium. Try the excellent Scalloway Hotel in Scalloway instead.

Mammals: grey seal, common seal, otter.

Botany: interesting and varied.

Birds: gannet, Arctic skua, great skua, puffin, guillemot, razorbill, black guillemot, shag, fulmar, kittiwake, red-necked phalarope, whimbrel.

Other: Isle of Noss by boat from Lerwick beneath spectacular gannetry.

Speyside

The Spey Valley, for long a haunt of the discerning and dedicated, has had tourism thrust upon it. The Scottish charm of Aviemore has dis-appeared under a forest of glass and concrete, and what were once lonely hillsides are now flocked by skiers in winter and tourists in summer. For many the area has been spoilt beyond repair, and if they seek the feel of a former age they must seek it further north at Gran-town, Boat of Garten or Nethybridge.

Things are not really as bad as they sound. Most of the modern hotels are grouped west of Aviemore's main street and, with all the so-called contemporary amenities there as well, the rash is confined. Of course there are plenty of people, but they are concentrated by season and anyway tend to stick to the better-known spots. Loch Morlich is virtually overrun with campers, picnickers, canoeists, sailing dinghies and so on. The road onward to Cairngorm is full of cars, and the ski-lift seems to enjoy a booming business. Even the very top of Cairngorm is littered with people on a hot summer day. But take an anorak, a map and a compass and start walking in any direction away from modern transport and you are on your own in some of the finest countryside to be found anywhere. The traditional walk up the Lairig Ghru is as empty as ever, and if Cairngorm itself is avoided, the hills are occupied only by dotterel, snow buntings and golden eagles.

Even the lowlands are empty away from a few well-beaten paths. Take the nature trail from Loch Morlich itself and you quickly leave people behind. Instead you will find black grouse, crested tit (a real rarity that is difficult to find anywhere else in Britain), siskin and perhaps the odd buzzard. In winter you might find wildfowl including

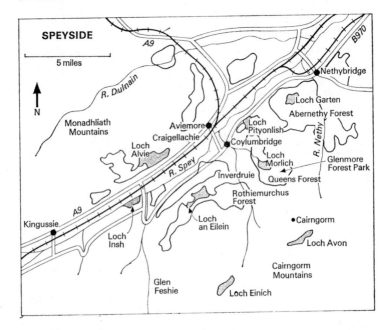

whooper swans on the lakes, and the countryside is alive with fieldfares and redwings.

Different forests offer different birds. To reach Craigellachie you must pass through modern Aviemore, but soon you are among the birches and the air is full of willow warbler song. From the top of the hill the whole of Speyside lies before you, the bowl of Glen More Forest Park with the Cairngorms behind, and Rothiemurchus Forest, scattered pines that have survived the onslaught of generations. Away to the north Abernethy Forest and the Spey below, full of salmon for those who can afford the right beats.

Speyside offers a variety of landscape and of possibilities for exploration; those that follow are highly selective.

Cairngorms National Nature Reserve
The Reserve covers 64,118 acres and is the largest NNR in Britain and one of the largest reserves in Europe. It includes most of the huge range of mountains that lie to the south of the Spey valley, though not the summit of Cairngorm itself. For the toughened hill walker it is the only place in the country where he can walk all day around the

4000 feet mark, but – perhaps more important – here he can walk vast areas of wilderness with a great chance of seeing red deer. Over 2000 acres are wooded, and a considerable proportion of this is made up of the old Caledonian Forest of Scot's pines. Higher up pines give way to birches, and in the high screes and corries there is an interesting Arctic-Alpine flora. Wild cat, red deer and roe deer are widespread, and golden eagles are quite numerous.

Access is virtually unrestricted save only in Mar and Glenfeshie in August, September and October, when the red deer are in rut. There are two nature trails. The one at Loch an Eilein is reached from the B970 a mile south of Inverdruie; there is a visitor centre, and the trail wanders round the Loch concentrating mainly on the botany of the area. The trail at Achlean is reached by leaving the B970 further south at Feshiebridge and following the track along the eastern side of the Feshie River. It enters the reserve at a higher level and there is a good chance of seeing red deer from an observation tower.

Craigellachie National Nature Reserve

Covers 642 acres, of which 250 acres are woodland on the steep slopes west of Aviemore. The nature trail leads from the modern Aviemore Centre through the birch woods, which are full of flowers in early summer. Views over the Spey can be obtained, but even better views are attainable by those who penetrate the open moorlands above the woods and the trail to the summit at 1700 feet. Though alive with willow warblers, the reserve is mainly known for its insect life, and in particular for its moths, which include Rannoch sprawler, Kentish glory and great brocade.

Glen More Forest Park

Over 3000 of the Park's 12,000 acres are woodland, and though much of this is planted foreign trees there is still a substantial area of Scot's pine around Loch Morlich. Unfortunately this area has now become a trippers' paradise and lost most of its appeal, but a good nature trail starts from the Loch, as noted earlier. Surrounding the Park the open moors are empty save only for the area around the ski-run and the roads. Thus wild mammals such as red and roe deer are often to be seen, along with blue hare and, more rarely, wild cat. A feature of Cairngorm slopes here is the introduced herd of reindeer, which have prospered and now number about a hundred animals. Visits are arranged every morning, leaving Reindeer House, Glen More, at

11.00 hours. Contact Mikel Utsi, Reindeer Company Ltd, Aviemore, Inverness PH22 1QU.

Loch Garten

After twenty years of regular osprey breeding, during which time over half a million people were able to see the recolonizing pair of 'fish-hawks', the Royal Society for the Protection of Birds finally purchased the Loch Garten area of Abernethy Forest. Now 1500 acres (£290,000) have been purchased and another part of the old Caledonian Forest has been protected. Ospreys, well signposted and reasonably reliable, are the main attraction, but the visitor may well come across crested tit and crossbill, capercaillie and blackcock, buzzard and sparrowhawk. In winter the lochs are a roost for whooper swans and greylag geese, and up on the moors above the forest in summer there are curlew and wheatear, merlin and passing hen harrier.

Mammals, best seen in the early morning, include red deer and roe deer, fox, stoat and weasel. There are even otters in the Loch. Contact the RSPB for further details of visiting this new reserve.

Visiting: there are excellent road connections both north and south and, via motorways, London–Aviemore is just a long day's drive. There are regular air services to Inverness, as well as overnight trains and car-train ferries from various parts of the south. Accommodation is plentiful and varied: write to the Aviemore Tourist Development Board, Aviemore, Inverness. The Coylumbridge Hotel is modern and excellent, and the Nethybridge Hotel traditional and comfortable. Small inns are rather scarce, but the Lynwilg south of Aviemore is good. There are camping and caravan sites and some good restaurants and fish and chip shops. As elsewhere the beer is served in hotels.

Mammals: wild cat, red and roe deer, reindeer, otter, fox, badger, stoat, weasel, wild goat.

Birds: osprey, golden eagle, hen harrier, merlin, buzzard, sparrowhawk, capercaillie, black grouse, red grouse, ptarmigan, curlew, common sandpiper, golden plover, dunlin, dotterel, snow bunting, redstart, dipper, wheatear, willow warbler, crested tit, crossbill, siskin.

Botany: crowberry, blaeberry, wavy hair grass, stiff sedge, heath bedstraw, starry saxifrage, dwarf cudweed, purple saxifrage, Alpine saxifrage, Alpine forget-me-not, rock speedwell, mountain bladder fern, club moss, Alpine meadow rue, Alpine cinquefoil.

246

Torridon and Beinn Eighe

Torridon, owned by the National Trust for Scotland, and Beinn Eighe (pronounced 'Ben-ay'), a National Nature Reserve, lie in the north-west Highlands immediately west of Kinlochewe. They have been described as the best mountain scenery in Britain: certainly their heights are among the most impressive. The Torridon sandstone has been eroded to show the layers of sediment previously laid down by rivers running off the hard Lewisian gneiss. The effect is startlingly beautiful. In contrast, the steep flanks of Beinn Eighe are a stark, hostile-looking grey. Between them the two massifs extend over an area twelve miles by four miles, much of it open to access by walkers. A number of routes have been established and are described in a guide-book called *Torridon*, available from the National Trust for Scotland or at their visitor centre at the head of Loch Torridon. Many of the walks are long and hard, but anyone can enjoy a few steps away from the road into these mountain fastnesses.

Though not as rich as the famous Ben Lawers in Perthshire, Torridon has an excellent Arctic-Alpine flora, particularly on the cliffs that are out of reach of the grazing sheep. Streams produce Alpine meadow rue, Alpine bistort, Alpine willowherb, and starry and mossy saxifrage. Drier areas have Alpine ladies mantle and Alpine clubmoss. High screes boast some of the rarer plants, including northern rock cress and Arctic mouse-ear, while on the tops there are least willow thrift and the rarest plant of all, the curved woodrush.

Deer are rather thin on the ground, and the other mammals are generally nocturnal and difficult to observe. But wild cat and pine marten (watch litter bins at dusk) occur, as do otters along the wilder streams and coast. Birds are more numerous, but it needs many hours and much hard walking to find great northern diver, golden eagle (try the mouth of the Kinlochewe River), peregrine, merlin, ptarmigan, corncrake and greenshank, all of which have bred. Redwings frequent the alder woods along Loch Maree.

Beinn Eighe is, perhaps, a more impenetrable place, but the main purpose in its establishment as a reserve was to protect the remnants of the old Caledonian Forest that lines the southern shores of Loch Maree. Here, signposted on the A832, is the Glas-Leitire Nature Trail ('Coille na Glas-Leitire' = 'Wood on the Grey Slopes' in Gaelic). There is a car park, and the trail leads up into the woodland picking out various features of the landscape, its fauna and flora. It is possible to see golden eagle, wild cat and pine marten, but most visitors will

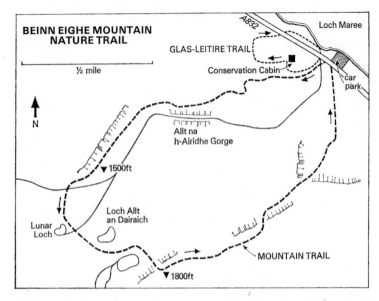

have to make do with wood anemone, wood sorrel, tormentil, woodruff and enchanter's nightshade. There are sundews, lousewort and bog asphodel all picked out with the aid of an excellent little trail guide.

Also starting from the Loch Maree car park is the much longer mountain trail. This follows the Glas-Leitire Trail up the hill but then continues southward into the interior of the reserve. Though the route is easy to follow and marked with cairns, it is four miles long and rises to 1800 feet. The track is rough and, in places, steep, but allowing four or five hours should be sufficient. The major climb is up the gorge that has been created along the Allt na h-Airidhe fault between 1000 feet and 1500 feet. Here pines cling to the precipitous slope, out of reach of browsing. Higher still the landscape becomes virtually lunar, with scant vegetation, and from the Conservation Cairn at the top of the trail, thirty-one peaks over 3000 feet may be seen. Watch for golden eagle, ptarmigan and red deer. On the way down watch for pine marten, moonwort, globeflower and dwarf cornel.

As if all of this was not enough, Loch Maree boasts some of the finest early sea trout fishing in the country. See the Fishing Record Books at the Loch Maree Hotel.

Visiting: the A896 and A832 out of Kinlochewe give access to the area.

There is good accommodation in crofts at Alligin and Lower Dia-baig, on Loch Torridon, and a delightful remote Youth Hostel at Craig. (But watch out for arriving, departing or fishing, etc., on the Sabbath.) There is a camp site for single nights at Taagan Farm, just off the A832 at Beinn Eighe, and a private longer-term site in Kinlochewe. Loch Maree Hotel is typically highland, built like a fortress and very hospitable.

Birds: great northern diver, black-throated diver, red-throated diver, fulmar, grey heron, eider, red-breasted merganser, goosander, golden eagle, common buzzard, peregrine, merlin, red grouse, ptarmigan, corncrake, ringed plover, golden plover, curlew, common sandpiper, redshank, greenshank, herring gull, common tern, Arctic tern, great spotted woodpecker, redwing.

Botany: cotton grass, crowberry, bearberry, dwarf juniper, lousewort, milkwort, bog asphodel, heath violet, royal fern, mountain sorrel, Alpine saw-wort, water avens, starry saxifrage, mossy saxifrage, Alpine meadow rue, Alpine bistort, Alpine willowherb, Alpine ladies' mantle, bog whortleberry, dwarf cornel, Arctic mouse-ear, spiked woodrush, least willow thrift, curved woodrush.

North and South Uist and Benbecula

This central section of the Outer Hebrides, or 'Long Island' as it is often called, is by far the richest part in terms of natural history. Like the other islands it is a strange contrast of rich shell-sand grassland (machair) in the west and tough peat-clad hills in the east. While the west coast is smooth, with headlands only here and there breaking up the run of golden beaches, the east is indented with deep fjords cutting into the heart of the islands. Naturally the road runs nearer the west coast, and as it goes it flirts here and there with the divide between fertile sheep-grazed slopes and rugged heather moors. In the east the nature of the land has created a maze of lochs and lochans the largest of which are the primary natural history attraction of the islands.

At Loch Druidibeg on South Uist, for instance, the largest flock of the native greylag geese breed and gather with their young. The area is a National Nature Reserve with a handy watchtower, but it is quite unnecessary to go through the formalities, for the geese can be seen from the roads. Just to the north is Loch Bee, which is really an inlet of the sea that all but cuts off the northern part of South Uist. Here swans galore loaf and feed – most are mute swans, but it's worth a search for the rarer species. Northward still runs the causeway across the straits that separate the island from Benbecula, notable for its airport and not much else. Continue to North Uist which, for the bird-watcher at least, is the most attractive of all. The shell-sand beaches are alive with waders in season, and in summer eiders, Arctic terns, redshank and, if you look in the right place, even the rare red-necked phalarope may be found. The best place to look is the Royal Society for the Protection of Birds' reserve at Balranald – ask the Warden.

To the east the hinterland with its bogs, hills and lochs is wild territory indeed. Here there are golden eagles, red-throated divers, some duck, buzzards and many other hill birds. It is perhaps the contrast that is so exciting in these outer islands, a contrast within such a small and manageable area.

To the north lies the Sound of Harris, one of the most treacherous stretches of sea in Britain. The tide races here have seen the demise of many who have risked the crossing. The small islands and rocks are a major haunt of seals, and they can be seen to advantage from the ferry that regularly plies between Newton and Leverburgh.

There are three ways to the islands: by air to Benbecula, by boat from Oban via Barra to Lochboisdale, or from Uig in Skye to Lochmaddy. Lochboisdale has the hospitable Lochboisdale Hotel overlooking the harbour and offers some of the finest sea trout fishing to be had in Britain. The back bar is the local, and a hard-drinking place it is too. The atmosphere is essentially male, but it is a genuine piece of Outer Island life.

Visiting: by air from Glasgow to Benbecula. By Caledonian Mac-Braynes steamer from Oban via Barra to Lochboisdale, or from Uig to Lochmaddy.

Botany: varied, with orchids in the west.

Mammals: grey seal, common seal.

Birds: greylag goose, red-necked phalarope, golden eagle, buzzard, Arctic tern, shelduck, oystercatcher, redshank, mute swan.

Other: rocket range on South Uist – no entry.

Common Seal

Index of Places

Places in bold type are those with main entries in the text; those in normal type are other wildlife areas mentioned.